LIFE UPSIDE DOWN

Reclaiming Autism and Neurodivergence Beyond Stereotypes

Solweig G. Habert

Mindwiz Media

MINDWIZ
MEDIA

ISBN: 979-8-9932381-1-1 (Paperback)
ISBN: 979-8-9932381-0-4 (Digital)
First Edition: September 2025
Mindwiz Media
https://www.mindwiz.com/

Cover design by: Solweig G. Habert
Printed in the United States of America

CONTENTS

FOREWORD

For years, I dismissed "self-compassion" as feel-good nonsense. How could I love someone I truly believed was flawed and always failing at the basics of being human? I performed a version of myself I thought the world would accept. I monitored my tone, managed eye contact, refrained from stimming, and apologized for my intensity. I was slowly disappearing into a performance that was killing me.

At thirty-one, an autism spectrum disorder (ASD) diagnosis gave me something I had never felt: genuine compassion for the child and young woman who struggled so hard in a world not designed for her brain. The ground didn't just shift—it stabilized. A decade later, when Attention-deficit/ hyperactivity disorder (ADHD) was added to my constellation of neurodivergence, I was already at peace with myself. The second diagnosis brought something deeper: I began to like myself. I wouldn't change a thing.

This journey from self-rejection to self-acceptance shows why diagnoses save lives. It's not about labeling or pathologizing differences. It's about giving people the knowledge and framework to understand themselves, rebuild their relationship with their identity, and stand up for themselves with the confidence that they were never fundamentally wrong.

This book invites you to make the same shift: from pathology to possibility. Whether you're neurodivergent yourself, or a friend, family member, educator, employer, or anyone who wants to understand and support our community, we'll replace deficit language with difference, shame with precision, and stereotypes with authentic understanding. The goal isn't for neurodivergent people to pass as neurotypical; it's for all of us to create spaces where everyone can thrive as their authentic selves—and benefit from the unique perspectives that neurodivergent minds bring.

Why This Book, Now

The stakes are real. Misunderstandings cost health, livelihoods, and, at times, lives. When I read about an autistic woman who died by suicide, I wondered: What if she had received the legal protections she deserved? What if people understood her need for cyberbullying protection and physical safety? What if society saw her sensitivity to certain struggles not as "issues no one could see," but as legitimate neurological differences needing understanding, legal protection, and accommodation?

This tragedy crystallized the emergency we face. While traditional systems debate a one-fits-all notion of inclusivity, real people are suffering from isolation, misunderstanding, and a criminal lack of support. We can't wait for slow pipelines to catch up. People need practical support now.

Why I Self-Published: Mission Over Market

Traditional publishing optimizes portfolios, not public need. Publishers evaluated my work based on its market positioning. Did my book fit their diversity initiatives? Was this topic already in their catalog? Not one asked whether my book could truly help people or solve urgent problems.Their incentives prioritize prestige and profit; mine is public impact. Self-publishing let me prioritize speed, access, and accountability to the people this book is for—not to a corporate catalog. Some messages are too important to wait for systems that never valued them in the first place.

How I Deliver Quality—Fast

Without a traditional publishing infrastructure, I built a modern editorial stack. AI gave me an editor, research aide, and language coach—English is my second language. The message reached you sooner without loss of quality. Technology didn't dilute the message; it amplified it, making it accessible at the pace urgent social change requires.

What You'll Get in These Pages

You'll get answers to the questions that matter. What makes autism and ADHD so hard to detect in women and intersectional groups? If people seem 'okay,' are their struggles real? Why shouldn't they hide their 'odd' behaviors to fit in? These answers come from my experience as a woman and mother with ASD and ADHD, backed by the most recent research and understanding of how medical history still affects our community.

You'll learn how educational systems, homes, and workplaces can be more inclusive—and why this benefits everyone, not just neurodivergent individuals.

My promise is simple: practical, respectful tools and insights you can use right away, and a voice that refuses to apologize for neurodivergent lives. I wrote this outside old gate-keeping systems so it could arrive on time. If you've spent years shrinking to fit spaces that weren't designed for you, this book offers you the extra leg room you need to sit comfortably in the world.

Let's take action. Start your journey now—own your story, share your voice, and help build a world where every story counts.

***

INTRODUCTION

Imagine waking up every day knowing your performance starts the minute you get out of your bed. Everything—from the way you dress to the way you talk, including your mannerisms, your eye contact, the length or lack of it, your tone, your enthusiasm—must be done perfectly according to a script. Your life depends on your daily performances. Not for applause, but to be accepted. Many autistic people, whether diagnosed or not, start this performance in childhood, responding to audience feedback to determine how to act in different situations. They learn quickly which behaviors are praised and which are punished, which parts of themselves are acceptable and which must be hidden. Over time, this becomes a mask. A carefully constructed version of themselves that helps them survive in a world not designed for them.

This book is for the women and minorities who've worn those masks so well they've nearly forgotten who they are beneath them. It's also for the ones who were misdiagnosed, overlooked, muted by a culture that ignores the very concept of mental health. Those who were told they were "just sensitive" or "too much." It's also for those seeking to understand them better—friends, partners, educators, clinicians, and curious allies.

We live in a world that subtly and persistently demands conformity. As autistic women or minorities, we often become experts at adapting to these expectations, building hidden mental frameworks and strategies designed to navigate social life without attracting attention. Like the electrical grids beneath our cities, these systems are complex, vital, and mostly invisible. But make no mistake: the effort required to appear "normal" is extraordinary, and it comes at a price.

My own story, like many others, begins with the dissonance of being human in a way the world doesn't expect. As a woman on the spectrum, I have spent much of my life studying the social rules others seemed to grasp intuitively. At times, this has felt like both a burden and a gift. I have observed Humanity's rituals from a vantage point, both inside and outside the system. And while I sometimes joke that this makes me a social scientist appointed to interpret the strange customs of the neurotypical world, the truth is that it has often felt lonely, confusing, and exhausting.

But before attempting to understand what it means to be an autistic woman or an autistic minority, we need to start with a fundamental question: what does it mean to be human?

The Philosophical Foundation: Humans as Social Animals

The concept of humans as fundamentally social beings dates back to ancient Greek philosophy. Aristotle famously wrote in *Politics*[1] that "man is by nature a social animal," and that anyone who is either unable to live in society or has no need for it is "either a beast or a god."

This idea suggests that our humanity is not just enhanced by social connection, but defined by it. We are not merely social creatures by habit or preference—sociality is embedded in the very structure of who we are.

Scientific Evidence for Human Sociality

Modern science supports this ancient view. Evolutionary biology tells us that human intelligence developed in large part to manage increasingly complex social relationships, a concept known as the social brain hypothesis. Neuroscience has identified systems like mirror neurons that are invaluable in the development of empathy and intuitive social understanding. Developmental psychology shows that even newborns seek out eye contact and voice, and that disruptions in this social pattern are among the earliest indicators of autism.

Research demonstrates this innate social orientation from birth. Newborns typically prefer faces with open eyes and direct gaze. At the same time, children with autism often display significantly decreased visual fixation on faces compared to their neurotypical peers. By six months, infants later diagnosed with autism already show atypical gaze preferences and slower orientation to social stimuli, highlighting how fundamental social connection is to typical human development.

One particularly striking finding: toddlers who spend more than 70 percent of their attention on geometric shapes instead of social stimuli can be accurately identified as autistic with near 100 percent accuracy.

Autism and the Nature of Social Connection

What does this mean for how we understand autism?

It means that people with autism are not antisocial. They are not uninterested in connection. Instead, their brains process social information differently. Many autistic individuals desire relationships just as profoundly as anyone else. Still, they experience difficulty with the mechanisms that neurotypical people take for granted. The desire is there. The expression is simply different.

If being social is central to being human, and people with autism are fully human, then we must recognize that they, too, are social. The difference lies in how that sociality is expressed, understood, and responded to.

What This Book Offers

This book is an invitation to rethink what we believe about autism in women. It blends philosophy, neuroscience, and lived experience to offer a more inclusive and nuanced picture of one that honors the deep humanity behind the mask.

We will explore the hidden systems autistic women build to function in a neurotypical world. We will examine the cost of constant masking and what happens when those masks finally fall away. We will look at how diagnosis can be both liberating and destabilizing, and what it means to reconstruct a self that was never allowed to form fully.

Most of all, this book is about returning to ourselves. It is about seeing and being seen, for who we truly are.

Scan this QR Code and enjoy your Bonus Content!

***

WHY AUTISM GOES UNSEEN

Being Social with an Autistic Brain: The Social Paradox of Autism

I take a deep breath as I stand outside the conference room. I've finally pieced together the puzzle of my life through two diagnoses: autism at 31, and ADHD at 42. Right now, I'm mentally rehearsing my presentation one more time, lips silently moving through my carefully memorized script. My hand clutches a small, smooth stone in my pocket—a discreet alternative to my usual hand ritual that would calm my racing thoughts but draw unwanted attention. "You've got this," I whisper to myself, straightening my uncomfortable pants. The fabric feels like sandpaper against my skin, but I've learned long ago that professional attire is non-negotiable, regardless of sensory discomfort. As I enter the room, my face transforms. The tension in my shoulders remains, but my expression shifts into what I call my "work face"—practiced smile, deliberate eye contact, and carefully modulated voice. No one would guess that the fluorescent lights overhead feel like needles in my eyes or that the overlapping conversations around the table register as unintelligible noise I have to work twice as hard to process.

Before finding my current online position, which I've maintained for over sixteen years now, my work history was a graveyard of short-lived jobs. Six months seemed to be my limit—whether in retail during my student years or later in office environments. Each time, the pattern was the same: initial success followed by a gradual erosion of my energy reserves until what looked to others like a nervous breakdown would force me to quit. The real problem wasn't the work itself —it was the constant masking, the sensory onslaught, and the exhaustion that came from navigating neurotypical social expectations without accommodations.

My current remote position has been life-changing. Working online means I can control my sensory environment. I can move freely between video calls, I do very little masking so I can focus on productive work. I can take breaks when my executive functioning hits a wall. I communicate primarily through writing, which gives me time to process information at my own pace. What looks to the outside world like a successful career is actually careful adaptation—finding the one work model that doesn't require me to sacrifice my well-being.

The presentation today is a rare in-person requirement. It goes well—it always does. I've spent hours analyzing successful presenters on YouTube, studying their gestures, intonation patterns, and forced humor. I've timed my pauses, rehearsed my answers to potential questions, and prepared fallback phrases for unexpected situations. My colleagues praise my confidence and poise, completely unaware of the exhaustion building behind my performance.

By the time I reach my car three hours later, the mask is crumbling. My carefully constructed persona has consumed every ounce of mental energy I possess. The drive home passes in a blur, I reject every single phone call, even from family and friends, I gave the presentation everything I had. Finally, as I close my house door, I start removing all those uncomfortable pieces of clothing to jump into leggings and a T-shirt. I lay down in the darkness of my bedroom with my sunglasses on, an ice pack on my head. Hopefully, my migraine medication will work sooner rather than later. I had it prepared next to my bed to allow myself to recover right after my meeting. My afternoon is fully blocked: No phone calls or meetings. If I manage to nap, I should be able to welcome my children with a smile after school and to enjoy a low-key family evening without too much talking.

**

When I received my autism diagnosis at 31, the psychologist was surprised, noting how "well adjusted" I appeared. I almost laughed. Well adjusted? I'd spent three decades building and maintaining a catalog of personas for every social situation, analyzing and mimicking others' behavior, suppressing my natural movements, and forcing myself to endure painful sensory experiences—all while burning through my limited energy reserves at an unsustainable rate.

The ADHD diagnosis at 42 completed more of the picture, explaining the executive functioning struggles that compounded my autistic traits in traditional workplaces. Together, these diagnoses helped me understand why conventional jobs had been so impossible to sustain—and why finding the right environment had made such a dramatic difference.

This is masking—the invisible labor that allows me to appear neurotypical to the outside world while concealing the true cost within. No one sees the Sunday spent entirely in bed, recovering from social events. No one counts the meltdowns behind closed doors. No one measures the cumulative exhaustion of living in a world not designed for minds like mine.

As I finally drag myself to pick up my children from school, I feel profound gratitude for my online career. For all those years, I've been able to sustain work while dramatically reducing the masking requirements that once led to repeated burnout. I still need to be "Professional Soly" for meetings and presentations, but now I can balance those demands with the space to be authentically myself for most of my working hours. Even if I never was offered a proper career with promotions and pay raises, I am still thankful for working, unlike most of us on the spectrum.

People on the spectrum are traditionally perceived as introverted or not social. The reality is more nuanced: Many of us want social connection but face significant cognitive and sensory challenges because of the cognitive demands of social interaction. This creates a fundamental misunderstanding when neurotypicals (NTs or non-neurodivergent population, in other terms... "regular people" if they exist) observe autistic behavior and conclude a lack of interest in socializing, rather than recognizing the underlying neurological differences at play.

Masking refers to the conscious or unconscious strategies used to hide, suppress, or compensate for autistic traits in order to fit in socially and meet neurotypical expectations. **Common masking behaviors include: Forcing eye contact** even when it feels uncomfortable or overwhelming, **Scripting or rehearsing** conversations and social interactions in advance, **Mimicking** the social behaviors, gestures, and speech patterns of peers, **Suppressing stimming** (self-soothing repetitive movements) in public, **Camouflaging intense interests** or only discussing them with select people, **Pushing through sensory discomfort** without showing distress, **Studying social rules** like an academic subject and applying them manually.

Girls are often socialized more intensely around social conformity and relationships, creating stronger pressure to mask. They may also naturally develop more sophisticated masking strategies earlier than boys, which led to underdiagnosis. They feel like they're "performing" or "playing a character" in social situations.

While masking can help navigate social situations, it's mentally and physically exhausting. Prolonged masking is associated with increased anxiety, depression, burnout, loss of sense of self, and delayed diagnosis. Many women don't receive an autism diagnosis until adulthood, after years of struggling to understand why socializing feels so draining despite appearing "normal" to others.

Masking in autism is not a conscious choice but a survival mechanism that develops naturally after experiencing repeated rejection and humiliation. For autistic individuals, especially us, girls, masking emerges as a response to understanding that we are "different" in ways that aren't socially accepted.

During kindergarten and early elementary years, I experienced rejection and mistreatment, sometimes even from teachers. During lunch recess, which lasted about an hour and a half in France, I would sit alone on a bench and observe other children playing, carefully watching their interactions while trying not to be noticed. I recall with clarity studying the games other children played, sensing the other children understood something instinctively that I did not naturally comprehend. On rare occasions when a player was missing, I would be invited to join. Inevitably, I would make mistakes by not understanding the game rules, resulting in further rejection. Those failed social attempts illustrate how masking begins— through necessity and survival.

The constant criticism came from all directions: children, teachers unhappy about behaviors like not raising a hand properly, giving inappropriate looks, using the wrong voice tone, or swinging in chairs in first grade (which I later recognized as stimming for sensory regulation) that led my teacher to spank me and have me standing as punishment in the first row of the classroom for the rest of the day, being humiliated for allegedly not appreciating "the luxury of a chair." Ironically, to this day, my preference remains sitting on the floor to work... I guess I still do not appreciate this luxury!

The masking process involves creating social personas by carefully studying and imitating those who appear socially successful. I used to spend my time alone at recess watching popular girls who were appreciated by peers and teachers, then meticulously studying how they dressed, fixed their hair, conversed, and expressed interests. This observation led me to develop special interests in psychology, acting, and stand-up comedy, as these fields helped me decode social rules. I also turned to animation, where emotional responses are clearly described or exaggerated, making social cues more obvious.

What is the Spectrum?

When we speak of autism as a "spectrum," we acknowledge a complex and diverse neurological reality that extends far beyond simplified categorizations. The Autism Spectrum is not a linear continuum from "mild" to "severe" as was once thought, but rather a multidimensional constellation of traits, abilities, challenges, and experiences that vary widely from person to person. Think of the spectrum as a color wheel rather than a straight line. Each autistic individual has their own unique profile across multiple domains: sensory processing, social communication, movement patterns, interests, cognitive abilities, and executive functioning. One person might have exceptional verbal abilities yet struggle profoundly with sensory overload. Another might communicate minimally through speech but navigate social dynamics with keen observation. A third might excel in pattern recognition while finding motor planning challenging.

This multidimensional understanding helps explain why no two autistic people present exactly alike. The outdated terms "high-functioning" and "low-functioning" fail to capture this complexity: an individual categorized as "high-functioning" based on verbal ability might still experience debilitating sensory sensitivities, while someone deemed "low-functioning" due to communication differences might possess extraordinary talents in other areas.

The spectrum also fluctuates within each individual. An autistic person who appears to manage well in certain environments might struggle tremendously in others. On some days, the resources to maintain social interaction may be abundant; on others, even basic communication might require extraordinary effort. This variability depends on numerous factors including stress levels, sensory environment, energy reserves, and support systems.

It's important to understand that autism is not defined primarily by deficits but by differences in neurology that lead to different ways of experiencing and interacting with the world. These neurological differences are present from birth and remain throughout life. No one grows out of autism. The neurodiversity framework recognizes that "differences are not seen as deficits" and that there is "normal variation in development that forms the basis for neurodiversity/ neurodevelopmental differences." Neurodiversity is described as "the idea that people experience and interact with the world around them in many ways, with no one "right" way of thinking, learning, and behaving, and differences are not deficits." Research supports that "the neurodiversity movement does not face variations in neurological and cognitive development in ASD as deficits but as normal non-pathological human variations" and that "ASD is not identified as a neurocognitive pathological disorder that deviates from the typical, but [...] neurodiversity is described as equivalent to any other human variation, such as ethnicity, gender, or sexual orientation." In fact, a 2020 research by Both and Frost supports the idea that many challenges faced by autistic individuals stem from minority stress and environmental factors rather than the autism itself. Moreover, on the ontological status of autism, the Milton (2012) "double empathy problem" supports the idea that communication and social difficulties in autism may be mutual rather than one-sided deficits.

The autism spectrum also intersects with other aspects of human diversity. Gender significantly impacts how autism presents and is recognized, with girls and women often developing more sophisticated masking strategies that can delay diagnosis. Cultural context shapes both autistic expression and how it is perceived by others. Coexisting conditions such as ADHD, anxiety, or sensory processing differences further influence an individual's experience.

The medical model of autism, which has historically dominated discourse, positions autism primarily as a pathology or deficit to be remediated. However, contemporary neurodiversity perspectives recognize autism as a natural variation in human neurocognitive functioning—different, not lesser. Just as we acknowledge the uniqueness of every neurotypical individual, it is both scientifically accurate and ethically necessary to recognize the distinct neurological profiles of autistic people.

Autism represents a natural variation in human neurology, not a deficit—much like left-handedness, different languages, or biological sex differences. Just as a cello isn't a broken violin, Spanish isn't failed English, and a woman isn't a defective man, autistic brains aren't malfunctioning neurotypical ones —they're distinct operating systems processing the world differently. Like how left-handers struggle with right-handed scissors or Spanish speakers navigate English-speaking environments, autistic people face challenges primarily because the world is designed for neurotypical brains. This isn't pathology; it's the natural cognitive biodiversity that makes human populations resilient and innovative. The difficulty lies not in autism itself, but in the compatibility gaps between different neurotypes trying to interface without proper understanding or accommodation.

Research in neuroimaging and cognitive science has consistently demonstrated that autistic brains show different, not simply deficient, patterns of connectivity, sensory processing, and information integration. These differences lead to diverse manifestations of autistic traits that vary widely between individuals. The assumption that all autistic people should exhibit identical characteristics contradicts both scientific evidence and lived experience.

As long as autism continues to be primarily framed as a medical condition requiring "cure" rather than a neurological difference requiring appropriate support, autistic individuals will continue bearing the disproportionate burden of conforming to arbitrary neurotypical standards. This pathologizing framework not only misrepresents the neurobiological reality of autism but also contributes to psychological harm through the implicit message that an autistic brain is fundamentally broken rather than differently organized. A more scientifically accurate and ethical approach recognizes varied support needs without positioning autism itself as inherently problematic. Neurodevelopmental differences in autism may lead to specific challenges that can qualify as disabilities in certain contexts, just as neurotypical individuals may experience disabilities from various causes.

Therefore, understanding autism as a spectrum means recognizing that each autistic person has a unique profile of strengths and challenges that cannot be reduced to a single label or position on a linear scale. Research notes that "borrowing this concept has led to the misleading idea that autism is a linear scale with profoundly affected individuals at the 'low' end and less affected individuals at the 'high' end" and that "a person with good intellectual and language skills, often known as high-functioning, may nevertheless be profoundly disabled by repetitive behaviors and routines." This nuanced perspective allows us to move beyond simplistic notions of autism as merely "severe" or "mild" toward a more accurate appreciation of neurodivergent humanity in all its complexity.

Unlike legitimate medical distinctions such as Type 1 versus Type 2 diabetes—which have clear physiological definitions and specific treatment protocols—autism "functioning labels" have no consistent medical definition and vary arbitrarily between professionals (Sparrow, 2024). We would never deny insulin to someone who "looks Type 2" or assume someone's diabetes management needs based on their appearance, yet this is precisely what happens with autism support. A student who appears "high-functioning" may lose crucial sensory accommodations and subsequently fail academically—not due to intellectual inability, but because sensory overload prevents them from processing auditory information in an overwhelming classroom environment (Sultan, as cited in Healthline, 2023). This is equivalent to denying insulin to someone based on appearance rather than actual medical need.

If it's common knowledge that each neurotypical individual is unique, why should neurodivergent individuals be expected to exhibit identical profiles? As long as autism spectrum disorder is viewed as a medical condition requiring "cure" instead of a neurological difference requiring individualized support, autistic individuals will continue bearing the disproportionate burden of conforming to arbitrary neurotypical standards. This approach makes them appear inadequate in a world that compares their behaviors to a single neurotype. If a square is the norm, then a triangle or a circle shall be deemed "abnormal"—yet we don't question a diabetic person's legitimacy based on whether they "look" Type 1 or Type 2 during casual conversation. Not to mention, it would be considered "rude" to proclaim that one looks more Type 1 than 2 and vice versa!

So, please, whether you are uncomfortable talking about autism, are on the spectrum, or care for someone on the spectrum, please stop using this "functioning model." Not only does it mean nothing medically speaking, but it does a huge disservice to our community, often stripping us of essential accommodations in the name of our undeserving looks.

I may not look like I am struggling, but I am still on the spectrum. Think about how much effort and energy it takes me to behave the way I do in public. Just like an Olympic athlete, I was not "gifted" with my social performance, it came with decades of practice, failures and "injuries" to look perfectly "normal" during the timed period I interact with you, after which I have to recover. Did Usain Bolt happen to just show up one day, at the Olympics, to take home the Gold? Or did he trained, day after day, week after week, year after year, and allowed himself to recover between trainings to reach this level? Same here, except for a tiny detail: We never get any recognition for our consistent efforts whatsoever. They are just expected. So, we sure make a point in keeping our noise-canceling headphones in public!

The Cognitive Experience of Social Interaction

For many of us, social interaction requires four main simultaneous activities:

1. Consciously analyzing facial expressions, tone, and body language that neurotypicals process automatically

2. Manually filtering irrelevant sensory information that neurotypical brains filter automatically
3. Explicitly reasoning through social rules and expectations without intuitive understanding
4. Managing overwhelming sensory input while attempting to focus on conversation

Research has demonstrated significant differences in how autistic brains process social information compared to neurotypical brains. Social-cognitive neuroscience has identified that brain systems of the medial frontal cortex, temporal cortex, parietal cortex, and reward centers enable mentalizing (understanding others' thoughts and intentions). In autistic individuals, differences in these neural networks can lead to alterations in the spontaneous use of mentalizing abilities and the motivation involved in social interactions.

The processing demands are substantial and multilayered. While neurotypical individuals process social cues implicitly and automatically, autistic individuals must engage in explicit, conscious processing of the same information. This difference is now well documented in literature. Research indicates that autistic individuals show more challenges with implicit social cognition—the automatic, unconscious processing of social cues—than with explicit social cognition tasks that allow for conscious reasoning. Dr. Temple Grandin, a professor with autism, has described this experience as feeling like "an anthropologist on Mars," *An anthropologist on Mars: Seven paradoxical tales.* Knopf. having to explicitly study and decode human social behavior that others understand instinctively. This description resonates with many autistic adults who report exhaustion from the constant mental calculations required during social interactions.

A particularly telling metaphor compares neurotypical and autistic brains to computers running different operating systems with different resource allocations. Autism and

Asperger syndrome: The facts. Oxford University Press.. The neurotypical brain might be like a computer optimized for social processing, with dedicated hardware and automatic background processes that handle social information efficiently, leaving plenty of processing power for other functions.

In contrast, the autistic brain is like a computer with multiple resource-intensive applications running simultaneously. Each social task—interpreting facial expressions, filtering sensory input, analyzing tone of voice, maintaining appropriate body language—functions as a separate demanding application consuming significant processing power. When too many of these "applications" run at once, the system becomes overwhelmed. Basic functions that should be simple—like formulating a verbal response or remembering what you were about to say—begin to lag or freeze entirely as the processing resources are depleted. Eventually, the computer will crash: This would be your autistic shutdown (internal overwhelm leading to withdrawal), or meltdown (external expression of overwhelm leading to self-injury in my case), during which an individual with ASD has lost control of their basic applications. Keep entering input and you'll only delay the restarting process. In other words, stop overwhelming us with words, sounds, light, touch. Any sensory input is adding to the overload. As a woman with ASD, when I "shut down" during social interaction, it's not a matter of unwillingness or lack of skill, but rather a processing overload where even simple cognitive tasks become impossible because all available resources are being consumed by the effort of managing the social situation. At this point in my life, I recognize when I am approaching this point, and simply close the extra running applications... In other terms, I remove myself from the social situation until my active memory reaches an acceptable running level. In my book, no one is worth an autistic meltdown or shutdown, and the recovery that comes with it.

Consider the sensory aspects as well. Many researchers, including Kovarski et al. (2017), recognize that "a mismatch in sensory abilities across individuals can lead to difficulties on a social, i.e., interpersonal level and vice versa". This interrelationship between sensory processing and social interaction creates additional cognitive burdens. While attempting to process and respond to social information, autistic individuals must simultaneously manage potential sensory overload from background noises, lighting, or tactile sensations that neurotypical brains automatically filter out.

Studies found that "individuals with ASD often experience intense sensory processing, which makes it difficult for them to adapt to the changing sensory environment" and that "communication involves multiple social cues that are often combined, requiring individuals to process multiple sensory modalities simultaneously." What does that represent exactly? Just picture trying to have a conversation while simultaneously monitoring your facial expressions for appropriateness, analyzing the other person's tone for hidden meanings, consciously maintaining eye contact (but not too much), trying to filter out the sound of air conditioning, distant conversations, and traffic outside, remembering social rules about turn taking in conversation, and calculating when to nod or make affirmative sounds. For an individual with autism, this experience is not sporadic—it is continuous. This multitasking daily task represents a tremendous allocation of cognitive resources that neurotypical individuals can dedicate to other aspects of interaction, such as forming deeper connections or expressing themselves more freely.

Social Interactions: Cognitive Experiences with Limited Social Energy Resources

Picture entering a room, already overwhelmed by unfiltered sensory input from lights and sounds, while simultaneously having to analyze the social context, determine which of your prepared "masks" is appropriate, and select the right scripted responses for each interaction. This mental calculation happens continuously as you move through environments and encounter different people: professional approachable mask with your coworkers, professional formal mask with your boss, casual formal mask with acquaintances (by the way, when do they enter your friend's circle?), casual informal mask with your friends while making sure you match their interests, casual formal with the lady who just bumped into you at Starbucks... A day constantly assessing the context and interactions, switching from one mask to another, while doing everything else! Just think about the number of social contexts you encounter on a regular basis and how much energy it would cost you if you had to solve a hard equation on the fly for each context and individual interaction: Close family circle, building acquaintances in the elevator, holding the door leading to the street, driving or walking your kids to school (parents, teachers, etc.), grabbing a cup of coffee on the go, meeting with clients, then meeting with coworkers, work in your cubicle with colleagues popping up here and there for a "quick" something (question, chitchat, venting session, request), all while trying to get your work done.

The cost of masking is severe and cumulative. It inevitably leads to shutdowns, meltdowns or burnouts which means having to resign from jobs or studies, withdraw from relationships, and lose touch with friends due to depleted energy resources. When this happens, social judgment follows: "She's a quitter," "She's a loser," "She couldn't handle the pressure," "She thought she was so smart," "She doesn't care," "She's not a good friend." This creates a devastating cycle when recovery from burnout is complicated by having to also recover socially from others' negative judgments and rejection.

This represents the fundamental dilemma of masking: It is the solution for social acceptance, the source of profound exhaustion and the reason why people minimize the diagnosis: Masking becomes so effective that even after diagnosis, autistic individuals face disbelief: "I don't think you are [autistic], because you don't look like it", or "You're fine, you don't look like it" or "I'm not worried for you, you'll be fine", and the repulsive: "Do you really want to reduce yourself to a label? You could be so much more if you didn't make excuses..." The painful irony is that we "don't look autistic" precisely because we've mastered masking as a survival strategy, to make everyone else comfortable in our presence, but it's also destroying us. Not only is it depleting our energy level, but it is erasing our own identity that we must constantly suppress.

The Hidden Cost: When Social Effort Goes Unrecognized

What neurotypical individuals may not understand is that, for us, social interactions are never automatic or effortless. This complex exercise demands simultaneous collection, analysis, and interpretation of data from all senses. Mistakes in this process can be harshly penalized by society, resulting in workplace rejection, damaged reputation, character assassination, or relationships loss. The cruel paradox is that despite these extraordinary efforts, as autistic individuals, we rarely receive validation for our social exertion. Instead, we face criticism when we make mistakes, with little forgiveness offered for social missteps. Not to mention the additional pressure that the most recent culture of cancelation brings: One social faux pas and you can be publicly taken down, criticized and "stoned" on social media.

Another terrible consequence of "hiding" is the energy dedicated to masking that literally takes away from developing one's authentic identity, self-respect, and pride. Precious time that should be spent on cultivating special interests or personal growth is consumed by suppressing one's true self out of shame. Even outside social hours, recovery becomes the only focus, leaving little energy to simply exist as oneself —to enjoy preferred activities or environments without exhaustion.

For those who also experience sensory-related conditions like sensory overload-induced migraines, recovery might mean isolating in a dark room with ice packs, unable to tolerate any noise or light. Imagine living this cycle day after day, week after week, even on vacation. As energy reserves diminish and recovery becomes increasingly difficult, having to solve the social equations that still mean nothing to you, repeatedly, daily, while still expected to perform at school, work, and in your relationships. It becomes overwhelming, if not impossible: Focus on everything at the same time, multitasking as a lifestyle, and being expected to deliver each and every time.

This explains why social anxiety, generalized anxiety disorder, depression, burn out and PTSD are common byproducts of being on the spectrum while attempting to meet neurotypical standards. The sensory processing differences compound these challenges: while trying to identify all the social data from interactions, an autistic brain cannot filter irrelevant sensory information that neurotypical brains remove automatically such as background noises. The ambulance passing by, cars driving, wind blowing through leaves, nearby conversations, background music, or air conditioning blowing through a vent are all processed with equal intensity as the primary social exchange. In fact, I cannot count the number of times I ask someone to repeat themselves in a day which is aggravating for everyone.

Imagine taking your SAT exam standing up at a bar, surrounded by overwhelming distractions like glass clinking, chatter, laughter, football games on TVs, live music, and the occasional drunk tapping your shoulder to tell you their last joke. Yet, you are still expected to provide an appropriate response in a timely manner. Day after day, you would show up for a different exam in the same conditions. This exhausting process, repeated throughout life, explains why many autistic people eventually resort to basic scripted interactions out of sheer survival instinct.

The final heartbreak comes when disclosing a diagnosis to someone important in our life, only to hear: "You don't look like it" or "Don't let people put a label on you." These dismissive responses leave us feeling invalidated, unappreciated, and fundamentally misunderstood, with little to no hope of getting some kind of help or basic understanding from anyone.

So next time you feel compelled to tell someone on the spectrum that they don't look like it or come up with a blanket statement such as "People on the spectrum are not social," please realize that isolation is, for most of us, our only left recovery mechanism. It's depressing because we crave social connections like everyone else. Our brain is just not naturally equipped for them, but our heart is. And we sure feel intensely the pain of isolation.

The simple fact that we share our diagnosis with you is our attempt to connect with you, to show you that you are indeed important enough in our life that we feel compelled to share a part of our true self with you. Its denial is extremely painful and even more isolating. So, please, ask yourself: if you were disclosing autism or another condition you may have to someone who would question or reject it, why would you ever attempt to open up again about it?

The Core Misunderstanding

The fundamental misunderstanding isn't about whether autistic people want social connection, many of us desperately do. It's about recognizing that the neurological equipment for socializing works differently, imposing significant cognitive and energy costs that necessitate careful management of social resources.

This difference has been supported by numerous studies in social neuroscience. Rather than demonstrating "social skills deficits," research suggests that we may possess "a distinct mode of social interaction style". This perspective shifts the narrative from one of deficit to one of difference, a crucial distinction for understanding autism.

Sure, we walk upside down on a planet in comparison to most people, but isn't the pull of gravity designed to secure all of us on the planet to begin with? And what if upside down was the norm? A perspective down up instead of up to down sure helps uncover details missed by the latter. While autistic and neurotypical individuals may navigate the social world differently, as if walking from opposite orientations, both are operating within the same fundamental reality governed by the same physical laws. The capacity for human connection exists for both, even if the approach differs dramatically.

In that perspective, challenging the assumption of what constitutes "normal" seems perfectly relevant: Didn't we used to think Earth was flat? Accepting the fact that it is indeed a sphere means the concept of "up" and "down" are merely relative positional constructs, not absolute truths. In space, there is no universal "up" or "down"—these orientations only have meaning relative to a gravitational reference point. Similarly, in neurocognitive terms, there is no objectively "correct" way to process social information.

Who determined which orientation of cognitive processing is "standard" and which is "atypical"? This determination largely stems from statistical prevalence rather than functional superiority. Neuroimaging studies have confirmed that autistic and neurotypical brains process social information using different neural pathways and resource allocations, not inherently better or worse ones. If the majority of humans suddenly processed information like us, with heightened detail perception and pattern recognition but increased demands on executive function during social processing, then the current neurotypical processing style would be considered atypical and potentially disadvantageous in certain contexts.

Normalcy is not an objective neurological truth, but a statistical construct based on an assumed majority experience. This is supported by research showing that we often demonstrate superior abilities in specific cognitive domains, including pattern recognition, detail orientation, and logical reasoning—advantages that would be considered "normal" in a predominantly autistic population. The field of neurodiversity acknowledges this reality: different cognitive styles offer unique advantages and challenges depending on environmental demands and social contexts.

Finally, and perhaps most profound, is the suggestion that the autistic perspective offers unique value precisely because it differs from the typical orientation. By viewing the world from a different angle, "down up instead of up to down," we often notice patterns, details, inconsistencies, and possibilities that remain invisible to those processing information in the conventional manner. Many scientific and artistic breakthroughs throughout history have come from individuals thought to have been on the autism spectrum, whose different perceptual orientation allowed them to see what others missed.

Therefore, we need to move beyond tolerance of neurodiversity toward genuine appreciation. The autistic mind isn't merely a defective version of the neurotypical mind —it's an alternative cognitive orientation that contributes valuable perspectives precisely because of its difference.

Just as astronomers gain new insights by viewing celestial bodies from different angles, humanity benefits from the full spectrum of neurological orientations.

Dr. Damian Milton's "double empathy problem" provides further context for this understanding. This theory proposes that the social communication difficulties between autistic and non-autistic people are bidirectional, stemming from different ways of experiencing and understanding the world. It's not simply that autistic people lack understanding of neurotypical social norms; neurotypical people equally struggle to understand autistic ways of being.

Evidence supports this reciprocal view. Studies show that we experience high interactional rapport when communicating with other autistic people, and external observers can detect this comfort. Both autistic and non-autistic observers show similar patterns in how they rate the rapport of autistic, non-autistic, and mixed pairs. In fact, Autistic people share information with other autistic people as effectively as non-autistic people do with other non-autistic people, but information sharing is significantly poorer in mixed neurotype chains, accompanied by significantly poorer self-rated interactional rapport. The social difficulties autistic individuals experience when interacting with non-autistic individuals may at least partly be attributed to a mismatch in neurotype, suggesting that social difficulties for autistic people may be relational in nature, rather than an individual impairment. This contradicts the idea that autistic individuals universally struggle with social connection—rather, the difficulty arises from the mismatch between different neurotypes.

The limited energy resources for social interaction are particularly relevant here. Each social encounter depletes a finite reserve of cognitive and emotional energy. When this reserve is exhausted, we may experience shutdown or meltdown—not because we don't value social connection, but because the cognitive demands have exceeded available resources. This isn't asocial behavior; it is strategic social engagement based on different neurological constraints. Understanding this distinction is crucial for creating more inclusive environments and relationships that accommodate neurodivergent social needs.

Parents, educators, partners, and clinicians who grasp this fundamental aspect of autism can adjust their expectations and approach. Instead of perceiving withdrawal, or recovery, as rejection or lack of interest, they can recognize it as necessary energy conservation and management. Instead of pushing for more socialization, they can focus on creating quality interactions with lower cognitive demands.

The implications extend beyond individual relationships to how we structure educational and clinical interventions. Rather than focusing exclusively on teaching autistic individuals to adapt to neurotypical social norms—which incurs tremendous cognitive costs—we might also consider how environments and expectations can be modified to reduce unnecessary social processing demands. By respecting these different neurological constraints and working with them rather than against them, we could create the possibility for meaningful connections across neurological differences, connections that honor the authentic autistic experience rather than demanding unsustainable masking.

***

DIAGNOSTIC BIAS AND GENDERED ASSUMPTIONS

Common Myths About Autism

The most pervasive myth about autism is that it manifests as a set of obvious external behaviors that follow the classic male presentation: poor eye contact, obsessive interests in mechanical systems or numbers, social awkwardness, and limited emotional expression. This cliche ignores many less visible traits, such as auditory processing differences and alexithymia, revealing the broad range of autistic internal experiences. Those stereotypes keep clinicians from looking beyond surface behaviors.

Before exploring these experiences, it's crucial to understand that, as autistic women, we employ three adaptive strategies. We may or may not be aware of them, but one thing is certain: if we manage to go unnoticed, it's because of the active deployment of one of those:

- Compensation or learning strategies for social situations (rehearsing a joke before a meeting)
- Masking/Camouflaging or hiding autistic traits to appear neurotypical
- Assimilation or changing behaviors to fit social norms

These strategies are often used together, making autism nearly invisible even to medical professionals. To spot masking, clinicians can look for discrepancies between a woman's reported and observed behaviors. For example, signs might include a delay in emotional responses, inconsistent eye contact, or stress responses such as fatigue or anxiety after social interactions. Medical professionals should consider asking questions about the individual's social preparation habits (even in a form to be filled out before an appointment), such as:

- Do you find yourself rehearsing conversations before or after social interactions?
- Do you feel exhausted after social engagements?
- Do you find group conversations and dynamics difficult?

These insights can help recognize masking behaviors and provide a better understanding of the individual's condition.

When I told my physician I was autistic and suggested my migraines could be related to sensory overloads, she dismissed me, citing my eye contact and relationships as proof I couldn't be autistic. This reflects a broader pattern of gendered diagnostic scripts where women's social abilities are often used to question their autism diagnosis. According to Research by Ratto et al. (2018), the tendency to interpret female sociality as incompatible with autism can result in overlooked or misdiagnosed ASD cases in women. I felt invalidated and exhausted from the effort to appear "normal." Her ignorance led me to seek another doctor since she clearly couldn't treat my needs.

A groundbreaking study by Hull et al. (2020) found that autistic females engage in significantly more camouflaging behaviors than males. The study used "a newly developed self-reported measure of camouflaging (Camouflaging Autistic Traits Questionnaire) in an online survey to measure gender differences in autistic (n = 306) and non-autistic adults (n = 472) without intellectual disability for the first time.

Controlling for age and autistic-like traits, an interaction between gender and diagnostic status was found: autistic females demonstrated higher total camouflaging scores than autistic males (partial η^2 = 0.08), but there was no camouflaging gender difference for non-autistic people." In the article Why Many Autistic Girls Are Overlooked by Beth Arky, Gabriela Fiszbein explains that girls with autism are "sometimes better at controlling their behavior in public" and may have "learned early on to smile or make eye contact," leading to missed diagnoses.

When taking the Camouflaging Autistic Traits Questionnaire, women and girl's answers validated that social masking is not absent in autistic females but is certainly more sophisticated and exhausting. The previously mentioned groundbreaking study found that "autistic adult females endorse higher masking and assimilation as compared to males. Based on the CAT-Q, "Autistic females and non-binary and gender-diverse Autistic people typically score higher than Autistic males in camouflaging behaviors." Often underestimated, the CAT-Q is indeed a valuable tool in clinical settings: it can help clinicians identify camouflaging behaviors that are often overlooked. By using this questionnaire, healthcare practitioners can achieve a more accurate understanding of autistic women's experiences, leading to better-informed diagnostic and treatment decisions. You may check the questionnaire yourself, and you will see that relying on "typical" objective masculine traits, such as lack of eye contact, and "obvious" autistic behaviors, without any insight on internal processes, will almost always miss female autistic key signs.

Social Performances: Females with ASD vs Females without ASD

As females with ASD, we do not fit the stereotype that doctors expect. The difference between my social performance and the neurotypical social experience is as simple as the difference between two students scoring excellent on a prepared standardized test. Student 1 understood, learned and applied the concepts, while Student 2 relied solely on the formulation and patterns of the questions and their possible answers to look for the context cues that will hint them toward the desired approach or answer. In fact, Student 2 never learned or understood the course.

For example, based on my observation of the behaviors of people perceived as "kind" and "polite," I know that when something "bad" happens to someone, I am expected to say that "I am sorry." The reality is that I would not typically feel compelled to say anything, not because I don't care or don't feel for them, but because expressing that "I am sorry" does not mean anything to me in this context. Seriously, what am I sorry for?... If someone break their leg and I was not personally involved in the event leading to a broken leg? Now, apologizing for accidentally bumping into someone makes perfect sense to me.

I have also managed to maintain eye contact through a form of assimilation, by suppressing my natural communication style from a young age under societal pressure. In addition, I developed compensation strategies by cultivating socially acceptable interests such as literature and psychology, while masking my intense engagement with these topics. Outwardly, I may appear emotionally responsive, but this is often the result of carefully orchestrated compensation and masking.

I used to rely heavily on learned scripts, actively suppressing authentic reactions to mimic neurotypical behaviors. I would often apply the wrong script, not having fully identified the required conditions for an adequate social response in a particular situation. In fact, I often struggled to understand fiction, frequently missing emotional cues implied by lengthy physical descriptions. Novels were often extremely confusing and intellectually draining to me. This is why I tend to rely more on non-fiction, which is more tangible and accessible to me.

My autistic mannerisms were hidden behind years of compensation strategies to navigate social situations. Depending on context, I often suppressed my core autistic self-regulation needs to meet expectations from family and friends. At the end of each day, I was exhausted, desperately needing solitude to recuperate from the constant demands of performance. Being alone was not a reflection of what some saw as "my autistic personality," it was a biological need like sleeping is essential for recovery.

Misogyny in Medicine: The Enduring Impact on Autism Diagnosis

Healthcare professionals often misinterpret autistic traits in women as personality disorders, anxiety, depression, or even attention-seeking behavior. Autistic women like me end up in inappropriate, therefore inefficient, treatments for years, wasting precious time to get the help they need, eroding further their self-esteem and mental health. A study found that "one in four autistic adults, and one in three autistic women, reported at least one psychiatric diagnosis, obtained prior to being diagnosed with autism, that was perceived as a misdiagnosis." In other terms, about 33% of women's ASD diagnoses are initially missed. And they are often overlooked for years. In fact, an Italian study found that "75.4% received their ASD diagnosis average eight years later than the first evaluation by mental health services" and that "females were less likely to be correctly diagnosed and more likely to be misdiagnosed at first evaluation than men." In 2025, how is this even possible? Such massive medical overlook is just unacceptable. This critical gap in understanding autism in women and intersectional communities requires urgent attention from the medical community, with the implementation of multidisciplinary assessments that promote at least gender-sensitive training for clinicians, ideally with a cultural component as well since social behaviors are also influenced by culture. By incorporating diverse expertise from neurologists, psychologists, and gender studies specialists, healthcare systems can develop a more holistic understanding of autism in women and less represented communities. Additionally, training programs that emphasize recognizing gender-specific presentations of autism can empower future clinicians to improve diagnostic accuracy and patient outcomes. All the practical steps previously identified and taken to properly identify males should be covered, offering females the same level of diagnostic accuracy, followed by proper care.

After describing my sensory sensitivities, my psychiatrist dismissed me as overly sensitive and diagnosed me with Generalized Anxiety Disorder. Later, with an ASD diagnosis, I learned that accommodations for sensory processing would have been more appropriate than only anxiety treatment.

The persistence of misogynistic approaches in medicine and psychiatry continues to shape how practitioners approach diagnosis and treatment, in particular for conditions like autism that have been historically studied through a male-centric lens.

The Ghost of Freud in Modern Practice

Despite being largely discredited in many scientific circles, Freudian theories still haunt medical and psychiatric education, including in the United States, parts of Latin America, and some European nations. Meanwhile, countries like Sweden, Norway, and increasingly the UK have drastically reduced or eliminated Freudian psychoanalysis from their main medical curriculum, recognizing its lack of empirical support and problematic gendered assumptions.

When medical students are still taught Freudian concepts,

even in a historical context, without sufficient critical analysis of their misogynistic foundations, these ideas can subtly influence clinical reasoning. To foster analytical skills and awareness of bias, educators should encourage students to critically examine these historical theories, considering their ongoing impact on current practice. Freud's theories pathologized women's bodies and minds, suggesting that psychological distress stemmed from women's reproductive anatomy, like the infamous 'wandering uterus' concept that evolved into 'hysteria', rather than legitimate neurological differences or responses to trauma and societal pressures. As Dr. Andrea Tone and Mary Kaziol (2018) note in their research on gender bias in medical education: "The disproportionate use of lobotomies and tranquilizers by doctors as therapies for female patients exemplify how gender bias has shaped twentieth-century medicine" and "most lobotomized patients were women, although most institutionalized patients at the time were men."

From Hysteria to Modern Misdiagnosis

The etymology of "hysteria" itself reveals the deeply rooted gender bias in medicine. This pejorative term is indeed derived from the Greek word for uterus (hystera). Therefore, it implies the offensive concept according to which psychological disturbances are intrinsically linked to female reproductive organs. In other terms, psychological issues are a female problem. While we no longer officially diagnose "hysteria," its derivative adjective, hysterical, is still used daily to refer to an emotional feminine reaction or behavior. And its legacy continues in how women's health concerns are often dismissed as psychosomatic or emotional rather than physiological or neurological.

This bias manifests particularly strongly in the diagnosis of conditions like autism. When women present with autistic characteristics, their experiences are frequently reframed as anxiety, depression, or personality disorders—modern incarnations of 'hysteria' that locate the problem within women's presumed emotional instability rather than in neurological differences.

A study by Krahn and Fenton (2012) critiques Baron-Cohen's "extreme male brain theory" and argues that it is misled by an unpersuasive gendering of certain capacities or aptitudes in the human population" and "this may inadvertently favor boys in diagnosing children with Autism Spectrum Disorders with "serious consequences for treatment and services for girls (and women) on the Autism Spectrum. In fact, a study found that women waited an average of 10 years longer than men to receive an autism diagnosis after initially seeking help, with females showing a significantly greater delay in referral to mental health services and significantly higher age at diagnosis compared to males... So much for early detection and intervention! Some medical professionals even believe that a female should present high levels of testosterone to be diagnosed with autism, thanks to the "extreme male brain" theory. In this perspective, I guess I never was "hairy" enough to be considered anywhere close to "the spectrum." Clearly, gender bias in diagnostic practice continues to reflect historical assumptions about women's psychological makeup that can be traced directly to 19th and early 20th century psychiatric theories. Sadly, this is 2025, just about time for everyone to update their textbooks. Let's finally level up the field for girls and women and consider this data from Organization for Autism Research a starting point:

- Only 8% of girls with autism are diagnosed before age 6 versus 25% for boys
- 50% of boys with autism are diagnosed before age 11, versus only 20% of females

The "Refrigerator Mother" Theory and its Modern Echoes

One of the most damaging misogynistic theories in autism's

history was Leo Kanner's and later Bruno Bettelheim's promotion of the "refrigerator mother" hypothesis in his 1943 and 1949 papers. This theory blamed autism on mothers for supposedly being cold, unloving, and detached, effectively holding women responsible for their children's neurodevelopmental conditions. Although officially debunked, this idea persists in subtle critiques, such as "over-coddling" or "helicopter parenting." Social media also perpetuates mothers' guilt with hashtags like #mommyblame.

Mothers of autistic children, particularly those who themselves display autistic traits, still report being scrutinized for their parenting and interaction styles by medical professionals. No longer directly accused of causing autism, their behaviors are suggested as "exacerbating" symptoms or "enabling" their children's autistic behaviors.

McDonnell and DeLucia (2019) observed in their research on maternal blame in developmental conditions that, even though formally rejected, the refrigerator mother theory continues to receive scrutiny "on maternal interaction styles in comparison to paternal contributions, particularly when mothers themselves exhibit traits that diverge from neurotypical social norms." Even more disturbing, when comparing Kanner's case studies with case records of Kanner's patients to understand the origin of "the so-called 'refrigerator mother' caricature" Eyal (2019) found that Leo Kanner engaged in selective reporting when developing his characterization of autism families. Despite encountering autistic patients whose parents did not match his preconceived notions, Kanner chose not to include these cases in his published work. This selective publication pattern suggests that Kanner's influential description of the "autistic parent" was shaped by confirmation bias rather than comprehensive clinical observation. The lasting impact of this biased representation continues to affect autism recognition today, as it created a persistent association between autism and upper-class, highly educated families, and cold mothers while simultaneously making it more difficult to identify autism in children from families that don't fit this stereotypical profile.

Female Clinicians and Internalized Misogyny

Perhaps most insidiously, female practitioners are not immune to perpetuating these biases. Having been educated in systems designed by and for men, and having succeeded within those systems, many female clinicians have internalized the same biases that would disadvantage them as patients. Thanks, ladies!

The Cycle of Medical Misogyny: When Female Physicians Perpetuate Gender Bias in Autism Diagnosis

In the course of my life, consulting medical practitioners, I often noticed that female physicians or specialists reproduced misogynistic diagnostic approaches toward autistic women. Those strange behaviors reflect a sociological pattern where marginalized individuals sometimes enforce discriminatory systems more rigorously than their privileged counterparts. This paradoxical behavior stems from several interconnected psychological and institutional factors.

Female physicians undergo medical training in systems designed by and for men. Clinical diagnostic frameworks overwhelmingly reflect male presentation of conditions. According to sociologist Pierre Bourdieu, this "symbolic violence" subjects its victims to an insidious discriminatory system that they come to accept and reproduce, marginalizing their peers. In medicine, this could manifest as female physicians sometimes becoming stricter adherents to male-centric diagnostic criteria than their male colleagues. In addition to Pierre Bourdieu's symbolic violence, the Queen Bee Phenomenon (Derks et al., 2016) would also suggest that women in male-dominated fields like medicine distance themselves from other women and adopt masculine norms to succeed.

To address this issue, it is important to encourage self-assessment among healthcare practitioners. By reflecting on their own potential biases and understanding how institutional culture shapes diagnostic habits, practitioners can cultivate greater self-awareness. This enhanced understanding can significantly contribute to professional growth and improve diagnostic accuracy, ultimately benefiting both physicians and their patients. Let's add another layer of interiorized discrimination with the notions of Cognitive Dissonance and Defensive Attribution: for female physicians who have succeeded in medicine despite gender barriers, acknowledging gender bias in diagnostic criteria creates cognitive dissonance, particularly if they've internalized the belief in medical objectivity.

Understanding how medical professionals respond to evidence of bias in their field requires consideration of the psychological mechanisms that protect professional identity. When individuals have invested significantly in a system and achieved success within it, challenges to that system's fairness can create substantial psychological tension. The cognitive dissonance theory (Festinger, 1957) explains that such conflicts between belief and evidence motivate individuals to reduce discomfort through various cognitive strategies. This dissonance could become particularly acute when female physicians encounter potentially autistic women whose experiences might mirror unrecognized aspects of their own neurodivergence. Additionally, defensive attribution theory (Shaver, 1970) suggests that people tend to assign responsibility for negative outcomes in ways that maintain psychological distance from those affected, particularly when the alternative might implicate systems they value or depend upon.

Drawing on these theories of cognitive dissonance (Festinger, 1957) and defensive attribution (Shaver, 1970). we can theorize that female physicians who have succeeded despite gender barriers may experience psychological conflicts when confronting evidence of gender bias in diagnostic practices

"The aim is not to criticize female medical practitioners, but to encourage reflection that can break the cycle. This dynamic is not unique to autism and has parallels in other historical contexts where members of marginalized groups have enforced existing systems. Research on the anti-suffrage movement demonstrates that some women actively opposed voting rights for women, often because they had found ways to exercise influence within existing patriarchal structures and feared that political changes might undermine their established positions (Marshall, 1997). This pattern reflects what Fanon (1952/2008) identified in colonial contexts—the tendency for those who achieve success within oppressive systems to become psychologically invested in maintaining those systems, having internalized the dominant group's values and worldview."

I suffered from severe jaw pain for two years, lost mouth opening and weight, yet a maxillofacial surgeon insisted my symptoms were mostly psychological, suggesting I start practicing yoga, "smelling the roses," and breathing exercises. Despite my research and suggestions, another doctor prioritized therapy for suspected eating disorders and an inability to manage my stress over physical causes. Finally, a social worker I consulted to express my frustration with the medical system and my debilitating pain referred me to Miami School of Medicine, where I was diagnosed with a dislocated jaw requiring surgery within 5 minutes. I had lost about 60% of my mouth opening and my jaw was clearly sliding left when open... by about an inch. Turns out my "eating disorder" and panel of psychological issues were fixed by a single surgery out of which I was immediately able to chew my food, sleep, and manage my "stress"... Luckily for me, it happened in 2020, I suppose fifty years prior my life-altering surgery would have been a lobotomy!

The question haunted me: how many men would endure years of excruciating pain and obvious symptoms without doctors investigating real, physical causes such as a jaw injury? As a woman, and especially one with an ASD diagnosis, I had to fight to be heard, spending countless hours looking up my symptoms to find a specialist willing to listen and investigate the source of my pain instead of discounting it because of both my gender and neurology.

Toward Gender-Inclusive Medical Practice

Recognition of this cycle provides pathways to intervention. Based on established principles of bias reduction in medical education and the psychological theories discussed above, we can theorize that when medical training explicitly addresses gender bias in diagnostic criteria and creates supportive environments for self-reflection, physicians may become more accurate in identifying autism across gender presentations.

The key insight from this theoretical framework is that breaking the cycle of gender bias in autism diagnosis requires acknowledging and addressing systemic issues embedded in medical practices. These must be exposed, discussed, and addressed at institutional levels, rather than focusing solely on individual practitioners. Female physicians may not be inherently more biased than male colleagues; rather, they may face unique psychological pressures within systems that have historically devalued both women and neurodivergent presentations.

Impact on Autism Diagnosis in Women

These persistent frameworks have concrete consequences for autistic women: Diagnostic overshadowing occurs when women's autistic traits are attributed to their gender or to other conditions. Women struggling with sensory overload or communication differences may be reframed as "attention-seeking," "self-centered," or "manipulative," echoing historical views of women as inherently emotionally unstable.

Higher diagnostic thresholds are applied for women: Research by Dworzynski et al. (2012) found that girls needed to have more severe symptoms or additional problems to receive an autism diagnosis compared to boys with similar underlying autistic traits. The tendency to view autism through a male-typical lens means that female-typical manifestations (such as special interests in literature or psychology rather than mechanical systems) are overlooked, leading to a lack of recognition for different manifestations.

Research on late-diagnosed autistic women reveals the ongoing impact of these biased frameworks. Bargiela et al. (2016) documented how diagnostic practices continue to be shaped by gendered assumptions about behavior and emotional expression, contributing to delayed or missed diagnoses in women.

Breaking the Cycle

Progress in correcting these historical errors requires multiple simultaneous approaches that involve each one of us.

Medical professionals should conduct a critical examination of medical education. Medical and psychiatric curricula need a thorough review to identify and eliminate lingering misogynistic frameworks. Representation in research should be reevaluated to include diverse participants across genders and presentations. Medical institutions need to recognize how misogynistic approaches have harmed women by delaying or preventing proper diagnosis and support.

Autistic female voices must be heard, including our lived experiences of the world, our sensory processes, and our feelings and emotions. The cycle will not be broken unless the diagnostic criteria and clinical understanding of female ASD are based on the actual experiences of females with ASD. Who else could possibly articulate how we experience the world?

To finish, the path forward requires not just adding knowledge about female autism presentations but actively unlearning deeply embedded misogynistic assumptions that have shaped medical practice for centuries. Only then can we develop truly gender-inclusive approaches to understanding and supporting autistic individuals across the spectrum of gender and presentation.

Changes if diagnostic tools were created from women lived experiences

One psychiatrist mentioned that I was "too articulate" to be autistic. My need for routine was persistently framed as obsessive-compulsive. Each misdiagnosis added layers of self-doubt, lowering my self-esteem, increasing my shame, and perpetuating inappropriate treatments, including the prescription of an antidepressant under which I started a self-injury behavior I never presented before (or after stopping this medication). I would later learn that this medication had been discontinued after getting stitches for cutting my left wrist was later removed from the market. Let's just say that with proper early diagnose, I could probably have avoided sexual, emotional and physical abuse, a couple of stitches, my parents and family members scrutinizing and vilifying some of my self-regulating behaviors, pushing me to hide and isolate myself further... Leading to easier victimization.

Current diagnostic tools primarily reflect observable behaviors identified in studies of autistic boys and men, missing the nuanced presentation common in women and girls.

During my first assessment, the clinician asked about my special interests. When I mentioned my passion for stop-motion animation and Tim Burton, she said that it didn't count because it wasn't "unusual" enough. She didn't ask additional details about that interest, such as "Are you watching his movies often or is this more than just a passion with daily rituals?"... such as repeating the same couple of frames for hours to soothe my mind. This repetitive frame-rewind can be understood as a "self-regulation stimming behavior," highlighting its relevance for those assessing autistic traits. I also used to seek information on anything related to Tim Burton or stop-motion animation and watched Wallace & Gromit or Mary & Max (written and directed by Adam Elliot) for hours. Clearly, the assessment tools were not designed to capture the autistic nature of my interests because they happened to be in a socially acceptable domain.

Lai et al. (2015) demonstrated that current gold-standard diagnostic tools show gender biases in sensitivity. Their research found that the same level of autistic traits may lead to a diagnosis in males but be missed in females, suggesting that different thresholds or additional assessment criteria may be needed for accurately identifying autism across genders, particularly with tools like ADOS and ADI-R.

If diagnostic tools were built from our experiences, they would ask different questions. Instead of "Do you make appropriate eye contact?" they might ask, "How do you feel when maintaining eye contact, and what strategies do you use?" Rather than "Do you have friends?" they would also ask, "How do you feel after socializing?" "Do you need alone time between most social interactions?" They would explore how we've learned to compensate for social challenges, mask our autistic traits, and assimilate by changing core behaviors to fit neurotypical expectations. They would recognize our intense interests even when they're in stereotypically female domains, and understand that our communication challenges might be hidden behind compensation strategies, such as learned scripts and careful observation. They would capture the internal experience of autism, not just its external presentation.

It is time not only to question established narratives about autism, but also to take direct action: challenge missed or delayed diagnoses, advocate for updated diagnostic tools that reflect diverse female experiences, and actively promote a more inclusive and accurate understanding of autism in all settings.

A woman sitting by came to me after I mentioned my Autism diagnosis and research on social skills to a friend. "You've just described my daughter perfectly," she said. "She's 14 and struggling with anxiety and depression, but the psychologist dismissed autism because she has friends and makes eye contact." I gave her resources on how autism presents in girls, in particular Tony Attwood, and encouraged her to seek a specialist who understands female autism. Six months later, she emailed me: Her daughter had received an autism diagnosis and was finally getting appropriate support. "For the first time, my daughter feels understood rather than broken." I could not help but wonder what my life would have been with a diagnosis at fourteen: So much time lost seeking help, wondering, giving up on studies, social life, and life itself, moving away from the pain to different cities, then regions, then country. Literally living and fleeing when the shame became so unbearable that I could not stand being seen by a single known soul. What a waste of my time, career, studies, energy, and relationships. A waste that almost cost me my life. The truth is, autism misdiagnosis and delayed diagnosis take away our mental health, our physical health, and sadly, still too often, our lives and those of our loved ones.

Loomes et al. (2017) conducted a meta-analysis revealing that the true male-to-female ratio in autism is likely closer to 3:1 rather than the previously estimated 4:1 or higher, suggesting that diagnostic biases contribute significantly to the under-identification of autistic females. This research implies that thousands of women and girls remain undiagnosed and unsupported.

If you are a potentially autistic woman, parent, educator, or clinician: demand that diagnostic approaches move beyond stereotypes. Challenge dismissal based on social success or compensation strategies, such as maintaining eye contact or having friends. Insist on thorough, individualized assessments, and advocate for further education among professionals about female autism. Listen deeply to autistic women's voices and stop dismissing their lived realities. Above all, know that neurodivergence is not a sign of brokenness— join the effort to replace forced normalization with genuine understanding and accommodation. Your voice and action can help ensure that no more women are left unsupported, misunderstood, or misdiagnosed.

***

CHILDHOOD CLUES AND MISSED MOMENTS

I was five years old, standing frozen in the doorway of a classmate's birthday party. The noise was unbearable and confusing: children laughing, music blaring, movement everywhere as children tried to hit a piñata, harsh fluorescent lights reflecting off colorful decorations, the elastic band of the birthday hat scratching my neck and pinching my ears. Her mother gave me a gentle push forward to enter the room, but my feet wouldn't move. My heart raced and I ran away, removing the pointy cardboard hat and throwing it on the way. It was a moment that would later reflect a pattern—a visceral sensory overload starkly mirrored in the diagnostic process. These early signs of sensory sensitivities and disorientation in social situations often get misinterpreted or overlooked as mere shyness, rather than potential indicators of autism. This foreshadows the later discussion on how such experiences contribute to the critical gaps in understanding autism in women that persist into adulthood.

"She's just shy, and it's her first birthday party," my mother explained to the other parents. "She'll warm up."

But I didn't warm up and spent the next hour in a corner trying to make sense of the children playing. Why were they having fun? How? I just couldn't comprehend their thrill in all this confusion. What could possibly make their social interactions so effortless? How were they not irritated by all those sounds? They were not even covering their ears! When the time came for musical chairs, I participated mechanically, following the rules perfectly, until I was the last one standing. Rather than celebrating my win, I retreated to my corner, overwhelmed by the fact that I suddenly became the center of attention. That was the last thing I needed.

"She's so sensitive," the adults whispered. "Such a little perfectionist."

No one, not even me, had the words to explain what was really happening: I was an autistic girl overwhelmed by sights and sounds and confused by social situations, with no way to understand or deal with my own experiences.

***

The Missing Pieces: How Autism in Girls Goes Unrecognized

Many women who think differently show clear signs of autism as children. But expectations about how girls should act and ways of hiding their struggles often cover up these signs. Many of those girls, and later women, are described as shy, quiet, perfectionists, or highly sensitive. But is that really true for all of them? This chapter highlights the early, often-overlooked signs of thinking differently and demonstrates how missing these signs can have a profoundly negative impact on girls' and women's lives. We will explore historical data that reveals enduring diagnostic biases, weave in personal narratives that bring these statistics to life and discuss the urgent need for reform in diagnostic practices to ensure no woman has to endure life without the understanding and support she deserves.

To understand autism in girls, we need to realize that the ways we diagnose it present significant blind spots, as discussed in the previous chapter.

Gender bias has tangible consequences. Research shows that while autism occurs in all genders, girls and women are diagnosed significantly later than boys and men, often missing the opportunity for early support and understanding. According to a comprehensive study by Rutherford et al. (2016), girls receive autism diagnoses an average of 2-3 years later than boys with similar traits, with many not receiving a diagnosis until adulthood or ever. To illustrate, consider Emma, a bright, curious girl who struggled silently through school without understanding why social interactions felt like an insurmountable challenge. Had she been diagnosed earlier, interventions could have been put in place to support her social development, help her form meaningful friendships instead of becoming an easy prey for bullies. She could have built her self-esteem and confidence, and reduced the anxiety that plagued her teen years. She could have avoided the permanent mark that this delay in diagnosis left on her educational journey, which she left abruptly. Ignoring the fact that her inability to learn in class was due to her sensory disorder, and not to her intellectual abilities, Emma entered frequent periods misdiagnosed as "depression," while she really was going through autistic shutdowns. Unable to leave home for even a simple trip to the grocery store, Emma turned suicidal around thirty, when she finally was diagnosed after her children's placement in special education classes.

The Lost Generations: Women Born Before 2000

For women born before the early 2000s, autism was hardly ever noticed. These "lost generations" had to deal with a system that saw autism mostly as something that happened to boys, leaving many women to go through life without a diagnosis or help.

Historical record reveals this diagnostic gap in astonishing terms. Kanner's 1943 original description of autism had a

4:1 male-to-female ratio (Kanner, 1943). By the 1980s, when autism first appeared in diagnostic manuals, the reported ratio had skewed to 10:1 or higher (Wing, 1981). Needless to say, such gender disparity wasn't questioned as potentially reflecting diagnostic bias until decades later.

Dr. Judith Gould, who co-developed the first diagnostic interview for autism, reflects on this period: "In the 1980s and 1990s, we were working with a male-centric diagnostic model. Many clinicians genuinely believed autism was essentially a male condition, with the few diagnosed females representing 'extreme' cases. The possibility that we were systematically missing female autism simply wasn't considered" (Gould, 2017).

This bias extended beyond clinical settings into research methodologies themselves. Kreiser and White (2014) conducted a landmark meta-analysis of decades of autism research, finding that before 2000, 83% of studies either included only males or had fewer than 15% female participants. This led to a cycle where theories of autism, derived from predominantly male samples, were codified as diagnostic criteria favoring male presentations. As these male-centric diagnostic criteria were used in further research, they reinforced the exclusion of female perspectives; thus, new research continued to overlook female autism traits, perpetuating the cycle.

The consequences were profound for women of earlier generations. A retrospective study by Lehnhardt et al. (2016) examined the records of women diagnosed with autism after age 35 and found that before receiving the correct diagnosis, 68% had experienced at least three major psychiatric misdiagnoses, with an average of 6.4 years of inappropriate treatments. Researchers calculated that women born before 1975 were nearly four times less likely to receive appropriate autism diagnoses than those born after 1990, even when controlling for symptom severity. As someone born in 1982, I witnessed firsthand the alignment with this data trend, exemplifying the substantial under-diagnosis my cohort faced. Adding my story to these statistics not only confirms the research but also highlights the personal impact of these diagnostic discrepancies.

As if we were not ignored enough, History further compounded these challenges. Dr. Lorna Wing noted how societal expectations shaped diagnosis: "In the 1960s and 1970s, the behavioral expectations for girls were much more rigid. Quiet, socially withdrawn girls were not considered problematic; they were considered ideal. The same behaviors that might trigger concern in boys were actively encouraged in girls" (Wing, 1981).

The psychiatric establishment itself enforced these gendered expectations. In a critical analysis of psychiatric textbooks published between 1960 and 2000, Bishop et al. (2017) found that autism descriptions overwhelmingly used male pronouns and male-typical examples, with many explicitly stating autism was "rare in females." More troublingly, when female presentations were mentioned at all, they were often pathologized differently, with terms like "emotionally disturbed" or "schizoid personality" applied to behaviors that, in males, would warrant autism evaluation.

The pharmaceutical and healthcare economic landscape also perpetuated this gender bias. Historically, research funding for conditions predominantly diagnosed in males has received significantly more investment than those affecting females. Pellicano et al. (2014) documented how autism research between 1970 and 2010 received disproportionate funding compared to conditions with similar prevalence but higher female diagnosis rates. "The allocation of research dollars reflects and reinforces gender disparities in diagnosis," they concluded. "Conditions conceptualized as 'male' disorders attracted substantially more research investment, creating better diagnostic tools and recognition for those conditions."

For women born in earlier decades, all these things together created what autism researcher Dr. William Mandy calls a "perfect diagnostic storm"—where real differences in how autism shows up, unfair rules, pressure to hide problems, and doctors not seeing autism in women all came together. This meant generations of women lived with undiagnosed autism, often developing other mental health problems because their autism was missed.

This historical context helps explain why so many women in their forties, fifties, and beyond are only now receiving autism diagnoses, often after decades of misdiagnosis and inappropriate treatments. As psychiatrist Dr. Meng-Chuan Lai notes: "For these women, diagnosis often comes as both revelation and grief—illuminating a lifetime of unexplained challenges while highlighting how different life might have been with earlier identification and support" (Lai et al., 2015).

Even in the 2010s, despite growing recognition of gender disparities, diagnostic rates continued to reflect significant bias. A large-scale study by Loomes et al. (2017) found that while true autism prevalence is likely closer to 3:1 male-to-female, actual diagnosis rates remained at 4:1 or higher, with the disparity greatest among those without intellectual disabilities—precisely the profile most common in undiagnosed autistic women.

Only in the past decade has this started to change significantly, as more people have become aware of the problem and more women have been identified. More autistic women speaking up, better research methods, and doctors learning more have slowly changed things. But for women like me, born before the early 2000s, getting a diagnosis still often happens only after a long struggle to be heard and to fight old ideas.

The Cost of Gender-Exclusive Research: A Medical Parallel

To understand the devastating impact of male-dominated autism research, consider cardiovascular disease, a condition where research inclusion of both sexes has proven essential for women's survival. Heart attacks in women often present with "atypical" symptoms like fatigue, nausea, and back pain rather than the "typical" male-pattern chest pain (Mehta et al., 2016). Had cardiovascular research followed autism's gender-biased pattern (85% male subjects), diagnostic criteria would miss these female-typical presentations entirely. The consequences would be catastrophic: Mosca et al. (2011) estimate that recognition of sex-specific presentations reduced female cardiovascular mortality by 30% between 1997 and 2009. By contrast, in autism, where female-specific manifestations remained unrecognized for decades, Bargiela et al. (2016) found that 66% of late-diagnosed women reported serious mental health crises directly attributable to missed diagnosis. This comparison demonstrates how gender-inclusive research methodologies literally save lives, while their absence creates generations of undiagnosed, unsupported individuals struggling to understand their own experiences. The cost of these missed diagnoses isn't merely clinical; it's deeply personal, shaping how girls understand themselves during crucial developmental years.

The Hidden ASD Profile in Girls: Internalization vs. Externalization

To understand why autism is often missed in girls, we need to look at the very different ways it can show up in boys and girls.

At age nine, while other children were collecting rocks or trading cards, I was meticulously collecting words. My teachers and parents marveled at my "advanced vocabulary," attributing it to being an avid reader and praising my apparent literary aptitude. This was a comforting narrative that fit neatly into gendered expectations: The quiet girl with her nose in books, destined perhaps for academic achievement or literary pursuits.

The reality inside my mind was profoundly different. The thick art history, philosophy, and metaphysics books that lined our home weren't sources of stories to me; they were treasure chests filled with linguistic gems waiting to be discovered. I would spend hours poring through these adult texts, not following narratives or arguments, but hunting for unfamiliar words with the focused intensity that characterizes autistic special interests.

Each newly discovered word would be carefully logged in my journal, along with its definition (which I would look up in our huge encyclopedic dictionary) and potential contexts, not to enhance communication, but because words themselves were the objects of my fascination. They weren't tools for connection but rather building blocks for my internal universe. Since words were the architecture of thought, each new acquisition expanded the possible structures I could build within my mind. I was particularly entranced by etymology; the story of how words evolved felt like uncovering hidden pathways between concepts.

This deep love of language exhibited all the signs of a strong autistic interest: intense focus, careful collecting, happiness in sorting things, and a profound knowledge of one topic. However, because it appeared in a way that people thought was good for girls, no one questioned whether it meant I thought differently. If this had been about memorizing train timetables, would it have been labeled as autistic? This question highlights the bias in how gendered expectations can mask identical behaviors, obscuring how these interests might truly indicate a difference in thinking.

What no adult noticed was that this "literary gift" did nothing to help me connect with peers. In fact, when I would excitedly use one of my collected words on the playground, it created distance rather than closeness. I became an oddity to other children, someone who spoke in a strange and formal manner. The sophisticated vocabulary that earned praise from adults marked me as different among children.

Most tellingly, no one ever asked me why I was interested in words or how I experienced them. Had anyone inquired, they might have discovered that my relationship with language was not what they assumed. I wasn't reading for stories or communication skills; I was collecting and categorizing in a way that was intensely fulfilling to my autistic mind.

This experience exemplifies how autism in girls often hides behind gender-compatible interests. A boy with an encyclopedic knowledge of train schedules might raise diagnostic questions, but a girl with an elaborate word collection system is simply considered "bookish" or "academically inclined." The external behavior—interest in language—looked neurotypical through a gendered lens, while the internal experience—systematic collection, categorization, and the joy of patterns—was classically autistic. My word collection reveals a critical flaw: people often look only at what a child is interested in or does, rather than at how they approach it.

At eleven, I became very interested in stand-up comedy, acting, and classic theater. My teachers praised my "exceptional memory of lines and quotes" and "academic focus," but no one saw this as the classic autistic habit of getting deeply focused on one thing. It was also the perfect way for me to perform a precise act according to a script in social settings, avoiding faux pas or blaming those on the skid.

Dr. William Mandy's research team has documented how autism often presents differently in girls compared to boys:

"Autistic girls tend to internalize their struggles rather than act out. While boys with autism might express distress through disruptive behavior, girls are more likely to turn anxiety inward, developing physical complaints, anxiety, or withdrawal behaviors that don't trigger the same level of concern or intervention" (Mandy et al., 2016).

This way of turning feelings inward has roots in the brain. Studies using brain scans have found differences in how autistic girls and boys handle social situations. Research by Lai et al. (2019) showed that "female brains may be better equipped to compensate for certain autistic traits through activation of additional neural circuitry not typically seen in autistic males" (p. 478). This brain compensation helps create what doctors call the "female camouflage effect," where girls learn to hide their autistic traits.

The consequences of this internalization and camouflaging are profound. While boys externalized behaviors often trigger evaluations and interventions, girls' internal struggles frequently go unnoticed until they reach a crisis point, often in adolescence or adulthood, when the demands of compensation become overwhelming. According to a study by Hull et al., prolonged camouflaging is linked with significant mental health challenges, including heightened levels of anxiety and an increased risk of self-harm (Hull et al., 2021). Like so many others, I ended up cutting my arms in my twenties (the stitches on my left wrist and lacerations on my left arm became permanent scars), banging my head against the walls to the point of having to hide for days because of the bruising, swelling of my face, knocking myself out or dislocating joints (two bumps on my skull, that I like to call my "horns," remind me of some of my finest head banging episodes during which bone growth was stimulated). I later had to undergo surgery to fix an untreated dislocation or injuries for which I hid instead of seeking medical help out of fear of being labeled unstable. Because I knew deep down that I was not. I knew there was an explanation for who I was and how I processed the world; I just needed to find it. Generalized anxiety disorder and its path of self-harm and destruction were a way of life since childhood... until the skies parted and a halo of light descended on me, when I finally got on anxiety medications! I woke up one morning and experienced what most people experience: Not living on the verge of losing it every second. So yes, misdiagnosis has real consequences, and they're not pretty. Most of us never discuss them because of the shame we carry. But here is my truth: shame is a privilege because I am lucky enough to be alive to talk about it, unlike too many others. So, I will show up with my shame any day if it means preventing the suicide of other undiagnosed women like me who just need some compassion and the attention and tools required by the care professionals to give them the gift of a proper, unbiased diagnosis.

Neurobiological Differences Beyond Gender Stereotypes

When we really think about it, it is baffling that people thought autism was the same in boys and girls, even though there is strong proof that male and female brains develop differently. Brain scan research reveals that the brains of typical females and males utilize distinct networks to process information. Ingalhalikar et al. (2014) found that female brains typically have more connections between the two hemispheres and greater activity in areas associated with emotions during social tasks, whereas male brains have stronger connections within each hemisphere and more activity in areas related to visual and spatial tasks. González-Gadea et al. (2018) found that women often utilize more parts of the brain simultaneously to solve problems, engaging both thinking and feeling areas. The idea that men and women communicate and show feelings differently because of biology became well known after Gray's (1992) "Men Are from Mars, Women Are from Venus." Different wiring demands different diagnostic lenses. Given this, it is surprising that scientists kept ignoring gender in autism research. These well-known brain differences make it a big mistake to assume autism looks the same in everyone. As Lai et al. (2017) say, this mistake probably led to years of missed diagnoses, because doctors did not see that autistic traits could show up differently in boys and girls.

Social Camouflage: Learning to Fit In

In third grade, I had already developed a detailed strategy for navigating social situations. I watched other girls closely, noticing how they talked, laughed, what they wore, and how they did their hair. I would practice these things in the mirror at home and try them out the next day. By the end of the school year, I finally had friends and played with other children at recess. Children liked me! I kept a list in my head of what to say or do in different situations, basically making up lines for myself:

If someone shows you something they made, say "That's so cool!" with wide eyes. If a friend is talking about something sad, tilt your head and raise your eyebrows; say something like, "Sorry to hear that." When adults ask how you are, always say "Good, thank you," regardless of how you actually feel. No one ever cares.

All this hard work to hide my real reactions made people call me "polite," "so well behaved," and "mature for my age," but no one saw how tired and anxious it made me feel.

Dr. Meng-Chuan Lai's research helps explain this phenomenon: "Social camouflaging in autism represents a compensatory strategy rather than the absence of autism itself. These compensatory behaviors require tremendous cognitive and emotional resources, often leading to exhaustion, anxiety, and even loss of identity in the long term" (Lai et al., 2017).

The classroom environment often reinforces this

camouflaging. As education researcher Dr. Sarah Cassidy notes:

"Schools typically reward compliance, quiet behavior, and academic achievement—all areas where many autistic girls excel through camouflaging. Teachers may interpret a girl's rigid adherence to rules and routines as model student behavior rather than recognizing it as a potential indicator of autism" (Cassidy et al., 2018).

This creates what developmental psychologist Dr. Svenny Kopp terms "the invisible autistic girl"—one who struggles profoundly but flies under the radar of traditional special education screenings: "These girls often perform adequately or even excellently academically while experiencing significant social and sensory challenges. Their good behavior and academic achievement become a mask that obscures their neurodevelopmental differences" (Kopp et al., 2010).

My own experience reflects this perfectly. While I managed to develop friendships in elementary school, middle school sent me back to square one. No more playing at recess meant no more organized socialization with clear rules to rely on. It also meant fewer opportunities to study my peers' behaviors: girls became more secretive, calling me a "stalking weirdo" when they caught me observing them to grasp the social cues I was missing. Boys were no longer playing with girls. So I gradually stood out, walking or sitting alone. I still excelled academically, but recesses were alone, overwhelmed by the chaotic social environment. In high school, I would spend my one-and-a-half-hour lunch break either hiding in the bathroom or sitting on top of the stairs leading to the highest classroom in the building, which was rarely used, to retreat and hide from everyone. For my teachers, my discretion and reluctance in interacting with my peers were signs of maturity rather than a social difficulty. Often, I would tell my parents that I was "an old soul" rather than a child struggling with sensory processing and social communication. When I disclosed my late diagnosis to my history and geography teacher in high school, he told me he always thought something was off: He came to question later if I could have been autistic, and remembered me vividly sitting still on my chair, "like a cat," barely moving at all to breathe during the entire class.

The Praise Trap: When Autism Gets Mistaken for Good Behavior

One of the hardest and most upsetting parts of being an undiagnosed autistic girl is getting praised for things that actually show you are struggling. This "praise trap" makes you hide your true self and prevents people from acknowledging your genuine challenges. I also reinforced your belief that something is fundamentally wrong with you. Shame then takes over, convincing you to hide who you are even further, because you will be rejected and are not worthy of love.

I was consistently praised for being "so good" in waiting rooms, restaurants, and other public places. What adults didn't recognize was that my stillness wasn't a virtue, it was overwhelming mixed with the sheer fear of being exposed. I wasn't being patient; I was frozen in sensory overload, desperately trying to process the cacophony of sounds, smells, and visual input bombarding my nervous system. I was also desperate to control every visible inch of my body: Were my hands in the right place? Was my facial expression betraying me? Were my clothes fully covering my body? I soon decided to wear large pants, men's hoodies, and anything that could cover me like a social shield, ensuring my protection in my most vulnerable moments. Headphones with a visible "Walkman" (the equivalent of an iPod for the younger generations) helped me showcase my unavailability to the world as an additional layer of preservation to avoid any unplanned interactions. The minute I left my bedroom, I was exposed and "ready to be seen" with all my tools (full covering clothes, Walkman, etc.) and excuses to dismiss socialization (homework, exams, etc.). The minute I left my building and emerged into the streets, I was "ready to flee," accelerating my pace if I saw familiar faces, looking down, with my hoodie on, fully hiding my frame. Ideally, people should not have been able to identify whether I was a boy or a girl. I wanted to be nothing, to disappear and become invisible to everyone. The cost of visibility was too high, and I stopped fighting to have a social life. It was not worth it.

Dr. Tony Attwood, a leading researcher in female autism presentations, explains this phenomenon:

"Girls with autism are often praised for characteristics that actually represent coping mechanisms. Their compliance, quietness, and apparent maturity can be misinterpreted as personality traits rather than recognized as adaptive responses to being overwhelmed. This praise inadvertently encourages further masking rather than addressing underlying challenges" (Attwood, 2018).

This praise trap also extends into social settings. As psychology researcher Dr. Rachel Hull notes, "Autistic girls are frequently praised for being 'sweet,' 'helpful,' or 'caring'— traits that may actually represent learned scripts and careful observation rather than intuitive social understanding" (Hull et al., 2020).

I became the classroom helper, the quiet kid who always did what I was told. Teachers loved me because I never caused problems. What they didn't see was how I would go home and cry from the stress of pretending all day, or how I would have big outbursts over small changes that disrupted my sense of safety. When I was younger, people just thought these outbursts were tantrums: "She just can't stand it when things are not going her way!"

The praise trap creates a painful paradox: The better an autistic girl becomes at hiding her authentic responses, the less likely she is to get the understanding and support she needs. Gendered expectations compound this effect, rewarding traits commonly encouraged in girls, regardless of the personal cost.

Recognizing the Signs: What We Know Now

With growing awareness of how autism presents in girls, we can now identify early indicators that were once overlooked. These signs don't always match the stereotypical autism checklist developed primarily from observations of boys.

Common signs of autism in girls that often go unrecognized include:

Social mimicry: Rather than appearing obviously uninterested in social interaction, many autistic girls study and copy their peers. As Attwood (2020) notes, "They develop what I call a 'social echolalia,' borrowing entire personas or interaction styles from peers or characters they observe."

Rule-following: Extreme adherence to rules, particularly social rules, is common. I was devastated by any suggestion I had broken a rule or disappointed an authority figure, a trait common in autistic girls that is often misinterpreted as simple conscientiousness.

Hyperfixation on socially acceptable topics: Instead of the usual interests, such as trains or memorizing facts, autistic girls often become very focused on topics like animals, stories, psychology, or art. These interests seem normal, but they are pursued with the same deep focus and passion.

Imaginary friends or fictional worlds: Many autistic girls create elaborate imaginary worlds where they can control social rules and interactions. This creativity is often praised rather than recognized as a coping mechanism for social confusion. During my middle school years, I lost myself in an imaginary friendship with a fairytale-like character that would follow me everywhere, providing me the support I needed to face the isolation, mockery, manipulation, and even predatory behaviors I became the prey of at school or in my church group.

Sensory seeking or avoiding: Subtle sensory sensitivities might manifest as "pickiness" about clothing, food textures, or environmental conditions. I would wear the same soft outfit repeatedly and had elaborate rituals around food texture and arrangement, behaviors that were seen as quirky rather than significant in terms of neurodevelopment. New pieces of clothing became a source of anxiety: As much as I wanted to wear trendy or pretty outfits, they would often trigger my sensory disorder to the point of having a meltdown. I would then be criticized for being "spoiled, unappreciative" or for taking for granted things that underprivileged children would love to have.

Emotional reactions that don't match expectations: What seemed like overreactions (melting down over a small change in routine or responding with apparent indifference to major events) often reflect autistic differences in emotional processing. A change in routine flips our entire safety system upside down. If it happens at the beginning of the day, it can compromise our ability to cope with everything else coming our way because we have exhausted our social and emotional resources by 9am. What looks like a small event to a neurotypical child quickly escalates into a major event for us.

Friendship difficulties: Rather than having no interest in friendship, many autistic girls desperately want connections but struggle with maintaining them, particularly in group settings. I could manage one-on-one interactions but became overwhelmed and confused in groups, leading to a pattern of short-lived friendships. Soon, looking back at my childhood through this lens, the signs seem obvious. But without this framework, parents, teachers, and even medical professionals missed what now appears clear. As neuropsychologist Dr. Susan White explains, "We can only recognize what we've been trained to see. When our understanding of autism is built around male presentations, female presentations remain invisible not because they're absent, but because they're outside our conceptual framework" (White et al., 2017).

Reflection: Connecting Past and Present

For many women diagnosed with autism as adults, looking back at childhood memories brings strong moments of understanding. Things they once saw as personal failures or problems with their personality now make sense as natural signs of being autistic. Realizing this can feel both comforting and painful. It raises the question of how life could have been if people had understood earlier, and also highlights how much extra struggle happened because a simple diagnosis was missed.

Reflection Exercise

Think back to your own childhood (or someone close to you). Were there behaviors that stood out—perhaps framed as quirks, anxiety, or giftedness—that may have been missed signs of neurodivergence?

• What were you praised for as a child?
• What behaviors were misunderstood?
• Who helped or hindered your self-understanding?

For parents, educators, healthcare providers, and employers reading this, these reflections highlight the importance of looking beyond surface presentations. The quiet, rule-following girl who seems to be coping might actually be struggling intensely beneath a carefully constructed mask. The seemingly "dramatic" reactions might represent genuine sensory or emotional differences rather than behavioral problems.

Recognition of these patterns matters not just for diagnosis but also for fostering environments where neurodivergent individuals can authentically exist without needing to exhaust themselves with camouflage. As educator and autism researcher Dr. Wenn Lawson notes, "The goal shouldn't be making autistic people appear non-autistic; it should be creating environments where autistic neurology is accommodated rather than pathologized" (Lawson, 2018).

Moving Forward: From Missed Moments to Understanding

Understanding the often-hidden signs of autism in girls means we need to change how we think about differences in brain development. Instead of only looking at what we can see, we need to consider how girls feel inside, the ways they cope, and how expectations for girls impact them.

For women diagnosed later in life, connecting these childhood dots provides crucial context for understanding their lived experiences. For parents of young girls showing similar patterns, early recognition can lead to support and validation.

For educators, this understanding creates opportunities to identify students who are struggling and might otherwise go unnoticed. A quiet, academically successful girl who isolates herself at recess deserves attention just as much as a disruptive student—her suffering is no less real for being less visible.

For employers and colleagues, recognizing these patterns helps create more inclusive workplaces where neurodivergent individuals can contribute their unique strengths without the exhausting burden of constant masking.

Most importantly, for autistic girls themselves, recognition offers the profound gift of self-understanding, the knowledge that their experiences are real, valid, and shared by others.

As I moved into adolescence, the cost of masking grew heavier. The expectations became unmanageable, the rules more complex, and I was no longer a child quietly blending in. To maintain my grades, I had to choose between prioritizing my social life and academic performance. I decided to maintain my grades while trying to survive the noise. The strategies that had somewhat worked in childhood began to crack under the increased social and sensory demands of teenage life, leading to new challenges and deeper questions about who I really was beneath the masks I'd learned to wear.

***

THE COST OF LIVING UNDIAGNOSED AND OVERLOOKED

At nine, I developed debilitating stomach aches before school. The pediatrician found nothing physically wrong and suggested I was "just anxious." My parents were advised to be firm and not "enable" my behavior. No one recognized that these physical symptoms stemmed from the sensory and social demands of the classroom environment, demands that were particularly challenging for my autistic nervous system. Soon, I started crying every Sunday thinking of Monday at school. I was unconsolable. Relentlessly, I was told that it was not worth it to make such a big deal at going back to school. Most people did not like to go to school, or to work. But people do what they must do, and crying over it won't make it go away. I eventually stopped crying and started having episodes during which I would bang my head against the walls. If school was not going away, my distress was not going to disappear either. It was just going to manifest in different ways.

***

This pattern of misdiagnosis is remarkably common. Research by Bargiela et al. (2016) found that 80% of women diagnosed with autism as adults had previously received at least one incorrect psychiatric diagnosis. The most common misdiagnoses were anxiety disorders, depression, personality disorders, and eating disorders, all conditions that can represent secondary responses to the experience of being autistic in a world designed for neurotypical individuals.

Research on autistic masking reveals how suppressing authentic neurological experiences creates profound psychological harm. Studies consistently show that when autistic individuals are forced to camouflage their natural responses to avoid misinterpretation, they experience "exhaustion, isolation, poor mental and physical health, loss of identity and acceptance of self" (Cage & Troxell-Whitman, 2021). This constant suppression of authentic self-expression, rather than accommodation of natural autistic needs, creates a foundation for long-term mental health challenges.

When autistic traits go unrecognized, they don't disappear. They get relabeled, often pathologizing natural autistic responses as character flaws or different conditions entirely.

The emotional toll of this misunderstanding represents what researchers describe as systematic invalidation of autistic identity. Studies show that camouflaging behaviors emerge as responses to "autism-related stigma" where autistic individuals' fundamental ways of experiencing and interacting with the world are consistently discredited or pathologized (Perry et al., 2022). This ongoing invalidation forces autistic people to suppress core aspects of their identity to avoid social rejection.

I remember sitting in a fourth-grade classroom, covering my ears during a particularly loud activity, only to have the teacher remove my hands, saying, "It's not that loud. Stop being dramatic." This simple interaction carried a powerful message: My sensory experience wasn't real. My perception couldn't be trusted. There was something wrong with me for experiencing the world this way.

Over time, these messages accumulate. Research on late autism diagnosis reveals that identity formation presents significant challenges for those diagnosed in adulthood. Studies show that late-diagnosed autistic adults often struggle to incorporate autism into their personal identity, with some tending to externalize and view autism as separate from themselves, indicating difficulties with self-concept integration (Corden et al., 2021). Additionally, research consistently demonstrates that long-term masking of autistic traits creates what researchers describe as "exhaustion, isolation, poor mental and physical health, loss of identity and acceptance of self" (Cage & Troxell-Whitman, 2021). Studies with autistic children and adolescents confirm that camouflaging contributes to "mental health problems, confusion about identity, lower self-esteem, exhaustion, and burnout" (Hull et al., 2017).

Every beginning of the school year—in elementary school, middle school, high school, and university—I would start full of hope and goals: Great grades, having friends, being elected class representative. I would sustain those goals perfectly for the first month, often being elected to represent my peers, making a group of friends, shining in class, only to start slowly crashing around month two in what would look like a full-on nervous breakdown.

Very quickly, I would lose my "new girlfriends" as keeping up with their social expectations (check-in phone calls, meetings outside of school, respecting "girl code" which I did not know existed, understanding subtle tones, looks) was a full-time job on its own. Soon, they'd become nasty with me, making my isolation even more painful. I would end up hanging out with the boys (as usual, and still to this day) who are much more direct in their communication. But often, I would not realize some of them were looking for a romantic relationship and would accuse me of leading them on.

I would ultimately retreat altogether from any social life: Too complicated, too energy-taxing. My mother would tell me that I had to pick my battles, either my grades or being popular. I wasn't particularly looking for popularity... there had to be a middle ground between popularity and complete marginalization. But then my grades would start to tank. My mother would explain this by a homework load that was too heavy.

At thirteen, after taking an Intellectual Quotient test with a specialized psychologist, we found out that not only was my IQ above average, but it was high enough that I could integrate into the MENSA society. Maybe this could explain my odd behaviors—perhaps I just needed to accelerate my curriculum as I was probably not stimulated enough. I ended up eventually three years ahead of my peers, feeling exactly the same.

This time, the verdict was clear for everyone: I thought I was so special that I wasn't making the slightest effort to study. It was time I dropped my "obnoxious attitude." Meanwhile, my self-esteem was disappearing to the point of non-existence. Not only was I a complete loser, unlovable, but I was also a self-centered monster who disappointed everyone.

I wanted to disappear. Everywhere I turned, I faced the specter of blame for every single one of the behaviors I could not predict nor explain myself. I was ashamed and terrified that I would react embarrassingly at any time. I stopped talking altogether without realizing it. My head was so busy with thoughts, second thoughts, and more of what to say or not to say to someone, that by the time I was ready to articulate a word, my opportunity had vanished. And I was okay with it. Were my thoughts worth sharing anyway?

I spent months listening to people's conversations in disbelief: What was the point of small talk? I could not bear the thought of entertaining those useless conversations. It seemed like people were talking to feel seen because they were just faking laughter at their own jokes or loudly stating the obvious: "Oh, it's a beautiful day!" "It's going to rain, isn't it?"

Was socialization all an act? Did I have to go through a life of acting and pretending? Had I missed a memo? I couldn't stand the sound of those forced laughs and fake surprises... not only were they annoying by nature, but they were so loud that they triggered debilitating migraines. I would end up locked in my room, in the dark, with sunglasses on, covering my ears, in complete utter pain.

Clearly, I was not designed for the crowd. If humans were social animals, maybe I was lacking humanity. Maybe I was some kind of social monster and should hide my true nature. I always had to hide and pretend in social contexts; maybe there was a reason for it: I was embarrassingly inhuman, unlovable, disappointing, insensitive, selfish. No wonder my parents were embarrassed, and kids were making fun of me at school. I was the definition of an embarrassment; I should be ashamed of myself.

The Silent Struggle

"Everyone says I'm fine. I don't feel fine."

In this chapter, I'll take you inside the quiet crisis of living undiagnosed: The confusion, the masking, the emotional aftermath of never having the language or validation for what was really going on. Living without a diagnosis creates invisible wounds—self-doubt, chronic anxiety, imposter syndrome, and a fragmented sense of self. The emotional toll of being overlooked is deep, compounding as the years go by.

The years before my diagnosis at 31 were filled with a sense of being perpetually out of step with the world around me. I knew something was different, but without the framework to understand it, I blamed myself. It was like trying to solve a puzzle without knowing what picture I was supposed to be creating.

For many autistic women and girls, this experience is all too common. Research indicates that girls with autism are diagnosed, on average, two to three years later than boys, with many not receiving diagnosis until adulthood—if at all (Bargiela et al., 2016). This diagnostic delay creates a uniquely painful experience, where we're expected to function in a world that wasn't built for our neurology, all while being told we should be able to manage just fine.

The difficulty many of us face is connecting our diverse experiences to a condition we may have only heard described in stereotypically male terms. As Hull et al. (2020) found, "The conceptualization of autism was largely male-centered until recently, resulting in diagnostic criteria that may miss females who present differently."

Internal and External Emotional Gaslighting

"You're just sensitive." "You're overthinking." "Everyone feels overwhelmed sometimes." "You're unappreciative and spoiled." "Stop being such a drama queen."

These dismissals aren't merely annoying, they're insidious. They lead to internalized guilt, eroding self-esteem, and profound shame. When you're constantly told that your perfectly reasonable needs are excessive, you stop advocating for yourself. You begin to believe that your feelings are invalid, your perceptions unreliable, your needs unreasonable.

The pattern is sinister in its simplicity. First, deny that there's anything different about a girl's neurology. Then, criticize her for her naturally occurring autistic behaviors and sensitivities. Finally, when she inevitably struggles, blame her character rather than recognizing the unseen disability.

As Kreiser and White (2014) noted, "Females with ASD are at heightened risk of having their symptoms missed or misunderstood due to the expectation that females are inherently more socially skilled than males." This misreading of our struggles as character defects rather than neurological differences set up many of us for a lifetime of masking our true selves.

This conditioning creates the perfect foundation for future victimization and abusive relationships. We learn that our feelings and impressions are never legitimate, that we should never trust our instincts—including our core survival instincts. The red flags we cannot explain are dismissed as overreactions. It is profoundly detrimental to our safety, both physical and mental.

Unfortunately, parents, educators, and adults foster this victimization very early by denying a formal diagnosis and refusing the fact that there is indeed a fundamental difference in us that is actually explainable, legitimate, and should be respected. Respect, in general, is implicitly denied to us. How could we then develop proper self-respect and learn to stand up for ourselves?

We are raised to be victimized after being denied any natural reactions or instincts, only being praised for our masking behaviors. The message is clear: We are not worthy of love, friendships, or social life "as is." We must hide and be ashamed of our true selves to be worthy of human connections. How destructive can this message be in a girl's and woman's life? How could it possibly lead to anything else but self-destructive behaviors, depression, chronic anxiety, PTSD, or even suicide?

Burnout Before the Diagnosis

For most of us, each time we experience epic autistic shutdowns, burnouts, or meltdowns, we (or our parents, partners, caregivers) seek help. Eventually, one day, we're lucky enough to be diagnosed. So, the diagnosis doesn't come from us "trying to feel special" or "hiding behind a label"—it comes from a place of true desperation, helplessness, and urgency.

When we share our diagnosis, it comes from a place of relief, hope, and a genuine desire to build authentic connections while healing from years of denying our very sense of self. This sharing represents an act of courage and self-advocacy that deserves to be received with understanding and respect.

Consider how we would never expect left-handed people to write exclusively with their right hands, then criticize them for poor penmanship or coordination when they struggle to adapt to tools designed for right-handed use. We understand that left-handed individuals function optimally when provided with appropriate tools and accommodations that work with their natural wiring, not against it. This same principle applies to neurological differences.

The impact of understanding versus expectation became strikingly clear to me through an unexpected comparison. When I could no longer tolerate living undiagnosed in France —a country where autism awareness was severely limited during my formative years—I made the difficult decision to move to the United States. Paradoxically, despite not speaking English fluently and being unfamiliar with American culture, I found myself thriving in ways I never had in my home country.

The difference was revolutionary: Americans knew I was foreign, so they naturally accommodated my differences. When I was invited to a baby shower, colleagues didn't assume I would intuitively understand this cultural tradition. Instead, they explicitly explained what a baby shower was, what gifts to bring, what to wear, and what to expect. They broke down social rules and cultural expectations in clear, concrete terms because they recognized I was navigating an unfamiliar system. The accommodation felt natural and helpful rather than condescending because everyone understood that being foreign meant needing explicit guidance about unspoken cultural codes.

This experience illuminated a profound irony: I received more support and understanding as a foreigner in America than I ever had as an undiagnosed autistic person in my home country. In France, the expectation was that I should simply "know" how to navigate social situations, cultural norms, and unspoken rules because I had grown up there. My struggles were interpreted as personal failings or character flaws rather than as signs that I might be operating with a different neurological framework that required explicit explanation and support.

The willingness of Americans to serve as cultural interpreters for a foreign visitor contrasted sharply with the lack of recognition that some people—regardless of their country of origin—might need similar explicit guidance to navigate social and cultural expectations. In essence, being seen as foreign provided me with the accommodation I had needed all along as an autistic person, but which had never been offered because my differences weren't visible or understood.

As someone who experienced firsthand the challenges of being left-handed in a Catholic school environment where students were required to write with their right hands, I can attest that expecting people to function against their natural neurology creates unnecessary struggle and often leads to unfair judgments about their capabilities. What seemed like a reasonable expectation at the time—that all students should write the same way—actually prevented left-handed students from demonstrating their true abilities and potential.

The parallel to autism is striking, and my international experience deepened this understanding. When we recognize autism as a different neurological operating system rather than a deficit, we can begin to see how environmental modifications and understanding, rather than attempts to change the person, create the conditions for authentic thriving. Just as Americans naturally provided cultural interpretation for a foreign visitor, we can develop approaches that offer explicit social and cultural interpretation for autistic individuals who may be navigating neurotypical environments as foreigners in their own land.

This understanding opens up possibilities for genuine connection and mutual growth. When autistic individuals share their diagnosis, they're offering you insight into how their mind works and what they need to function at their best —much like how sharing one's foreign status provides context for why certain cultural guidance might be helpful. This information is a gift that can deepen relationships and create more inclusive environments for everyone.

The goal isn't to change fundamental aspects of how autistic brains work, but to create environments and relationships where different neurological styles can flourish naturally with the same kind of explicit support and cultural interpretation that we readily provide to visitors from other countries. This benefits not only autistic individuals but entire communities, as neurodiversity brings unique perspectives, problem-solving approaches, and innovations that enhance collective wisdom and capability.

The irony of my experience—thriving more easily as a foreigner than as an undiagnosed autistic person in my home country—highlights how simple awareness and willingness to provide explicit guidance can transform someone's ability to participate fully in community life. When we approach autism with the same generous spirit of cultural interpretation that we offer to international visitors, we create space for authentic connection and mutual understanding that enriches everyone involved.

Raymaker et al. (2020) defined autistic burnout as "a syndrome conceptualized as resulting from chronic life stress and a mismatch of expectations and abilities without adequate supports." Many of us experienced multiple burnouts long before we ever had the words to describe what was happening. These periods were often misinterpreted as laziness, moodiness, or poor coping skills.

One woman described to me her pre-diagnosis burnouts this way: "I'd push myself to be 'normal' for as long as I could, sometimes months at a time. Then I'd crash. I couldn't get out of bed, couldn't speak, couldn't function. My parents thought I was being dramatic. My doctor diagnosed depression, but the antidepressants didn't help. No one recognized that I was in autistic burnout because no one knew I was autistic."

The Social Perception Problem

The very perception of what "being social" means is a problem. The minute you can interact with people and enjoy interaction with them, you are considered "social" and therefore "not autistic." The problem is not our ability or even our desire to be social; it is the ability of our brain to handle such exercise.

Our brains are not wired to handle socializing with ease— filtering out extra noise, naturally reading social cues, body language, facial expressions, etc. It demands intense focus and exhausts us quickly. Stop telling us that "we are fine" because "we are social." We know that! Sure, we are social, we want social connections and a social life, just like everyone else. Our brains just get overwhelmed very quickly.

Imagine having to constantly socialize with your family, friends, or coworkers in a nightclub with the music bursting at full volume, people dancing around you, constantly bumping into you, having to ask people to repeat what they were saying, over and over again, attempting to read their lips, interpret their face expressions to avoid asking them to repeat one more time... Too late, someone else already understood what they were saying; their brain is better equipped than yours. They just answered and are moving on to a conversation that you lost track of.

You're now just a spectator, feeling like an outsider and getting a serious headache. Don't you think that, day after day, week after week, dealing with this at home, at work, with your friends, at school, at the coffee shop, at the restaurant, you would need to retreat alone to a quiet room to sleep and recover?

Friendship Struggles and Exploitation

As a child, I had multiple one-on-one friendships that would inevitably collapse, and I would enter some kind of depression phase. It wasn't that I lacked the social skills or empathy to become a friend, but I was lacking the social energy that a friendship needed to be fueled in the long term.

When I would not follow up, call, touch base with people, or check in, it wasn't out of lack of interest—my friends were always on my mind. I just didn't know that I was supposed to reach out often to maintain the connection. For me, once the connection was established and we both knew I was going to be there for them at any time, it didn't matter how long we hadn't seen each other. But on their end, that wasn't the case. I came to realize later in life that they looked at me as someone who was too self-absorbed or did not care about them enough to reach out during key moments of their lives.

Unfortunately, friendship is the best-case scenario. We also very easily become prey to all types of predators, including criminals.

The Missing Mirror

I remember sitting in my third-grade classroom, surrounded by posters of famous scientists and historical figures, none of whom looked like me. The other children talked about the TV shows they watched and the characters they liked—again, none of them liked me. These moments created a profound sense of isolation that lingered with me for years. Growing up without seeing anyone like me in the media, at school, or in my social life made me feel even more alone. Not seeing myself represented made me question who I was and where I fit in. If none of the labels I saw matched my experience, how could I understand myself?

The absence of representation meant that I constantly questioned my own reality. Was I really experiencing the world differently, or was I just struggling to be normal?

As Kanfiszer et al. (2017) found in their research on women with late-diagnosed autism, "Many women described a sense of 'not fitting in'... without a frame of reference or explanation, this often led to feelings of alienation."

Without that mirror, many of us constructed elaborate personas in an attempt to approximate what seemed to work for others. We became social chameleons out of necessity.

Social and Career Consequences

The cost of pretending to be like everyone else at work is huge and very hard on our mental health. Research by Cage and Troxell-Whitman (2019) found that "Camouflaging Autistic traits was associated with significantly higher rates of mental health difficulties and suicidal thoughts." Yet for many of us, hiding our true selves felt like the only way to keep our jobs.

In relationships and motherhood, the pressure to perform like a neurotypical individual intensifies. Many women report exhausting themselves trying to manage the sensory and social demands of parenting while also maintaining a mask of neurotypical behavior. I personally never understood the need to discuss diaper brands and potty training among mothers. Did I really need to know what others favor to properly take care of my children? Did I need their approval? More importantly, what was the point of discussing something so evident (and uninteresting) in the first place?

The Grief and Relief of Diagnosis

For many women, getting an autism diagnosis as an adult brings both sadness and relief. These feelings are not opposites, but both are true and show how much it hurts to go through life without understanding or seeing yourself represented. There is sadness for the years we spent blaming ourselves, for the hurt we went through and are still trying to heal from, for the help we missed out on, and for the self-understanding that could have changed everything. At the same time, there is relief in finally having an explanation that makes sense of our lives. Accepting both feelings at once can help us understand ourselves and others better.

I cried after my diagnosis. Not because I was sad about being autistic, but because I wasn't broken, mean, narcissistic, not worthy of love, inhuman after all. There was a reason, and it wasn't my fault.

If I had been diagnosed earlier, I could have had more support and understanding. I might have done better in school, understood myself instead of blaming myself, and learned ways to work with my brain instead of against it. Meeting others like me could have stopped some of the hurt and loneliness, and maybe even kept my family together. Even though I still feel sad about what I missed, I am proud that I got through these hard times without a diagnosis. Despite all the challenges, I persevered and made my own way. I might have even loved myself and tried to have relationships I thought I did not deserve.

So, yes, grief quickly follows relief. And later, the diagnosis, the longer the grief, and the longer the road to rebuilding our sense of self, reclaiming every aspect of our life under the light of our newly discovered identity, tastes, desires, and talents... naturally leading to respect and self-esteem.

With this new understanding of ourselves, we realize we need to set boundaries that we never felt able to set before. If we did not think we deserved respect, we would not feel entitled to say no or ask for space. We learned for a long time not to trust our own feelings and that our needs were too much to handle. Our struggles often stem from differences in how our brains function, particularly when it comes to understanding other people's emotions. People with autism can find it hard to read social signals that others pick up on easily. This can cause confusion, where our boundaries are not seen as real but as our own mistakes. How could we have thought it was okay to ask for boundaries when we believed these struggles were our fault?

I remember my mother always being upset that I could not stand her kissing the back of my neck. To this day, I have a very hard time dealing with my neck being touched in certain ways. It's a sensory thing. My mother would always "force" herself on me to kiss my neck because "she was my mother and as such, she was allowed to kiss me the way she wanted," violating my boundaries because I was "overreacting" and denying me the very right to trust my own sensory perception. Who was I to trust my own instincts to touch when I had so many problematic reactions, such as autistic meltdowns, that I couldn't even explain myself?

Moving Forward

Living without a diagnosis causes emotional pain that others cannot see, but it is very real. Not being understood or represented leaves deep and lasting hurt. The self-doubt and tiredness build up, especially for women who are taught to blame themselves for their problems.

Getting a diagnosis does not fix everything, but it can help us start to be kinder to ourselves and understand ourselves better. It is like finally tuning a radio so you can hear clearly instead of just noise. It gives us the words to ask for what we need and helps us make sense of our experiences.

In the next chapter, we'll explore how one of the most misunderstood aspects of autism—sensory differences—shapes our experience of the world in ways that go far beyond simply being "overwhelmed."

***

SENSORY INTELLIGENCE AND OVERLOADS

The Breaking Point

The fluorescent lights buzzed overhead like angry insects. Each beep of the scanner three aisles over landed like a physical blow. Someone walked by trailing a cloud of perfume that felt like acid in my nostrils. My skin crawled under the scratchy tag of my new shirt. The background music—which apparently no one else even noticed—made it impossible to remember what I needed to buy.

I abandoned my half-filled shopping cart in the middle of the cereal aisle and fled to my car, where I sat with my head against the steering wheel, trying to breathe through what felt like my fifth panic attack that week.

What was wrong with me? Why couldn't I handle a simple trip to the grocery store when everyone else seemed fine? The shame was suffocating. My mother's voice echoed in my head: "You're just being dramatic again." My ex-partner: "No one else has a problem with restaurants—why do you always have to make things difficult?"

***

It would take fifteen more years before I understood that my nervous system wasn't broken. It was just different —processing everything at a volume and intensity others couldn't comprehend.

In this chapter, we'll explore what it means to live in a world that constantly bombards our senses—and how that isn't a flaw, but a form of intelligence. We'll reframe sensory sensitivity as insight, not pathology. What many call "too sensitive" is often an advanced sensory processing style, misunderstood and pathologized in women with ASD.

Understanding sensory overwhelm requires distinguishing between three adaptive strategies that autistic women employ. Compensation involves learning specific strategies to navigate sensory challenges like carrying noise-canceling headphones or developing exit strategies. Masking involves actively hiding sensory distress to appear neurotypical, like forcing a smile while experiencing painful overstimulation. Assimilation involves suppressing core sensory needs to fit social norms, such as enduring fluorescent lighting without complaint to avoid being seen as "difficult." Sensory overwhelm often forces all three strategies simultaneously, creating exhausting cycles that can be eliminated with proper environmental accommodations.

What Is Sensory Intelligence?

Sensory intelligence refers to an evolved way of perceiving the environment—processing details, patterns, and stimuli that others automatically filter out. It's the heightened awareness many autistic people experience across some or all sensory channels: sound, light, touch, smell, taste, proprioception (body position), and interoception (internal bodily sensations).

Research demonstrates that autistic individuals exhibit enhanced perceptual processing capabilities that allow them to attend to sensory information typically filtered out by neurotypical brains.

Recent neuroscience research reveals fascinating differences in how autistic brains handle every day sensory experiences. A groundbreaking study by Green and colleagues (2015) used brain imaging to watch what happens when an autistic youth encounters common sensory experiences like sounds and touch. What they discovered was remarkable: while most people's brains quickly learn to "tune out" repeated sensory information—like how you stop noticing the hum of an air conditioner after a few minutes—autistic brains showed a very different pattern. Instead of filtering out these sensory details, the emotional and sensory processing centers of autistic participants' brains remained highly active and engaged, continuing to thoroughly process information that neurotypical brains would typically dismiss as unimportant background noise. This suggests that what might appear as "oversensitivity" is actually the brain doing an incredibly detailed job of analyzing the sensory world, picking up on patterns and subtleties that others might miss entirely. Rather than a deficit, this represents a fundamentally different—and often more thorough—way of experiencing and processing the rich sensory information that surrounds us every day.

Later, Brinkert and Remington (2020) found that autistic adults demonstrate "increased perceptual capacity – the ability to process more information at any one time," which results in "increased susceptibility to distraction" as individuals may notice subtle environmental details such as "a fly in a room while on a conference call or hearing music that is set to the lowest setting while listening to a coworker." This enhanced processing extends specifically to background auditory information, as Tillmann and Swettenham (2017) demonstrated that while "visual perceptual load reduces auditory detection in typically developing individuals," this filtering mechanism does not operate in the same way for "individuals with autism spectrum disorders," who continue to process auditory stimuli even under high cognitive load conditions.

Together, these findings suggest that the autistic brain's tendency to process sensory information with remarkable thoroughness represents a fundamental difference in attentional capacity rather than a deficit, allowing for the registration of patterns and subtleties in the environment that neurotypical cognitive systems would typically discard as irrelevant background noise. This processing difference isn't a malfunction—it's an alternative operating system that actually handles more information. Just as some computers are optimized for graphics processing while others excel at data analysis, neurotypical and autistic brains have different specializations.

For many women with autism, this sensory intelligence manifests as noticing subtle changes in environments, detecting sounds others can't hear, heightened awareness of textures, perceiving emotional undercurrents through sensory cues, and strong reactions to stimuli that seem minor to others.

At school, I knew which light bulbs in a room were about to burn out by their particular buzzing frequency. It was an odd ability that I was quite proud of, except when it started buzzing in a way that was overwhelming and I couldn't turn off the light, nor my ability to hear its debilitating buzz.

The Spectrum of Sensory Sensitivities

Sensory processing in autism isn't one-size-fits-all. It exists on a spectrum with two main variations: hypersensitivity (over-responsiveness) and hyposensitivity (under-responsiveness). Many autistic people experience both, sometimes even within the same sensory channel.

Hypersensitivity occurs when sensory input feels amplified or intensified. Common experiences include auditory pain from loud sounds or inability to filter background noise, visual discomfort from bright lights or overstimulation in busy environments, tactile discomfort with certain clothing textures or light touch, strong reactions to smells others barely notice, limited food choices due to sensitive taste receptors, discomfort with certain body positions or spatial awareness challenges, and heightened awareness of internal sensations like heartbeat or digestion.

Hyposensitivity occurs when sensory input feels dull or requires greater intensity to register. Common experiences include not responding to name being called, seeking visual stimulation through lights or bright colors, seeking deep pressure or not noticing pain changes, craving movement or pressure, and missing hunger or bathroom signals from the body.

Many autistic women experience a mix of both hypersensitivity and hyposensitivity. I might be painfully sensitive to sounds and smells, yet under-responsive to pain or temperature. This complex sensory profile often confuses healthcare providers who expect more consistent patterns.

Research by Crane et al. (2009) found that "Women with autism frequently display complex sensory profiles that may be overlooked in clinical settings. This is particularly true when hyper and hyposensitivities co-occur, as the presentation can seem contradictory to clinicians unfamiliar with the nuances of autistic sensory processing."

Why Sensory Differences Are Misunderstood in Women

As with many aspects of autism, sensory differences in women and girls often go unrecognized for several critical reasons. First, girls are typically socialized to prioritize others' comfort over their own, to "be good," and not make a fuss. This social conditioning means many of us learn to hide our sensory discomfort, sometimes so effectively that even we don't recognize the toll it takes.

Research reveals a troubling pattern in how autistic girls learn to navigate sensory challenges within social contexts. Tierney and colleagues (2016) conducted in-depth interviews with ten adolescent girls with autism and discovered that these young women developed explicit masking and imitation strategies to cope with their social environment, motivated primarily by an intense desire to form and maintain friendships. The study found that girls described the social environment as uncertain and exhausting, yet they persisted in using techniques to mask their autism-related difficulties, including sensory responses, rather than seeking accommodations or expressing their needs. This masking behavior comes at a significant psychological cost —participants reported exhaustion, anxiety, and depression as consequences of constantly camouflaging their authentic responses to overwhelming sensory experiences. The research suggests that the increased social demands of adolescence, combined with gender-based expectations about how girls "should" behave, create particular challenges for autistic girls who feel pressure to endure sensory distress rather than advocate for their comfort needs.This pattern of self-suppression not only impacts immediate well-being but can also delay proper diagnosis and support, as girls become skilled at hiding the very symptoms that would indicate their need for help.

By the time many women seek diagnosis in adulthood, they've spent decades overriding their body's sensory signals—often at significant cost to their mental and physical health.

Second, sensory overwhelm in boys might manifest as visible meltdowns, aggression, or hyperactivity—behaviors that trigger referrals. Girls, however, tend to internalize their distress, showing subtler signs like withdrawal, silence, perfectionism, anxiety, or physical complaints like headaches and stomach issues.

My sensory overwhelm usually presented as becoming extremely quiet and withdrawn. Talking became so painful that even my favorite topics were not worth the effort. I could feel my blood pulsing in my temples, debilitating pain intensifying with each pulse. I would develop sudden headaches and nausea from natural light hitting my eyes as I walked outside, which is why I wear sunglasses even on rainy days. They became debilitating weekly migraines that could last between 24 hours to four days during which I could not eat, would vomit after drinking, and would need to constantly wear sunglasses. I could lose eight pounds during a typical migraine. Every day as I woke up, I feared that a sudden migraine would paralyze me. As I grew older and still had to face my daily activities despite the pain, I started to appear "spacey" or dissociated, disengaged. I was just going through the motions despite the pain, trying to avoid any trigger that could aggravate my symptoms: talking, socializing, noise, light. To remain in control of triggers, I needed to observe a rigid routine where plans had to be followed, and any change was a direct threat to my health. I would face those threats with tears, complete shutdowns or meltdowns. For my close circle, I was impulsive, unstable, overstressed, overworked, oversensitive, over the top. My survival quickly meant removing myself from any kind of social life and even my family life. Outside of work, I was mostly lying down in a dark room, with sunglasses on and ice packs on my temples. My life was pain and obligations. I couldn't stand it.

None of these behaviors screamed "sensory processing issue" to anyone around me. Instead, I was labeled as shy, sensitive, a perfectionist, or anxious—all characteristics often seen as normal personality variations in girls and women rather than potential signs of autism.

Third, many autistic women develop elaborate compensation strategies to manage their sensory environment, while simultaneously masking their distress and assimilating by suppressing their natural sensory needs to avoid drawing attention. Compensation strategies include carrying emergency items like sunglasses and headphones and creating routines to manage sensory triggers. Masking behaviors involve developing excuses to leave overwhelming situations instead of stating sensory needs directly, or forcing participation despite pain. Assimilation patterns include building their lives around avoiding sensory challenges rather than advocating for sensory-friendly environments and suppressing natural sensory responses to appear "normal."

Research confirms that many autistic adults who appear most "successful" in neurotypical environments are often those who have developed sophisticated but largely invisible compensation systems. Livingston and colleagues (2019) conducted the first quantitative study of compensatory strategies in autism, identifying that autistic adults employ complex repertoires of social strategies ranging from surface-level masking to deep compensatory approaches that provide alternative cognitive routes to social understanding. In another study, qualitative this time, they revealed that compensation typically results in a lack of support because participants appeared "too normal," with employers and colleagues holding them to neurotypical standards while their autistic characteristics went undetected.

Their studies found that because autistic characteristics went undetected by others, many participants reported difficulty requesting workplace accommodations, and following disclosure of their autism diagnosis, they were often disbelieved and poorly supported due to their neurotypical presentation. This "compensation" involves individuals consciously employing alternative cognitive strategies to demonstrate neurotypical social skills despite continuing to experience autism-related cognitive difficulties, creating an exhausting behind-the-scenes effort to appear socially competent. The research demonstrates that this extensive masking and compensation leads to frequent exhaustion and burnout, as these individuals must maintain constant vigilance about their presentation while never receiving the environmental modifications that would actually support their sensory and cognitive differences.

Sensory Triggers and Shutdown Patterns

For many autistic women, sensory overload doesn't build gradually—it accumulates invisibly until a sudden tipping point is reached. This pattern often confuses others, who only see the "overreaction" to what seems like a minor trigger, not the compound effect of the sensory load that preceded it.

Common sensory triggers for autistic women include auditory triggers like multiple conversations happening simultaneously, background music while trying to converse, unexpected loud noises, high-pitched sounds, repetitive noises, and echo-y environments. During a birthday party, I was seated at a table near both the DJ speakers and the kitchen entrance. By the time the toast began, I had endured two hours of overlapping conversations, clinking glasses, periodic music, and the swinging kitchen door's squeak. When the husband of the birthday girl tapped his glass with a spoon to begin his speech—a sound everyone else barely noticed—I felt like each tap was a physical blow to my skull. I naturally covered my ears and inserted my noise-canceling headphones. Later in the evening, I overheard a guest mentioning my "dramatic" behavior about "just a little tapping," completely missing how that small sound was the final straw after hours of accumulated auditory stress. I decided to ignore the comment, but it still stung to be judged for reacting out of genuine discomfort.

Visual triggers include fluorescent lighting, bright overhead lighting without dimming options, visual clutter and excessive movement, flashing lights or screens, and certain patterns or visual repetitions. My first part-time job was in an office with fluorescent lighting that had a subtle but persistent flicker. By mid-afternoon each day, I would develop severe headaches. My coworkers couldn't perceive the flickering at all, and I was denied a request to use a desk lamp instead of the overhead lights, suggesting I was being "high maintenance." I eventually resorted to wearing tinted glasses, claiming they were for screen protection rather than light sensitivity. The day I forgot my glasses, I vomited at my desk. A coworker suggested I might be pregnant.

Tactile triggers include clothing tags, seams, or certain fabric textures, unexpected touch or hugs, temperature extremes or rapid changes, certain fabric weights or pressures, and sticky, greasy, or wet sensations. As a child, I would only wear certain clothes and would have meltdowns over others. My mother, thinking I was being defiant, once forced me into a wool sweater for a family photo. What she saw as stubbornness was actually a response to what felt like thousands of tiny needles stabbing my skin. I dissociated during the entire photo session, appearing vacant-eyed in all the pictures. My grandmother blamed me for grimacing rather than smiling. Later, my mother found scratch marks where I had tried to relieve the sensation under the sleeves. Still, this was interpreted as me "being difficult" rather than experiencing genuine tactile distress.

Olfactory triggers include perfumes, colognes, and scented products, certain cleaning chemicals, food odors in closed spaces, body odors, and artificial scents. Social-sensory triggers include maintaining eye contact while processing speech, facial expressions that don't match verbal content, navigating physical proximity in social situations, and processing emotional information during sensory stress.

As a child, my mother would get upset at what she would call my "attitude" during serious conversations. She would ask me to look at her in the eyes instead of looking away. When I would do so, I was so focused on looking at her eyes that my intense eye contact would make her uncomfortable to the point that she would accuse me of "having daggers in my eyes." What she didn't understand was that I could either look at her or process what she was saying —not both simultaneously. I had developed compensation strategies like looking away to better process information, but I was forced to assimilate by maintaining eye contact even when it prevented comprehension. When I tried to use my compensation strategies, my mother interpreted them as defiance, so I learned to mask my confusion while assimilating to her expectations, often losing track of the conversation entirely. If social connection seemed more important at that moment, I would force eye contact but often lose track of the actual content being discussed, eventually being punished for not being able to repeat what she had just said. This trade-off is something many autistic women navigate constantly in personal, professional and academic settings.

From Trigger to Shutdown: The Invisible Pathway

What makes sensory processing issues particularly confusing for outside observers is that the pathway from trigger to shutdown isn't always linear or visible. Research has identified several common patterns that explain these complex responses. The accumulation effect occurs when sensory overload "can build up over time due to the effort it takes to cope with sensory sensitivities in daily life," depleting coping resources until a seemingly minor input causes shutdown. This can be triggered by a single event, like an unexpected loud noise, or it can build up over time. The accumulation effect occurs when multiple smaller triggers add up throughout the day, depleting coping resources until a seemingly minor input causes shutdown.

When my children were little, I worked online while my husband went to the office. I had created a carefully calibrated routine that balanced my work, childcare, and sensory needs —structured mealtimes, designated play periods, and most importantly, the children's nap, which served as my essential sensory recovery period. Occasionally, my husband would surprise me by coming home for lunch with a coworker. While this seemed like a pleasant social break to him, it completely disrupted my sensory management system. Instead of my quiet lunch routine followed by their nap and my crucial recovery time, I suddenly had to process loud adult conversations echoing through the house while managing my children's excitement about the unexpected visitors. By the time my husband and his colleague left, nap was derailed, and the children were overstimulated. With my recovery period eliminated, I'd still have to complete work deadlines and take the children to afternoon activities. By this point, my sensory system would be in overdrive—the sound of other parents chatting at drop-off felt physically painful, my children's voices seemed amplified to an unbearable degree, and even the ambient noise of the playground was intolerable. I would rush to drop my children off, then retreat to my car where I'd attempt to work on my laptop with sunglasses on because even the bright screen had become too intense. My husband was completely baffled by these episodes. "But you seemed fine during lunch! You even said you liked my friend—he's a nice guy." What he couldn't understand was that my daily schedule wasn't arbitrary—it was a meticulously designed system to prevent sensory accumulation by including recovery periods between triggering activities. His impromptu lunch visit wasn't the cause of my distress; it was the disruption of my essential recovery time that left me vulnerable to every subsequent sensory input for the rest of the day.

The delayed response occurs when sensory reactivity differences manifest in complex ways that may not be immediately apparent, with sensory overload sometimes feeling like "intense anxiety, a need to escape the situation or difficulty communicating" that appears hours after the triggering event.

Often, when I attend parties or go out for about two hours of loud laughter, voices covering background music, bright lights, and random ringtones, I seem perfectly fine during the event. I am engaged, smile and participate actively. But sometimes, it's not until the following morning that the sensory hangover hits me. I have a hard time getting out of bed, develop a migraine, and find myself on the verge of tears over minor frustrations. My family often connects this "mood crash" to work stress rather than to the intense sensory experience from the day before. In a way, I can borrow my social energy from the next day to get through the day, but the bill always comes due, with late fees. For an outsider, I may look manipulative: masking my sensory distress successfully during a family gathering but then experiencing the crash the next day when I can no longer maintain the masking and assimilation required to appear neurotypical.

The cross-modal effect occurs when "stress in one sensory channel can reduce tolerance in others," as children with autism "may have more difficulty with automatic processing of information and may already rely more heavily on already overloaded attention and working memory-based networks, such that when the stimuli reach and exceed capacity, the processing system fails." For example, coping with loud noises may lower my resistance to bright lights or touch. During a work conference, I was managing the noisy exhibition hall by wearing discreet earplugs. When a colleague unexpectedly touched my shoulder from behind, I jumped, which seemed like an extreme reaction to a gentle tap. My tactile sensitivity was heightened precisely because I was allocating so much energy to managing the auditory environment. It's like a circuit breaker—when one sensory system is overloaded, the thresholds lower for all others.

This complexity helps explain why many women with undiagnosed autism find their sensory reactions confusing. Before my diagnosis, I would be fine at a party I was eager to attend. Suddenly, after an hour enjoying myself, I would feel the desperate need to escape immediately. I instinctively wanted to push everyone out of my way to retreat to a quiet environment, alone. I would blame myself for being antisocial, when, in fact, my nervous system had been working overtime from the moment I arrived.

Another pattern many late-diagnosed women report is what some of us started calling the 'crumbling mask effect'—as sensory overload increases and our energy depletes, the ability to maintain masking behaviors and assimilation patterns decreases proportionally. At this point, even beneficial compensation strategies become impossible to implement because we lack the energy to use them effectively. In those situations, I run out of battery suddenly: I may be able to articulate words but without the appropriate speech pattern or facial expressions to support my speech. By that point, I am actually deep into overload. The real struggle had started earlier, but no one could see it because I was still able to mask in hope of "making it" to the end.

***

CAMOUFLAGING AND SOCIAL EXHAUSTION

I was complimented on how well I "handled" a three-day conference. No one saw me hiding in the hotel restrooms during lunch break or rehearsing my social performances each night, before crashing dead asleep, unable to form sentences, my head and back aching from the effort of being "on" for 12 hours straight.

The Performance of a Lifetime

The corporate networking event buzzed with conversation, laughter, and the clink of glasses. I stood by the appetizer table, glass of sparkling water in hand (alcohol intensifies my sensory issues), smiling and nodding at appropriate intervals as a group of colleagues discussed their weekend plans.

"What about you? Any exciting plans?" someone asked.

Without hesitating, I gave my practiced answer about a made-up brunch with friends, making sure to keep just the right amount of eye contact—enough to look interested but not so much that it seemed intense. I tilted my head a little, like I had seen other women do when they were curious. I changed my voice to sound just the right amount of excited—not too dull, not too over the top.

"That sounds lovely," a coworker responded, and the conversation moved on.

No one could see that under my carefully built mask, I was doing a lot of mental work: watching my own facial expressions, checking their reactions to see if they liked me or were confused, paying attention to the background noise that made it hard to hear, and fighting the strong urge to escape to a quiet place. No one knew I had practiced this exact conversation in the mirror that morning, or that I had looked up news stories to get ready for "spontaneous" small talk. The truth was: I couldn't wait for the weekend to stay home alone, comforting myself with an ice pack on my forehead and a Tim Burton stop-motion movie, in bed and in the dark. The last thing I wanted was for a social event to take away my much-needed time to recover before the next week.

Three hours later, I walked into my apartment, closed the door, and collapsed onto the couch. The smile fixed on my face disappeared, and my body, once posed to appear relaxed and confident, curled up on the couch. The voice that had maintained the proper inflection and volume now fell silent. I couldn't form words, much less sentences. It would take the entire weekend to recover from three hours of "successful socializing"—alone, in the dark, with no demands to be anyone but myself. I questioned whether I wanted to continue in a career where networking was mandatory. A successful event meant more invitations and even more social events. I eventually resigned. Management urged me to reconsider, highlighting my potential and the time it took to build a book of business. I struggled to explain my situation and eventually mentioned Autism. I was told, "Oh, honey, you're fine! Don't limit yourself to a label! It's all mental blocks. You're stronger than that!" I left feeling even more defeated.

This is camouflaging—the exhausting art of hiding your autistic traits to survive in a neurotypical world. And I had become a master at it long before I knew I was autistic. I began the exhausting work of trying to become someone else.

The Masking Marathon

By my twenties, I had become very good at hiding my true self. I watched other women closely, taking note of how they acted, talked, and moved through life. I built a version of myself that laughed at the right times, pretended to care about topics that I found boring, and hid the habits that helped me calm down when I felt overwhelmed.

Research using functional magnetic resonance imaging (fMRI) has revealed that autistic individuals show atypical neural patterns during social cognitive tasks. Studies demonstrate that while neurotypical individuals recruit cognitive control regions effectively during both social and non-social tasks, autistic individuals show marked hypoactivation in these areas specifically when processing social-cognitive stimuli, suggesting that social information interferes with cognitive control functioning. Meta-analytic evidence confirms that individuals with autism exhibit aberrant activation patterns in frontoparietal, dorsal attention, and other networks during tasks requiring effortful control, indicating the different neural strategies required for cognitive processing in autism.

But masking is exhausting work, and the cracks showed under pressure. In romantic relationships, partners were often initially drawn to my intensity, focus, and genuine interest in their lives. My way of connecting meant understanding someone completely—their thoughts, feelings, and preferences. The neurotypical idea of "casual" relationships didn't make sense to me; I seek depth and genuine connection, a level of commitment rarely reciprocated, especially by younger partners. Eventually, I would grow hurt by loyalty mismatches and exhausted from hiding my autistic traits. I would leave to recover, even as it meant breaking cherished routines that had been built around their lives. Leaving wasn't just ending a relationship—it uprooted one of the few connections I'd made and left me alone, routine disrupted. My sense of direction vanished; I had to navigate life in the dark.

Research by Sedgewick et al. (2016) explored friendship and romantic relationships in autistic women, finding that they often develop intensely focused relationships where individual best friends become "the sole focus of their social lives." Later research revealed that some autistic women describe their romantic partners as becoming their "special interest," reflecting an intense capacity for devotion and loyalty that stems from both social anxiety and a genuine desire for deep connection (Sedgewick et al., 2019). This pattern, while often misunderstood, represents an autistic strength in the capacity for loyalty and commitment.

The pattern repeated itself in friendships, at work, even within my own family. I would give everything—my time, energy, attention, care—only to find myself on the outside looking in, watching as others formed the effortless connections that seemed to elude me no matter how hard I tried.

As a result, everyone refused my diagnosis, and I had to maintain the hidden labor of camouflaging, the exhausting act of trying to pass as neurotypical.

You'll see why so many autistic women are misdiagnosed or dismissed and what happens when we prioritize belonging over authenticity. Camouflaging is the internal rewiring many autistic women do to survive socially. But it comes at a devastating emotional and physical cost. What appears to be social success on the outside often hides deep-seated exhaustion, identity confusion, and a growing disconnection from the self.

What Is Camouflaging?

After years of mastering these invisible performances, I began to understand the concept behind them. Camouflaging (also called masking) means hiding your natural autistic behaviors, sometimes without even realizing it, and copying the social behaviors of most people to fit in. It's a tiring process of watching and changing how you act, react to things around you, talk, and what you show interest in, just to seem "normal" to others.

Dr. Meng-Chuan Lai, a prominent autism researcher, discusses how "teenage girls reported that they developed explicit strategies to manage social relationships, in particular imitation and masking" (Lai et al., 2017), and describes camouflaging as involving "hiding behaviours associated with their ASC, using explicit techniques to appear socially competent, and finding ways to prevent others from seeing their social difficulties." However, for many autistic women, camouflaging goes beyond conscious strategies—it becomes so deeply ingrained that we lose awareness of doing it.

Dr. Devon Price's important work on autistic masking shows how harmful it can be. In their research on autistic burnout, Price describes masking as "a survival strategy that ultimately becomes a prison" (Price, 2022). We learn to watch every facial expression, change how we speak, and hide every "unwanted" behavior. The mental effort is huge, and the emotional cost is even bigger.

Common camouflaging behaviors include:

• **Social Mimicry:** Copying others' facial expressions, gestures, phrases, and intonation (once I started standup comedy, I began expanding my social circle, literally mimicking comedians' behaviors and using their lines to bridge the gap between my neurological differences and neurotypical brains to connect with my peers).

• **Scripting:** Preparing conversations in advance, including questions, responses, and anecdotes. This practice becomes so natural that I still surprise myself to this day replaying my daily conversations to analyze them, identify my "social faux pas" and anticipate a more appropriate answer to rehearse to perfection for the next similar conversation. It keeps my brain busy at night, instead of allowing me to relax and recover.

- **Forced Eye Contact:** Making deliberate eye contact despite discomfort. Eye contact became somewhat "normal" to me now, but I tend to have intense eye contact. Between childhood and my forties, I went from no eye contact to "intense eye contact" to the point of not being able to listen at the same time. My mother would order me to make eye contact, then accuse me of looking "furious" and "throwing daggers at her with my eyes," and would eventually slap me for my disrespect. So, yes, I eventually "learned" to soften my eye contact, even though, sometimes, when I get very into a topic, I might forget to look away here and there.

- **Interest Suppression:** Hiding passionate interests that might seem "odd" or "too intense" (for example, Noah's toilet or imaginary friends).

- **Sensory Pain Suppression:** Enduring painful sensory environments without showing distress. I once endured nine months of intense kidney pain ,as my left kidney tripled in size due to undiagnosed kidney stones.

- **Emotional Masking:** Displaying socially expected emotions that don't match internal feelings: faking happiness and excitement for a celebration like a birthday party, which is mostly a source of social anxiety or laughing at comments supposed to be funny without understanding second-degree humor.

- **Rule-Following:** Creating and adhering to detailed internal rules about social interaction, resisting the urge to talk about an intense interest that is not socially acceptable (toilets).

- **Persona Creation:** Developing entire personalities based on observed "successful" social behaviors. Often, multiple personas are created depending on the context or person: The goofy person, the polite with good manners, etc.

Many of us, particularly late-diagnosed, describe feeling as though our social selves are carefully constructed characters rather than authentic expressions of who we truly are: I spent years watching sitcoms to decode appropriate responses for everyday situations, practicing facial expressions in mirrors until I looked "natural," and memorizing a repertoire of socially acceptable answers. I became an expert at performing normalcy, timing my laughter to match others' reactions to jokes, replacing obvious autistic behaviors with more socially palatable alternatives. Instead of rocking, I learned to twirl my hair , a movement that served the same regulatory function but flew under the radar.

My diagnosis transformed everything. It gave me the framework to recognize these exhausting performances for what they were: toxic, energy-draining behaviors that kept me from expressing my authentic self. The revelation was liberating. Now I embrace who I am in my most genuine form, knowing that how others respond says more about them than it does about me. Like me or don't—that's your choice to make, not my burden to carry.

When and Why Camouflaging Begins

For most of us, camouflaging begins early—often before we have language to describe what we're doing.

The Polyvagal Theory

The Polyvagal Theory, developed by Dr. Stephen Porges, helps explain why masking becomes automatic for many autistic people (Porges, 2011). Our bodies are always checking for safety or danger. When our natural behaviors—such as stimming, needing routines, or having strong interests—

receive negative reactions, our bodies perceive them as a "threat to social connection." Over time, we become extra alert about our own autism, always watching and changing ourselves to avoid rejection. What makes this particularly insidious is that the masking works in the short term: People respond more positively when we force eye contact, when we laugh at jokes we don't understand (or don't find funny at all), when we pretend loud restaurants don't physically hurt us, and even enjoy our time. But each successful mask reinforces the belief that our authentic selves are unacceptable, while we continue to exhaust our energetic resources in hypervigilant states to scan our surroundings.

Research by Hull and colleagues (2017) examined camouflaging experiences in 92 adults with autism spectrum conditions, with questions focusing on the nature, motivations, and consequences of camouflaging. The research used thematic analysis to identify key elements of camouflaging, which informed development of a three-stage model of the camouflaging process. A later study by Hull and colleagues (2020) found that autistic females demonstrated higher total camouflaging scores than autistic males, specifically scoring higher on Masking and Assimilation subscales.

Multiple studies have found associations between camouflaging and mental health issues. Research shows that camouflaging was associated with greater symptoms of generalized anxiety, depression, and social anxiety, and autistic people consistently describe camouflaging as being exhausting and associated with feelings of anxiety, stress, sadness, and identity confusion.

Understanding this brain-body reality is crucial for individuals who work with neurodiverse peers. When you keep correcting autistic behaviors—demanding eye contact, pushing for typical social rules, or treating special interests as problems—you are not helping someone learn. You are teaching them that their way of being is wrong, which can lead to a lifetime of shame and feeling disconnected from who they really are.

Early Childhood: The First Masks

Even as young girls, many of us sensed we were somehow different from our peers. We observed others being naturally accepted while we faced confusion, rejection, or outright bullying. Without understanding why, we began to study our successful peers like anthropologists documenting a foreign culture.

Maeve, diagnosed at 36, shared: "I remember being about six years old, sitting alone at recess, watching the other girls play. I would catalog their behaviors—how they greeted each other, what made them laugh, and how they resolved conflicts. Then I'd go home and practice in front of my mirror. I thought everyone had to rehearse how to be a person."

Research by Dean, Harwood, and Kasari (2017) examined elementary school-aged autistic girls and found evidence of sophisticated camouflaging behaviors during playground observations. The study revealed that autistic girls used compensatory behaviors such as staying in close proximity to peers and weaving in and out of activities, which appeared to mask their social challenges. When observed from a distance, autistic girls looked like their typically developing peers, effectively masking their social difficulties. This camouflaging occurred in contrast to autistic boys, who typically played alone, making their social challenges more easily detectable to observers. These early compensatory strategies often go unrecognized by teachers and parents because the girls appear to be socially engaged, though closer observation reveals they are less successful at drawing on actual social skills when interacting with peers.

Adolescence: When Camouflaging Intensifies

For many autistic women, adolescence marks a dramatic intensification of camouflaging efforts. The already complex social world becomes exponentially more complicated with unwritten rules about everything from clothing choices to communication styles.

My own camouflaging reached new heights in middle school, when the friendly interactions of elementary school gave way to complex social hierarchies, in-groups, and changing friendship dynamics. I created detailed "friendship scripts" in my journal, documenting exactly how to initiate conversations, what topics were "cool" to discuss, and how to tell if someone was actually joking or being mean. I practiced facial expressions and vocal tones for hours, recording and analyzing them to match what I observed in popular girls.

Research by Tierney, Burns, and Kilbey (2016) reveals that adolescence presents particularly challenging circumstances for autistic girls as social dynamics become increasingly complex and demanding. The study found that participants were motivated to develop and maintain friendships, but during adolescence this became increasingly difficult, leading them to develop explicit strategies to manage these relationships, including masking and imitation. The research demonstrates that the complexity and intensity of social demands can become overwhelming during this developmental period, particularly when compounded by transitions to larger school environments with increased social expectations and an inability to interpret unspoken rules. As social expectations intensify and become more gender-coded during adolescence, autistic girls often amplify their camouflaging efforts to meet these evolving social and feminine behavioral demands, though these strategies come with both advantages and significant personal costs.

In my experience, teen girls often find themselves at one of two extremes: either retreating into exceptional discretion and invisibility or becoming strikingly conspicuous—loud in their opinions and reactions, dominating conversations, interrupting others, expressing themselves through bold clothing choices and intense emotions. This more visible presentation can appear almost caricatural, inadvertently pushing people away at the very moment when these girls are most desperate for genuine connection. The irony is profound: their most authentic attempts at social engagement often become the very irritating behaviors that create distance from the relationships they crave most.

Professional Environments: The High-Stakes Mask

By adulthood, many undiagnosed autistic women have developed such sophisticated camouflaging strategies that they can "pass" in professional environments—often excelling in structured settings with clear rules and expectations. However, the energy cost remains enormous.

Research by Black et al. (2020) examined employment facilitators and barriers for autistic adults across multiple countries, revealing that many autistic individuals, particularly women, thrive in structured work environments with clear expectations and predictable routines. The study found that autistic employees often excel in roles that capitalize on their strengths such as attention to detail, honesty, dedication, and unique problem-solving perspectives, with many gravitating toward fields that offer systematic approaches and defined protocols. This career pattern doesn't indicate reduced autism traits, but rather represents a strategic adaptation where autistic individuals can leverage their natural strengths while managing social and sensory demands through environmental predictability and clear role expectations.

My own career choices reflected this pattern. I excelled in roles with clear protocols and expectations, but struggled tremendously with "collaborative" environments where social navigation was constant. I remember one team-building retreat where I successfully played the role of the "enthusiastic team member" for three days straight, only to develop a massive migraine from the strain of constant masking, spending the following week bedridden pretending to have a cold.

The High Cost of Camouflaging

I remember the first time someone complimented me on my "social skills." I was in my twenties, attending a work event where I had spent two hours beforehand researching everyone who would be there, practicing small talk topics, and rehearsing appropriate responses to common questions. My boss told me I was "so good with people," and I felt simultaneously proud and hollow. She was complimenting my performance, not my authentic self. She was so pleased with me; she'll make sure to have me participate in most events... I wanted to cry; I knew I could never sustain social events on a regular basis. I had to find a way out, or I would have to resign.

Research increasingly shows that camouflaging extracts a devastating toll on autistic individuals, particularly women who may mask continuously from childhood through adulthood without support or understanding.

Identity Confusion and Loss

When you spend decades pretending to be someone else, who are you, really? Many late-diagnosed autistic women report profound identity confusion after years of camouflaging.

Hull et al. (2017) found that: "Many participants described feeling as if they were playing so many different roles for different people that they were unsure which, if any, was the real them. This led to an identity crisis for some, who felt they had lost sight of who they truly were after decades of camouflaging."

I experienced this acutely in my late twenties when, after a particularly social period in my life, I realized I had different personalities for different friend groups. With one group, I was the "intellectual one" who discussed philosophy and politics. With another, I was the "carefree adventurer" always ready for spontaneous activities (which I actually found deeply anxiety-provoking). With family, I was the "responsible, pragmatic one." None of these versions felt entirely genuine, yet I couldn't identify which—if any—was the "real me."

After diagnosis, I found journal entries from my teen years that broke my heart: "I don't know who I am when no one is watching." That teen didn't know she was autistic; she just knew she was constantly performing.

Mental Health Consequences

Camouflaging clearly links to poor mental health. Ongoing stress comes from constantly being on edge and suppressing emotions. People often feel excluded, even when they have tried hard. Comments like "But you seem so normal!" are dismissive. Deep fatigue drains energy needed for self-care and happiness.

Many people often reach a breaking point, even when they seem to be doing well at work. On the outside, they look successful, but inside, they may have panic attacks, emotional breakdowns, and stress-related health problems. Each time I reached my breaking point at work, I could barely get out of bed on weekends. I often ordered food in and took naps throughout Saturday. Meeting anyone or enjoying an activity was the least of my concerns. I needed to catch up on sleep just to get through the next week. My life became a depressing hamster wheel, and I was severely depressed.

Physical Burnout

In a groundbreaking study, Raymaker et al. (2020) identified "autistic burnout." It was the first formal academic research to define and characterize autistic burnout. The researchers used a community-based participatory research approach to conduct thematic analysis of 19 interviews and 19 public Internet sources. They ended up identifying it as the effects of prolonged masking, defining autistic burnout as chronic exhaustion, loss of skills, and reduced tolerance to stimulus.

After hiding my traits for a long time, I usually feel exhausted, lose abilities I once had, and find it harder to manage daily life. Physical signs may include being more sensitive to light, sound, or touch. I usually experience even more difficulty staying organized, communicating, or struggle to speak for a while. With autistic burnout, we may also become more susceptible to illness, get stomach problems, struggle to fall asleep even when tired, and find it challenging to take care of ourselves.

Why Women Become Camouflaging Experts

Research shows autistic women hide their traits more than men. Society expects girls to form friendships and maintain relationships. Boys who are awkward may still be accepted as "geeks." Girls who do not fit in often face harsher consequences.

Dr. William Mandy and colleagues (2012) note, "The social landscape for females is generally less forgiving of social difficulty. There are greater expectations for girls to be socially reciprocal, emotionally expressive, and attentive to others' needs from a young age." For women, social acceptance extends far beyond popularity—it encompasses issues of safety and survival. Research demonstrates that women are more likely than men to adopt "tend-and-befriend" responses to stress, which involve seeking social support and maintaining social networks for protection and resource sharing (Taylor et al., 2000). This evolutionary adaptation reflects how economic dependence and limited financial resources have been identified as compromising women's safety, including entrapping those who may wish to leave abusive relationships (Bybee & Sullivan, 2005, as cited in Adams et al., 2020). Current data demonstrate why social connection remains crucial for women's survival. Women may suffer isolation, inability to work, loss of wages, lack of participation in regular activities and limited ability to care for themselves and their children when experiencing violence (World Health Organization, 2024). Studies consistently show that women at greatest risk of intimate partner violence tend to be those in relationships where the couple has few economic resources, highly subjective stress about finances, experience higher unemployment and live in proximity to economically disadvantaged neighborhoods (National Institute of Justice, n.d.). These findings illustrate that for many women, maintaining social connections is not merely about belonging —it is a critical strategy for accessing resources, ensuring physical safety, and surviving in environments where isolation can lead to increased vulnerability to violence and economic exploitation.

Thus, camouflaging, masking, and assimilating are not just autistic strategies to blend in. They are tools of survival used to stay alive despite daily safety challenges.

How Camouflaging Prevents Diagnosis

As autistic girls and women, we face a troubling catch-22: we're so good at hiding our autism that doctors often miss the diagnosis entirely. For decades, autism was considered mostly a "boys' condition," with studies showing 4 boys diagnosed for every 1 girl. But new research reveals the real ratio is much closer—around 2 or 3 boys to every girl—suggesting thousands of women have been overlooked (Loomes et al., 2017). The problem is that girls learn early to copy their classmates' social behavior and mask anything that makes them seem different (Milner et al., 2019). The result? Countless women spend decades struggling with anxiety, depression, and feeling like outsiders—never understanding why daily life feels so exhausting—because they were too skilled at appearing "normal" to get the help they needed.

The 'social butterfly paradox' happens when hiding your traits makes people think you are not autistic. Doctors and other professionals often encounter someone who appears to possess good social skills. They may not notice the effort it takes. In social situations, camouflaging means planning what to say and learning what others like. It means keeping track of conversations to know when to talk. It also means setting aside time to recover after being social, realizing our own limits, but still pushing ourself until exhaustion.

In romantic relationships, camouflaging can mean tolerating discomfort to please a partner. It may include acting out expected emotions, pretending to share interests, and imitation. Many of us go through cycles: acting, exhaustion, revealing our true selves, and then confusing our partner, which can lead to rejection.

At work, camouflaging is adjusting our language to fit in, putting up with things like noisy office and hiding how tired social interactions make us feel from coworkers.

Recognizing Our Own Camouflaging

Signs include feeling exhausted after socializing when others appear energized. Acting differently in different situations, practicing conversations, and closely watching our own expressions and body language. We may feel as if we're acting, lose skills when alone, or be told we "look fine" even when struggling, and ultimately feeling out of touch with our own preferences and identity.

An exercise I often do is to list the places I hide my traits, noting what I change, which thoughts I hide, the uncomfortable feelings I tolerate, how long recovery takes, what I have practiced saying, and I decide if it's worth it. The older I get, the less I find people and situations are worth degrading my mental health and authenticity.

Building an Unmasked Life

Improvement means knowing the difference between hiding who we are in harmful ways and learning social skills that help us connect while being ourselves. Sometimes, adapting for short periods or safety can be necessary. Taking time to recover afterward matters.

To create places where we do not have to hide, and find people who accept us, we can start by setting up sensory-friendly spaces, making time to be genuine, being open with people we trust and join other autistic people for support and connection.

Simple changes can make hiding our traits much less stressful and help teams communicate more effectively. Written instructions and email updates, instead of spoken directions that can be missed or forgotten, help everyone. Research consistently demonstrates that workplace environmental and social accommodations significantly reduce masking behaviors and improve performance outcomes for autistic employees. Environmental modifications have been deemed to have the biggest impact on successful employment (Buckley et al., 2021) and could be a real improvement for all employees (Tomczak, 2022). In contrast, negative experiences that precluded full inclusion created and reinforced a need to mask or camouflage autistic traits (Morris et al., 2025).

For Parents and Professionals

As parents, watching for subtle signs is important. Is your child acting differently in different places or exhausted after socializing? Does your child observe other children playing or interacting? Is your child very self-critical about social mistakes (practicing conversations, or pretending to be someone else)? If so, your support should include accepting these differences, making space for their recovery, and teaching them to recognize and identify their own limits. Help them finding compatible friends (sharing a common special interest), encourage self-advocacy, and celebrate their authenticity.

As professionals or educators, we must look beyond appearances and consider the hidden cost of camouflaging, including assessing what someone can do and observe reactions in different situations. We should listen to their experiences to create supportive settings. When checking for autism, remember that effective communication does not rule it out. Inner feelings matter as much as what is seen.

Schools can help by establishing clear expectations, creating sensory-friendly environments, accepting different interaction styles, addressing bullying, and helping students connect based on interests rather than conformity.

***

EMOTIONAL DEPTH AND MISINTERPRETATION

I feel everything so deeply that it scares people. So, I learned to feel nothing on the outside, which scared them even more.

The Invisible Storm

I sat in my car, gripping the steering wheel as tears streamed down my face. All day, I had smiled through difficult meetings, nodded at complaints, and laughed at unfunny jokes—performing flawlessly.

Now alone, I couldn't hold back. The tears came from all the feelings I'd pushed down: sensory overload at work, the exhaustion of pretending, and the fear I might never fit in.

Twenty minutes later, composed, I walked into my apartment. My partner asked how my day was.

"Fine," I said automatically, moving toward the kitchen to start dinner.

He looked at me with concern. "You seem distant lately. Sometimes I feel as if you don't really care about anything."

If only he knew how intensely I cared, it felt like drowning. My "distance" was a desperate attempt to avoid being consumed by my constant inner storms. Saying "I'm fine" wasn't dishonest—it was survival.

Many autistic women live this reality: feelings so deep they can't be expressed, yet we're seen as distant or uncaring. Our emotions are often hidden, misunderstood by others, and sometimes even by ourselves. Let's explore this landscape and how misunderstanding shapes relationships, self-perception, and healing.

The Myth of the Cold Autistic Woman

One of the most damaging stereotypes about autism is the assumption that autistic individuals lack empathy or emotional depth. This myth is particularly harmful for autistic women, whose emotional experiences are often dismissed, pathologized, or misinterpreted.

Research by Lai and Baron-Cohen (2015) found that the common idea that autistic people have less empathy or emotion does not show the real emotional lives of many of us. I actually feel emotions more strongly than non-autistic people, not less. It's like a smoke detector that is very sensitive and goes off even with a little smoke, but if there is too much smoke, it stops working because it is overloaded. When emotions become overwhelming, it can appear as though I have shut down or I am not reacting, not because I feel less, but because I feel too much, and it's the only way I can keep functioning. I cannot stress enough how important it is to let go of this stereotype and recognize that shutdown, mutism, or apparent emotional detachment are signs of hidden overwhelm, not a lack of emotion.

Research on autism and emotions reveals that autistic individuals, particularly women, often experience intense emotional responses that may be misunderstood by others. Studies demonstrate that emotion dysregulation is particularly heightened in autistic females compared to autistic males, with this emotional intensity being mainly associated with alexithymia and psychological difficulties.

Clinical research describes autistic individuals as having "empathic attunement" - struggling with absorbing other people's emotional states, creating "a fog of emotions" that makes it difficult to differentiate one's feelings from others' emotions. This intensity often leads to protective mechanisms where autistic individuals may appear to have reduced emotional expression, when in reality they are managing overwhelming emotional experiences.

My own emotional experience has always been characterized by intensity rather than a lack of it. As a child, I would become so overwhelmed by injustice, even in fictional stories, that I would have to leave the room. I felt other people's pain as if it were my own, often to a degree that was incapacitating. Sad movies would leave me inconsolable for days. Arguments between my parents felt like physical wounds in my chest.

Because I felt emotional hurricanes, but didn't show them the "right" way, adults labeled me intense and punished my meltdowns. I had to learn to pack my emotions away, locking them in tight boxes, numbing myself until I no longer felt pain or joy. People called me "withdrawn" or "uncaring," because I would not cry when expected to. I just had shut down completely which made me drift even further from my feelings, as if I wasn't even living in my own skin.

The Complexity of Autistic Emotional Expression

The gap between how autistic women feel inside and what they show on the outside happens for many reasons, making their emotional world complicated and hard to manage.

Different Emotional Processing Timelines

Many autistic individuals experience delayed emotional processing—feeling the full impact of an emotional event hours or even days after it occurs. This creates confusion for both the autistic person and those around them. Additionally, autism spectrum disorder is "associated with amplified emotional responses and poor emotional control" due to compromised emotion regulation mechanisms (Mazefsky et al., 2013). This delayed processing can make emotional responses seem inappropriate or disconnected from the event that triggered them. The delay in emotional expression is therefore not due to absence of feelings but results from complex cognitive processing, sensory overwhelm, and the need to establish safety and certainty in confusing social situations (Lai et al., 2017).

I remember receiving news of someone's death and feeling... nothing. While people grieved around me, I appeared calm, almost clinical in my response to funeral arrangements and logistics. It was interpreted as a lack of genuine care or coldness. The grief hit me later. I found myself sobbing uncontrollably, overwhelmed by memories and loss that my brain had needed time to process. By then, the moment for "appropriate" grieving had passed, leaving me isolated in my delayed but intense emotional response.

The neurobiological basis for these processing differences lies in how "sensory processing" affects autistic individuals, as recent diagnostic criteria revisions have brought this "key domain of autistic experience into focus" (Robertson & Baron-Cohen, 2017). This processing delay means that emotion regulation impairments may be "inherent in ASD and may provide a more parsimonious conceptualization for the many associated socioemotional and behavioral problems in this population" (Mazefsky et al., 2013).

Research shows that people with autism often take longer to understand their emotions and have to think very hard about social situations. Autistic women often act like detectives with their feelings, not just to figure out what others mean, but to check if what they feel is real—especially when things are confusing or when someone is being tricky.

This habit of overthinking feelings is made even harder by alexithymia, which means having trouble identifying and describing emotions. Research demonstrates that "emotional processing difficulties reflect co-occurring alexithymia" rather than being a core feature of autism itself, with alexithymia present in approximately 49.93% of autistic individuals (Kinnaird et al., 2019). This is common in autistic people, especially autistic women (Kinnaird et al., 2019). So, the delay in showing feelings is not because there are no feelings, but because of complicated thinking, feeling overwhelmed, and trying to feel safe and sure in confusing social situations.

A helpful way to think about this is to imagine yourself as a detective at a crime scene. Imagine someone says something that sounds nice but actually isn't. In the moment, something feels wrong—like a quiet alarm you can't find. Instead of reacting immediately, your mind quietly recalls what happened. Then, over the next two days, you think about it, compare how the person usually acts to how they acted this time, notice changes in their voice or timing, and look for clues to explain why it felt wrong. This isn't just worrying too much; it's a way of thinking that compensates for not picking up on social cues as quickly as most people do.

Sensory-Emotional Overwhelm

For many autistic individuals, emotional and sensory overwhelm are intricately connected. Sensory overload can trigger intense emotional reactions, as research demonstrates that "youth with ASDs have greater neural responses to mildly aversive sensory stimuli" and show "sensorilimbic hyperresponsivity" particularly when exposed to multiple sensory modalities simultaneously (Green et al., 2015). Conversely, emotional distress can heighten sensory sensitivity, with neuroimaging studies showing that "the insular cortex receives input from sensory regions across modalities and is involved in emotional evaluation of sensory signals" (Green et al., 2023). This bidirectional relationship reflects shared neural mechanisms, as "a lower threshold for sensory information (hypersensitivity) may lead to intense and easily triggered reactions" while affecting emotion regulation processes (Mazefsky et al., 2013). This connection helps explain why many autistic individuals describe experiencing "intense anxiety" and feeling that "when the brain has to put all of its resources into sensory processing, it can shut off other functions, like speech, decision-making and information processing" (Autism Speaks, n.d.).

When I'm battered by bright lights, piercing sounds, and relentless social demands, my emotions flare and crash. The smallest problem swells to monstrous size, sometimes knocking me down with a sobbing collapse. People only see my outsized reaction—not the invisible storm of noise, pain, and pressure that makes every tiny challenge feel like drowning.

Alexithymia: When Emotions Have No Words

Approximately 50% of autistic individuals experience alexithymia—difficulty identifying, describing, or distinguishing between emotions (Kinnaird et al., 2019). This creates another layer of complexity in the emotional lives of autistic women. Research demonstrates that alexithymia in autism doesn't indicate absence of emotion, but rather difficulty with emotional introspection and verbalization. The emotions are present and often intense, but the individual may struggle to identify what they're feeling or communicate it to others (Bird & Cook, 2013).

For me, alexithymia showed up as not being able to say what I was feeling, even when my emotions were very strong. I might feel sick, jumpy, or unable to sit still, but not know if I am anxious, angry, sad, or excited. This makes it almost impossible to tell others what I need. However, studies indicate that alexithymia is not equivalent to a lack of concern or shallow emotional experiences (Bird & Cook, 2013). Many autistic people feel a lot, but can't easily name or show what they feel, especially right away.

When asked about my emotional state, my default response was always "I'm fine"—not because I was actually fine, but because I genuinely didn't have the words to describe what I was experiencing, and ultimately, I was alive... I might be in the midst of an emotional crisis, but unable to articulate whether I need comfort, space, help, or simply acknowledgment. This communication gap often leaves others, particularly romantic partners or close ones, feeling shut out or unimportant. They may interpret my inability to express emotions as a sign of unwillingness to share or a lack of trust in the relationship. The reality is that I am desperate to convey my inner experience, but I lack the emotional insight at the time to do so effectively. I eventually learned to say, "I don't know what I'm feeling, but it's overwhelming. I will let you know as soon as I can pinpoint it." This statement is actually accurate, and my family members now understand its meaning.

When I can't find words for my feelings, my body begins to scream. Anxiety tangles my stomach until I retch, sadness drags my limbs heavy and limp, anger bursts into splitting headaches, and overwhelm slams me into shutdown so hard my whole body aches. Physical pain erupts long before I realize what I'm feeling. Noticing the cold clamp of shoulders or burning ache in my chest became the only way I could decode my emotions—deciphering sadness in heaviness, anxiety in nausea, overload in pain.

The Rational Empath: Turning Alexithymia into Cognitive Intelligence

Even though alexithymia is often seen as a problem with

emotions, it can have a hidden benefit: it forces you to find a different way to understand feelings, one that is very careful, logical, and sometimes even more accurate over time. Imagine everyone else is using emotional GPS—fast, automatic, and usually right. I use a paper map, a compass, and a weather report. It takes longer, but when the GPS stops working, I can still find my way.

Because I struggle to quickly understand my feelings or read social situations, I've learned to think ahead and anticipate them. When something feels wrong, I examine it closely—remembering what people said, what they believed, and how they acted. I notice small changes in facial expression, voice, or behavior. What others see as chance, I keep as clues.

Often, this has meant picking up on the underlying truth behind a marriage falling apart, an affair beginning, or a betrayal brewing—long before anyone else noticed. I've been called paranoid, too sensitive, or even delusional... until the truth inevitably surfaced. When it did, those same people returned, asking me how I knew. Not because I have some supernatural ability, but because I have trained myself to notice what others overlook, and to compensate for my social difficulties with relentless rational pattern matching.

This is not mind-reading. It's understanding feelings by thinking them through. In this way, alexithymia, although challenging, can lead to a kind of careful empathy—one that utilizes logic, memory, and close observation. Research suggests that individuals with alexithymia may process emotional information differently, often relying more on cognitive processing of emotions rather than affective processing when attempting to understand emotions (Goerlich, 2018). This different path doesn't make it impossible to understand feelings—it just means it takes a different, slower route.

Where neurotypical individuals might feel an emotional undercurrent but dismiss it due to social norms or denial, I investigate. And in that investigation lies my strength—not paranoia, but precision.

The Masking of Emotions

As autistic women, we learn to hide our social behaviors, but we also often hide our real emotions to look more like everyone else. This hiding of feelings makes our emotional lives even more complicated. Research on camouflaging shows that autistic individuals use strategies to "mask or compensate for autistic characteristics" and may involve "portraying a non-autistic persona" during social interactions (Hull et al., 2019). Always pretending to be something we're not, or that we feel things we don't, is not only tiring, but also make us feel disconnected from our true selves.

Learned Emotional Scripts

Early on, I learned that certain ways of expressing feelings were not allowed or considered "wrong." Being very happy was "too much for others." Being very sad was "dramatic." Strong anger was "not reasonable." Fear was "silly." So, I devised ways to express my feelings that wouldn't bother other people.

I learned to show just a little interest instead of real excitement. I acted like I cared, but with "dignity." I started politely disagreeing in monotonous tone instead of showing any kind of agitation. These ways of acting helped me fit in, but they also made me feel disconnected from my true feelings. I started to wonder if my true feelings mattered at all.

The Smile Mask and Self-Defense

Perhaps the most insidious form of emotional camouflaging is what I call the Smile Mask, that automatic, socially conditioned expression of pleasantness, and calm, regardless of internal reality. For many autistic women, smiling becomes a survival strategy, not a reflection of how we feel. Autistic researcher Dr. Wenn Lawson describes the phenomenon of "adaptive morphing," explaining that it represents "a response, not of deceit, but one that is biological and not necessarily chosen" that serves as a protective mechanism for safety (Lawson, 2020). Often, we have been forced to adopt this response to appear socially acceptable. The problem? It may put others at ease, but it conditions us to disregard the way we feel and prioritize other's feelings, setting the perfect ground for abuse.

I smiled through suffocating panic attacks, through humiliation, through every trembling "no" I forced out, even when scared. I even smiled and apologized for asking again for pain management medication through the sharp pain of failed anesthesia during surgery, kidney stones, and a post-operative septicemia, all with a grin masking every flinch. This dangerous misalignment empowers those who cause harm: "She smiled," "She enjoyed it," "She wanted it."

But inside, I was frozen—quickly thinking through all the risks: Will I get in trouble if I say no again? Will they get mad? Will I lose a friend? A job? Am I going to be made fun of for overreacting? Will my parents be upset for damaging their friendship or work opportunity? For many autistic women, standing up for ourselves doesn't come easily—we have to think about it step by step. From a young age, we are taught to hide our real feelings, especially if they seem "inadequate" Remember, my own mother used to get upset because I could not stand her kiss on the back of my neck, thinking it was her right to kiss me anyway. And she kept doing it, saying, "I would eventually warm up to it." What else did I just needed to experience over and over again before warming up to it?

Let's take a minute and think about what this means and how someone could ignore a girl or woman's refusal to be touched, saying it is their right and that she will eventually want it. Let's think about how ignoring a girl's own feelings about her body as she grows up will affect her relationships and make her more likely to be abuse by others later in life. Even when these patterns are noticed after a diagnosis, women on the spectrum still have to work hard to protect themselves: They must figure out how they feel after years of prioritizing other's feelings, and still dealing with alexithymia, a condition making it hard to identify their own feelings. They also have to believe their feelings are valid to finally trust their instincts. Then, they might start feeling comfortable acting on them and standing up for themselves. Sadly, in emergency situations, this slow and analytical emotional process often takes too long to allow them to react quickly enough to stop someone from hurting them.

By the time I've analyzed my way to certainty—that my discomfort was real, that a boundary was shattered, and my defense would have been justified—I was left with the sting of violation and a storm of guilt. Why was I too slow? Why did I smile instead of scream? Why did I doubt myself when my body already knew the truth?

Studies on autistic women note that this kind of chronic masking significantly increases risk for victimization, delayed response in abusive situations, and PTSD. Studies on autistic women note alarming patterns of vulnerability and victimization. Research by Bargiela et al. (2016) found that 9 out of 14 autistic women participants reported rape, and many described experiences of victimization related to their autistic difficulties, including narratives of passivity and challenges with assertiveness. The Smile Mask is not a failure—it's evidence of conditioning, not consent; proof of Masking, not compliance.

Miscommunication in Emotional Language

Autistic people are widely known to often take things literally, so emotional conversations can be challenging, especially in close relationships where people expect them to intuit their feelings. Non-autistic people often use hints, figures of speech, and expect others to read between the lines. For example, "I'm fine" may mean "I'm upset but don't want to talk," or "Whatever" may really mean "I have strong preferences but don't want to seem demanding" or "I'm really upset."

This way of talking about feelings without saying things directly can be very confusing and upsetting for many autistic women, causing misunderstandings that make it hard to trust others in relationships. If we take "I'm fine" at face value, we might miss important signs about how someone really feels, while others might perceive our straightforwardness as a lack of concern. Dr. Peter Vermeulen's work on context blindness does align with the idea of literal thinking versus intuitive understanding, as the core concept involves difficulty using context to interpret meaning. In his work, Peter Vermeulen describes context blindness as a reduced ability to spontaneously use context to give meaning to stimuli. Literal, or acontextual, thinking is a direct consequence of this. He explains that people with autism tend to form fixed, one-to-one associations between a stimulus and a meaning, rather than using context to interpret flexible, situation-dependent meanings. Key examples from Vermeulen's work illustrating this concept include:

- **A "don't walk" sign:** He cites the famous scene from the movie *Rain Man* where the character Raymond Babbitt, a man with autism, stops in the middle of a street when the crosswalk sign changes to "don't walk," ignoring the context that he was already crossing.
- **Understanding emotions:** Crying is not always a sign of sadness. For those with context blindness, however, seeing a person cry after winning the lottery can be

confusing because the intuitive grasp of "happy crying" is missed.

- **Interpreting objects:** A boy with autism once described a pillow on a bed as "a piece of ravioli." He had correctly identified the bed and mattress but could not use the larger context of the bedroom to override the visual association of the square shape.

The previous examples are more obvious as they characterized a masculine representation of autism. Nevertheless, girls and women face the same challenges, handling them with more subtility. Understanding that "literal thinking" can help jumping to conclusions based on neurotypical emotional expected reactions. (Vermeulen, 2015).

The intuitive understanding that most people possess is dependent on a natural, unconscious sensitivity to context. This process allows for rapid interpretation of ambiguous situations by considering factors like body language, tone, and environment. For those with context blindness, this automatic process is impaired, so they must rely on explicit, literal information to make sense of the world. Vermeulen frames literal thinking as a result of an "intuitive gap," where contextually informed, higher-level meaning is not automatically constructed from lower-level information. This means a person with autism might "see" the context (a bed) but not "use" it to interpret the meaning of a detail within that context (the pillow).

During emotional conversations, I often asked directly for information that I am genuinely missing. Others may see this as cold or uncaring. If someone said they were upset, I would ask, "What exactly are you upset about? What would help? What do you need?" I asked these because I truly want to help, but people often think I am too logical. The truth is, I needed clear details to help. When people are vague, I just don't know how to respond.

The Pain of Being Misunderstood

When your emotions are misunderstood repeatedly, it causes deep emotional pain that can linger long after the moment has passed. If people keep misunderstanding or ignoring how you feel, it becomes hard to trust your own feelings. Many autistic women say they start to doubt themselves, wondering if they are "overreacting," "too sensitive," or "making things up."

While extensive research has examined how individual emotional characteristics and self-regulation techniques contribute to psychological distress such as depression and anxiety, considerably less attention has been given to how interpersonal dynamics—specifically others' responses to emotional expression—impact mental health outcomes. Schreiber and Veilleux (2021) addressed this gap by investigating perceived emotion invalidation, which occurs when individuals feel that others view their emotions as inappropriate or unacceptable. Through three separate studies involving both online participants and college students, the researchers examined whether perceived invalidation could predict psychological distress beyond well-established individual factors. Their findings demonstrated that when people perceive their emotions as being invalidated by others, this interpersonal factor significantly predicted increased emotional distress, even after accounting for personal characteristics such as emotional reactivity, emotion regulation abilities, self-compassion, and emotional intelligence. These results highlight that interpersonal responses to emotional expression may be more influential in determining psychological well-being than previously recognized, suggesting that how others react to our emotions matters as much as, if not more than, how we manage our emotions internally.

The "Too Much" and "Not Enough" Paradox

Many autistic women are told they are "too much"—too sensitive, too intense, too emotional, too reactive. This naturally leads us to hide our feelings, feel disconnected from them, and downplay their intensity. At the same time, we hear the opposite: that we're "not enough"—not caring, open, or responsive enough to others' needs.

This leaves us to feel that we are both too much and not enough, too emotional and too cold, too reactive and too quiet. These mixed messages reflect confusion about how we show feelings, not that something is wrong with us. As a child, I felt anxious about how adults saw my reactions. I was criticized for being everything and its opposite. So, I learned to stay quiet and controlled, and in control of every part of my body and face, almost like a creepy doll. I kept a careful smile that I could erase quickly if someone thought it was wrong, or develop further if everyone was smiling.

This double blind leads to questions about emotional numbness and the nature of our emotional experiences.

Are autistic women born without strong emotions, or have we learned to hide our feelings to protect ourselves? Research strongly suggests it is the second one. When autistic women and girls are repeatedly told their natural emotional responses are excessive or inappropriate, they begin to suppress these authentic reactions. Women and girls in studies reported strategies to mask and camouflage autistic behaviors, such as learning stock phrases or consciously studying eye contact. This emotional regulation is a learned response, not an innate trait.

Research by Gross and John (2003) provides compelling evidence that individuals who frequently suppress their emotional expression experience significant psychological costs. Their comprehensive five-study investigation found that people who habitually use suppression to regulate emotions experience less positive emotion and more negative emotions, including feelings of inauthenticity, compared to those who use suppression less frequently. This pattern occurs because suppression requires individuals to mask their inner feelings and clamp down on their outward emotional displays, which is mentally exhausting and prevents the natural emotional processing that contributes to well-being. The researchers also found that suppression is associated with poorer social functioning and reduced life satisfaction. For autistic women who may already struggle with understanding their emotional experiences, the added burden of suppressing emotions to avoid judgment can create a particularly harmful cycle, where concealing authentic feelings leads to increased distress while simultaneously making it more difficult to develop genuine connections with others who might provide emotional support and validation.

Gender-Specific Emotional Challenges

Autistic women have special emotional challenges because of what society expects from women and how girls are taught to act. Many autistic women feel they have to show perfect control over their emotions to be accepted. Trying to be perfect in this way can make us hide our feelings too much and feel more anxious about showing any emotions that seem "messy" or out of control.

The pressure to always show the "right" emotions made me constantly question how I acted and felt. I often changed my behavior to fit what I thought others wanted, rather than being true to how I felt. This constant self-checking became a form of acting, as I tried to avoid criticism or rejection.

Relationships and Emotional Misunderstandings

The emotional misunderstandings that autistic women go through show a bigger problem: these mix-ups can deeply affect relationships. In romantic relationships, a lack of understanding can lead to repeated hurt feelings. Partners might think shutting down emotionally means rejection, or see honest answers as not caring, showing how different the ways of showing feelings can be between autistic and non-autistic people.

Sarah, diagnosed at 29, shared: "My husband would tell me about his day, and I'd ask practical questions about solutions instead of providing emotional support. He felt like I didn't care about his feelings. I felt I was helping by solving problems. We were both speaking different emotional languages."

Friendships can be especially challenging because they often depend on unspoken emotional understanding and support. Since we struggle with these hidden rules, we may not check in when friends mention stress, or our practical advice can appear uncaring. Throughout my life, these emotional rules, especially with women, felt unclear and always changing, so I often chose activities with men to avoid these challenges.

For many autistic women, when we get too overwhelmed, our emotions can lead to meltdowns. These strong, automatic reactions to excessive stress are often perceived as tantrums, attempts to get our way, or a lack of control over our emotions. Research by Lewis and Stevens (2023) provides crucial insights into the neurological nature of autistic meltdowns. They are involuntary responses to overwhelming stimuli, characterized by individuals feeling completely overwhelmed by informational, sensory, social, or emotional stressors that exceed their processing capacity. During meltdowns, participants in the study described losing logic and experiencing challenges with thinking and memory, while simultaneously grasping for self-control yet feeling "out of touch with themselves." These accounts demonstrate that meltdowns represent a temporary loss of conscious control when the nervous system becomes overloaded, not deliberate behavioral choices. Understanding meltdowns as neurological responses to overwhelm rather than manipulative behavior is essential to identify our distress and the urgent need for environmental modifications or support.

My own meltdowns often happened after a long time pretending to fit in. The stress from trying to appear "normal" would build up until I lost control, causing strong emotional or physical reactions. Unlike tantrums, which are intentional, autistic meltdowns happen automatically when overwhelmed; we can't simply choose to stop them. The shame after a meltdown can be crushing, especially for autistic women who feel they must always control their emotions. The tiredness in the body and mind can last for days. I often had "meltdown hangovers"—times of numbness, exhaustion, and deep shame. I needed these times to recover, but others often misunderstood it as me pulling away.

In romantic relationships, the foundation laid during my formative years—that my natural emotions were wrong, inadequate, and shameful—created the perfect conditions for partners to weaponize my neurodivergence against me. These relationships typically followed a predictable pattern: partners would engage in unacceptable behaviors like lying or hiding important information, then when I responded with legitimate distress, they would dismiss my reactions as "overreacting." They learned to manufacture meltdowns by deliberately pushing my triggers, then used these neurological responses as evidence of my supposed instability. Rather than recognizing my meltdowns as valid communication about overwhelm and their harmful behavior, they reframed them as childish tantrums, denying me basic compassion, medical understanding, or even the right to name my own neurological experiences. This gaslighting was particularly effective because it built upon years of conditioning that taught me to distrust my own emotional reality and defer to "normal" people's interpretations of my experiences.

The systematic denial of care and validation unless I apologized for my neurological responses created a devastating cycle of control. Partners discovered they could manipulate me into compliance by threatening to use my meltdowns against me—suggesting my reactions could cost me my job, my children, my credibility, or future relationships. Gradually, I became increasingly "domesticated," suppressing my natural responses to mistreatment until I could no longer access my own emotions. The physical injuries from meltdowns—bruises, swollen face, dislocated jaw—I learned to hide with makeup and elaborate cover stories, treating my very survival and my children's well-being as dependent on concealing the evidence of my neurological distress. What I failed to recognize was that this concealment enabled partners with their own serious issues—narcissistic personality disorder, substance abuse, or other pathologies far more concerning than neurodivergence—to continue using my autism as a shield for their abusive behavior while systematically eroding my sense of reality and self-worth, while harming me.

Parents, siblings, educators, employers, partners of autistic women and girls, it is your responsibility to teach your children that their emotions, feelings, sensory reactions are valid. It is your responsibility to make sure you are not manufacturing future victims.

Healing Through Emotional Literacy

Healing from years of misunderstanding begins with developing emotional literacy: identifying, understanding, and expressing your feelings effectively. For many autistic girls, the first step is learning more words to describe different emotions. This can include using emotion wheels that assign names to complex feelings, checking our body for signs of emotions, tracking our feelings and causes in a journal, and expressing our emotions.

As we keep track of those, we can notice our own patterns, how long it takes to process certain feelings, what makes us feel overwhelmed, what our bodies do when we feel a certain way, and what we need to recover. Knowing these things about ourselves helps us assert our needs and communicate more effectively with others.

Learning to express emotions in ways that others can understand, while remaining true to ourselves, is crucial. This can involve coming up with things to say in common emotional situations, setting limits on what others ask of us emotionally, teaching close friends and family about how we express our feelings, and being kind to ourselves as we accept our emotions. We need to stop blaming ourselves for social mistakes, strong reactions, and embarrassing meltdowns that left us hurt, alone, and judged. For each of these, we deserve to take time to care for ourselves in every way.

Supporting Autistic Girls and Women

Understanding how autistic girls and women feel is key to giving good and respectful support. It is not only about accepting our strong feelings as genuine, but also speaking out against the notion that we are being childish. When autistic girls react strongly, they are feeling things deeply, and those feelings should not be ignored or treated as problems.

Believe and affirm the feelings autistic girls express or keep inside, and advocate for environments where emotions can be explored safely. Teach emotional vocabulary explicitly to help girls identify their physiological responses. Create spaces where autistic girls can feel and express their emotions freely, without conformity pressures, and recognize the critical importance of honoring emotional authenticity after years of invalidation.

Educators, don't assume that a student who appears unresponsive during emotional times refuse to participate. They may be overwhelmed. Emotional shutdown is not being stubborn—it is a way to cope with extreme emotional pain and stress so the person can keep going. When I have an emotional shutdown or can't speak, I feel a mix of so many emotions, tiredness, and pain that I can't articulate a single word. A shutdown feels like being put to sleep for surgery—you can't feel the pain even though you know it is real and sharp. Numbing allows you to act rationally and to recover facing a pain you really could not go through without anesthesia.

Recognize delayed emotional processing and do not rush students to explain themselves—instead, advocate for a culture where processing time is respected. Make social-emotional expectations explicit, and reject assumptions of universal common sense. Offer varied outlets for emotional expression, such as writing, art, or movement, to ensure that all students are supported.

Healthcare providers must center the experiences autistic women describe internally, advocating for their emotional voices to be heard regardless of outward expression. Recognize that difficulty naming emotions signals a need for support, not a lack of feeling. Offer practical, step by step emotional assistance and consider the profound harm caused by invalidation. True advocacy means treating emotional safety as a professional priority.

Reclaiming Emotional Truth

The repeated misinterpretation of autistic women's emotional experiences is the heart of this argument: it leads to profound disconnection and shame, and sometimes emotional shutdown. Reclaiming authentic emotional expression is key to identity healing and can transform both self-understanding and relationships.

Learning to trust our internal emotional experiences, communicate them effectively, and find relationships that honor our authentic emotional expression is an ongoing and vital process. It requires patience with ourselves and others as we navigate the gap between internal feeling and external understanding. For me, emotional healing has meant learning to trust that my intense feelings are valid, even if others don't understand. It means finding people willing to learn my emotional language, rather than expecting me to always translate. Most importantly, I've recognized my deep emotions are not flaws but strengths to be honored. By reclaiming the validity of my emotions, I not only started to reclaim my emotional identity, but also my emotional safety. At the end of the day, whoever is in my life must respect my feelings, the way I feel them, and listen to me when I express discomfort or pain. Whether my emotions or expressions of them are out of the norm is irrelevant. As autistic women, we spend most of our lives adjusting to neurotypical standards, forgetting that our experiences are ours to live, honor, and respect. Anyone denying our truth is not worthy of our trust.

When I received my diagnosis and started learning about autism traits, I realized that most of what I considered my qualities were inherent autistic traits: special interests with encyclopedic knowledge, extremely analytical abilities, strong rational thinking, and honesty to a fault. Most of my interests had been developed to cope with neurotypical demands (stand-up comedy, theater), while my authentic self had been buried under layers of performance. The emotional reclamation process involved not only accepting my feelings but also recognizing that my authentic self deserved space and respect.

***

THE COMPOUNDING EFFECT OF BULLYING AND TRAUMA

On June 21, 2025, Mikayla Raines, a 30-year-old autistic woman who had dedicated her life to rescuing foxes from fur farms, took her own life. Her husband said she had been "cyberbullied to death" by an online harassment campaign that spread rumors, personal attacks, and constant negativity. Mikayla had autism, depression, and borderline personality disorder—conditions that made her especially vulnerable to the psychological warfare that ultimately claimed her life.

We are not all equally capable of protecting ourselves from aggression. When someone faces conflict already carrying hidden pain from years of being left out, misunderstood, and criticized, they start off at a disadvantage. For the autistic and neurodivergent community, bullying is not just mean; it attacks a fragile sense of belonging that has already been worn down by years of hard social struggles in a confusing world. This chapter looks at why we are more at risk, why these hurts go deeper, and why society must see how much more bullying affects those already struggling because of how their brains work.

I was 31 when I found out I was autistic, but I was eight when

I first realized I was different in ways that made me a target. The bullying I went through as a child and teenager didn't just hurt—it almost broke me. The everyday meanness, being left out on purpose, and the sneaky insults that others seemed to ignore built up inside me like invisible scars. I wasn't just sensitive; I was someone fighting battles with old wounds that never got a chance to heal.

***

The Crisis in Numbers: A Public Health Emergency

The statistics tell a devastating story. Autistic children and teens are twice as likely to attempt suicide compared to their non-autistic peers, with 20% reporting suicidal ideation and 10% reporting attempts in the past year (Conner et al., 2023). The situation becomes even more dire for autistic adults, who are 25 times more likely to make suicide attempts than non-autistic adults, with 42% experiencing suicidal thoughts and 18% making attempts annually (Conner et al., 2023). When combined with research showing that 67% of autistic students experience bullying, these statistics paint a clear picture of a vulnerable population facing life-threatening discrimination and harassment.

The stark disparity in suicide rates—from double in youth to 25 times higher in adults—demonstrates that current anti-bullying measures and workplace protections are catastrophically inadequate. Legal recognition of autistic individuals as a protected minority class, with enhanced penalties for those who engage in bullying, harassment, or discriminatory practices, is not merely a matter of civil rights but a life-saving necessity.

More Vulnerable Brains

The Hyperresponsive Nervous System

My autistic brain does not just feel emotional pain—it amplifies it, focuses on it, and remembers it with devastating clarity. When classmates whispered about my "weird" behaviors or left me out, their cruelty didn't bounce off me like it might for other children. Instead, each act embedded itself in my mind, changing how I saw myself and my place in the world.

Research reveals the neurobiological reality behind this vulnerability. Studies by Basu and others (2005) found that in autistic subjects, the amygdala—an emotion center in the brain associated with negative feelings—lights up to an abnormal extent during direct gaze upon a non-threatening face. Dalton et al. (2005) connected the duration of eye fixation and the magnitude of amygdala activity in autism spectrum disorder. This amygdala hyperresponsiveness represents a neural indicator for heightened emotional arousal triggered by social interaction.

Unlike most people, who can often dismiss or rationalize mean behavior, our brains stay on high alert long after something bad happens. One bullying incident leading to hyperactivation of our amygdala results in heightened fear responses and prolonged emotional processing, causing lasting worry, overthinking, and emotional dysregulation for weeks or months. Rumball et al. (2020) found that about 60% of autistic participants reported symptoms of PTSD in their lifetime, compared to just 4.5% of neurotypicals. Critically, autistic people often develop PTSD symptoms even when criteria A of PTSD (Big T Trauma) is not met, meaning we are inherently more prone to traumatization.

This creates a devastating double vulnerability: because of autism, we are more likely to be victimized, and when victimized, our sensory profile and emotional dysregulation make us more likely to be traumatized.

The Compound Effect of Pre-Existing Social Trauma

Mikayla's husband said her autism made her already hard life even tougher. What he was describing is what researchers Monique Botha and David Frost call "cumulative minority stress"—the mental strain of living as someone different in a world made for most people. By the time most of us face undeniable bullying, we've already spent years being quietly excluded and criticized. We've watched friend groups form around us while we stayed on the outside. We've learned to believe that our natural selves are somehow flawed.

Jessica C. Kitchens (2025) explains how "untreated trauma is a primary trigger of autistic shutdown and burnout. However, many of the challenges autistic individuals face are chronic stressors rather than isolated incidents, making them more likely to experience ongoing, untreated trauma." This ongoing stress makes us perpetually on edge and exponentially more vulnerable when someone is cruel to us.

The Sensory Amplification of Trauma

For autistic individuals, sensory processing differences extend far beyond typical responses to lights and sounds—they fundamentally alter how emotional pain is experienced and processed. When social rejection or bullying occurs, the autistic nervous system doesn't simply register emotional hurt; it activates the same physiological alarm systems typically reserved for physical danger. Heart rate spikes, stress hormones flood the system, and the hypersensitive nervous system remains in prolonged hypervigilance that can persist for hours or days after the initial incident.

Research by Ben-Sasson and others (2019) indicates that individuals with sensory differences experience greater and longer-lasting stress in response to emotional threats. When bullies use loud noises, get too close, or create chaos to bother us, they cause changes in how we handle stress that can last long after the bullying is over.

Personal Account: The Breaking Point

During my second year in college, I lived in student housing and had just ended a three-year relationship. Despite my discomfort, my ex had somehow secured the studio apartment directly next to mine in the same residence. They insisted we could both benefit from the arrangement. I felt uneasy, but the decision was already made—so I went along with it, ignoring my instincts. Within weeks, they had rifled through my belongings and discovered I was seeing someone new. What followed was months of relentless psychological warfare. They spat on my door, surveilled my every movement, strategically "bumped into" me, and flooded my voicemail with disparaging messages. I became a prisoner in my own home. The harassment escalated when they forced their way into my studio as I opened the door, pinning me to the floor to "make me listen." I managed to break free and fled to the hallway, refusing to return until they left and I could lock the door behind them. But locks couldn't contain their obsession. They memorized my schedule, appearing suddenly in places I needed to be, forcing me to hide and abandon planned activities. Leaving away from my family, I soon lost all sense of safety. At year's end, I moved without telling anyone my new address, but it took years to stop constantly looking over my shoulder. I had learned to live in a state of hypervigilance— a survival skill that would later make me vulnerable to those who recognized my conditioned compliance.

Fast forward a good decade... When similar patterns of victimization emerged in my adulthood—through the toxic behavior of a partner's ex—my hyperactive amygdala didn't distinguish between past and present threats. The situation became exponentially more damaging when the very people who should have provided me with support became passive enablers of the abuse. The response from my partner and most of his family members—minimizing the abuse with phrases like "be the bigger person" or "don't make a big deal of it"— represented a profound betrayal that compounded the original trauma.

The abuse was multifaceted and calculated: public verbal insults, social sabotage, threats, and physical boundary violations. They also used covert bullying with manipulative tactics like rumor-spreading, social exclusion, or passive-aggressive behavior to cause psychological harm through damage to my reputation, self-esteem, and relationships. But the most insidious element was how they weaponized my own relationships against me. They sent berating texts about me to mutual friends and trusted acquaintances, transforming them into unwilling messengers of their psychological warfare. My trusted friends became conduits for their vile wishes and insults. They infiltrated my home, invaded my privacy, and parasitized my most sacred spaces—the conversations with people I loved. No relationship, place or moment was safe. No communication was sacred. This systematic assault created what trauma specialists call "complex trauma." Each incident didn't exist in isolation but built upon previous violations, creating a cumulative devastation that shattered both my mental health and my fundamental sense of safety. I developed hypervigilance so severe it resembled PTSD—because nowhere and no one felt safe anymore.

They didn't just abuse me; they corrupted my entire support system, turning my sanctuary into a battlefield.

That's precisely when neurological dam burst occurred —autistic meltdowns returned with a vengeance, unlike anything experienced since adolescence. These weren't products of weakness or immaturity; they were inevitable results of a nervous system pushed beyond its capacity to cope. Yet even these neurobiological responses—clear indicators of severe distress—were pathologized and punished rather than understood and supported.

The meltdowns were dismissed as "overreactions" and met with the cruelest possible response: abandonment. When explicitly requesting physical restraint—a recognized intervention for autistic meltdowns—these pleas for help were denied under the guise that "a man restraining a woman could be accused of abuse." The tragic irony is that this refusal to provide requested support constituted a far more serious form of neglect than the compassionate restraint desperately needed.

The consequences weren't merely emotional—they were devastatingly physical. To this day, permanent injuries sustained during those uncontrolled meltdowns continue to alter quality of life in profound and irreversible ways. Yet even these tangible, ongoing reminders of trauma were subject to denial and erasure. The expectation to lie about these injuries —to minimize or hide them to protect others from looking bad —represents perhaps the most insidious form of gaslighting: the denial of objective, physical reality itself.

How Bullies Target Our Vulnerabilities

The bullying that autistic people face is often more sophisticated than physical attacks or obvious insults. Bullies, whether consciously or not, seem to identify our specific weaknesses and exploit them with surgical precision through the following practices:

Relational aggression, a silent destroyer: Mikayla's husband described how "a group of people had been throwing dirt on Mikayla's name and the rescue," and that "they consistently spread ridiculous claims and rumors." This represents a classic pattern of relational aggression—bullying that targets relationships and social connections rather than using physical force.

Girls and women with autism are particularly vulnerable to this form of psychological warfare. Triantafyllopoulou et al. (2021) found that "high levels of social media use were associated with an increased risk of cyberbullying victimization amongst autistic adults." Maurya's (2022) study shows that people who are cyberbullied present higher rates of depression, anxiety, and thoughts of suicide than those who face more obvious bullying.

A teenager I was working with experienced this firsthand when she discovered that her supposed friend group had maintained a private group chat where they mocked her interests, imitated her speech patterns, and shared screenshots of her earnest messages with commentary. What made this particularly devastating was that it confirmed her deepest fear: that her real self was indeed laughable, that her attempts at connection were inherently flawed, and that even those who seemed to accept her were actually just tolerating her for their own amusement.

The corruption of special interests: Perhaps the cruelest form of bullying for autistic people is targeting our special interests —the things that make us happy, calm, and confident. When bullies attack these interests, they strike at the heart of who we are and our primary coping mechanisms.

Mikayla's passion for animal rescue was her life's work, but it also became a target for those who "spread ridiculous claims and rumors" about her nonprofit organization. Attacking special interests is especially harmful because these are often the only areas where we feel confident and in control.

Exploiting vulnerabilities: My son was fifteen when a friend discovered his detailed knowledge of toilets—a special interest that gave his life meaning. During tennis practice, his friend threatened to expose his passion to other players if he didn't comply with requests, calling his interest "weird and creepy." The more anxious my son became, the more his friend exploited this leverage. I spoke to parents and coaches, but they dismissed it as friendly teasing. For my son, it was constant torment. He obsessed over every possible scenario, searching for ways to handle bullies while still longing for companionship. It took months for him to realize this cruel boy was not a real friend.

Sensory and routine sabotage: Our sensory sensitivities and need for routine make us easy targets for bullies. In middle school, students discovered that loud noises made me jump and sometimes run out of the room. They started planning "jump scares"—slamming books, popping balloons, or shouting when I was working. All seemed like harmless pranks. But for my hypersensitive nervous system, each incident was a neurological assault that left me in hyperarousal for hours. The unpredictability meant I could never relax, never feeling safe enough to focus on learning or socializing.

Crane et al. (2018) research on sensory processing in autism reveals that unexpected sensory assaults can trigger trauma responses that persist far beyond the initial incident. When bullies exploit these differences, they're not just causing temporary discomfort—they're creating lasting changes in our ability to feel safe in the world.

Cyberbullying: When nowhere is safe: Mikayla Raines was "cyberbullied to death" according to her husband, who described how online harassment from "strangers, members of the animal rescue community, and people she knew personally" ultimately contributed to her suicide. Cyberbullying doesn't just move regular bullying online—it amplifies every aspect of the trauma.

Research by Nikolaou (2017) shows that cyberbullying leads to 8.7% more suicide attempts, with students almost twice as likely to attempt suicide if they have been bullied online. Because online harassment can happen constantly, there's no escape or safe space to recover. Hoover (2018) found that autistic children are three to four times more likely to be bullied by peers "with negative impacts on academic functioning and mental health symptoms, including increased risk for suicidality."

Multiple interconnected factors make us especially vulnerable to online attacks. Digital evidence's permanence is particularly difficult for autistic people—unlike spoken bullying we can only remember, online bullying leaves records we can review repeatedly, amplifying anxiety. Social media allows bullying to reach far more people than in-person harassment, magnifying shame for those already feeling isolated. Anonymity enables bullies to be even crueler than they would face-to-face.

Perhaps most challenging for autistic people is the sensory overload accompanying cyberbullying. Constant notifications, alerts from different apps, and information overwhelm can trigger sensory meltdowns that make clear thinking or effective responses impossible.

Personal Reflection

It took me about a decade to gather strength to write this book and expose myself "out there" in cyberspace because of how terrified I was of cyberbullying. I still am after years of school bullying and psychological, emotional, and physical abuse. But because I am among the lucky ones who survived those treatments, I feel responsibility to speak up for those who could not.

When Systems Fail: Institutional Betrayal

One of the most devastating aspects of bullying against autistic people is that institutions meant to protect us often perpetuate or enable additional harm. Schools, workplaces, and even mental health services frequently fail to recognize how vulnerable we are to social aggression.

The "Both Sides" Fallacy

Throughout my school years, when I reported bullying, the response was almost always some variation of "both sides need to work on their communication" or "maybe if you tried to fit in better, this wouldn't happen." This response isn't just unhelpful—it's actively harmful, suggesting that the victim bears responsibility for the aggression they're experiencing.

The idea of "both sides" being at fault ignores that bullying is not a conflict—it's abuse with intention to harm, a power imbalance between bully and victim, and repeated acts. Bullies have more power than their autistic victims. We are dealing with neurological differences, often facing people who understand social situations better than we do. Would schools ever tell a child with a physical disability to "change the way they move their body" to avoid being hurt during recess? The same logic applies here.

The Minimization of Harm

Teachers and school leaders often minimize how much bullying hurts autistic students by saying we are "too sensitive" instead of addressing the real problem. Comments like "they need to toughen up" or "they take everything too personally" reveal serious misunderstanding of autistic neurology. Would a teacher ever tell a child with Brittle Bone Disease to toughen up because it made it hard for other children to play with them? That would be clearly cruel and wrong, potentially exposing a teacher to criminal charges for negligence.

The minimization of harm done to autistic people reflects a broader cultural problem where we're considered partly to blame for how we're treated. This thinking allows bullying to continue and often makes teachers part of the problem by implicitly enabling bullying through refusal to impose actual consequences.

Personal Account: Systemic Failure

When my oldest son was in fifth grade, two girls were picking on him daily. As soon as he arrived at school, walking through corridors, they would deliberately push him around, telling him he was "taking too much space." Teachers were getting tired of hearing him complain, so I asked if he wanted me to meet with the teacher. He refused and said he would handle it. To my surprise, he went directly to the principal's office and told her about "the two bullies." She called them to her office and asked if it was true. They recognized their behavior. When asked why, they explained that "he deserved it because he's stupid." They felt very strongly about it and wanted to make sure my son understood his place. Thankfully, the principal did not tolerate such behavior and ensured consequences. During my own elementary and middle school years, I would never have imagined a principal would be interested in hearing about daily bullying. Realistically, I would probably have been punished for tattling and learned I was to blame.

The Suicidal Cascade: Understanding the Path to Crisis

Mikayla's husband described that "recently more of the rude words, accusations, and name-calling came from some of those she considered close friends, which led her to feel 'as if the entire world had turned against her.'" This represents a recognizable pattern in how bullying against autistic individuals can escalate into life-threatening crisis.

The progression often follows predictable stages. First, we become hypervigilant and anxious, constantly thinking about what happened and how to prevent it from recurring. This causes ongoing stress and sleep disruption. As Mikayla's husband noted, "She was so sensitive to everything, which is a double-edged sword because on one hand, it allowed her endless empathy for those in her care, but it also means that she took everything negative to heart."

Research by Patriquin et al. (2019) found that individuals with autism spectrum disorder demonstrated chronic autonomic nervous system hyperarousal, characterized by lower respiratory sinus arrhythmia and elevated heart rate compared to typically developing peers, indicating sustained biological threat response even in safe environments. Since our nervous systems already perceive threat even in "safe" contexts, it naturally switches to a high alert mode when bullying takes place daily.

The second stage involves social withdrawal and increasing isolation. Next, hearing repeatedly that they are "wrong" or "broken" causes loss of confidence and sense of belonging. This leads to feelings of hopelessness and belief that things will never improve. In the final stage, death may seem like the only escape from internal pain. Sadly, suicidal ideation often isn't a true desire to end life, but to "get a break" when our minds spiral out of control and we live in constant high alert where every noise, touch, or sudden event makes us jump like our lives are at stake. Sleep becomes impossible, and with lack of sleep, the cycle becomes nearly impossible to break without medication.

Holden et al. (2020) found that adolescents with autism spectrum disorder who experienced bullying had nearly double the risk of developing suicidal thoughts compared to those who had not been bullied. The study also revealed that females with autism showed nearly double the risk for suicidality compared to males. Therefore, individuals harassing, bullying, and tormenting populations like ours are not just "lacking care"—they are guilty of criminal cruelty and must be exposed as such by our legal system.

The Protective Silence That Endangers

One of the most dangerous aspects of bullying against autistic people is our tendency toward silence about it. We often don't report it because we've learned that people frequently ignore us, downplay what happened, or blame us instead. Sometimes, we don't even realize we're being bullied, assuming exclusion or mistreatment is our own fault.

I endured years of school and workplace bullying without reporting it because I had internalized the message that my social struggles were my own fault. When colleagues would exclude me from meetings, dismiss my contributions, or mock my communication style, I assumed these were natural consequences of my "difficulty" with social interaction rather than forms of social aggression.

This silence is extremely dangerous because it allows bullying to escalate while the person being bullied feels increasingly worse and isolated. Schools, workplaces, and healthcare providers need to make it safer and easier for autistic people to report bullying and get help.

The Legal and Ethical Imperative

The recognition that autistic individuals face aggravated harm from bullying isn't just a clinical observation— it's a legal and ethical imperative demanding immediate action from institutions and society. If children and senior citizens are treated as special categories with aggravated legal consequences for crimes perpetrated against them, the same should happen with special needs children at school and special needs adults. Enhanced penalties would serve as deterrents while helping the neurodivergent population feel safer and more likely to report misconduct.

The Disability Rights Framework

Both the Americans with Disabilities Act (ADA) and Section

504 of the Rehabilitation Act require schools and workplaces to make reasonable accommodations to ensure equal access and opportunity. This should include enhanced anti-bullying protections for autistic individuals who face documented increased vulnerability to social aggression.

Legal precedent is beginning to recognize that failure to address disability-related bullying constitutes discrimination. In Davis v. Monroe County Board of Education (1999), the Supreme Court established that institutions can be held liable for failing to address harassment that creates a hostile environment for students with disabilities.

The Duty of Care

Institutions supporting autistic people have greater responsibility to protect us from emotional harm. This doesn't mean we are weak or cannot handle challenges. It means our brains are different, so we need specific kinds of protection. Because we are more likely to be deeply harmed or attempt suicide, these institutions are obligated to provide enhanced protection. If they fail, it's not just a mistake—it's discriminatory treatment.

Breaking the Cycle: Intervention and Prevention

Just because autistic people are at higher risk doesn't mean they must suffer alone. Problems identified early and addressed promptly can prevent bullying before it escalates. This cycle can be broken to create safer communities for neurodivergent individuals.

Early Identification and Intervention

The best way to prevent bullying from causing lasting harm to autistic people is early recognition and swift action. This means training teachers, parents, and other students to recognize subtle signs of bullying targeting autistic people and how to intervene immediately. Students' awareness is key as they witness social dynamics firsthand. Valuing their voices and contributions through awards and Good Citizenship programs can motivate them to pay attention to everyone's well-being and support inclusivity.

Trauma-Informed Response Protocols

When bullying is detected, the response should be caring and focused on autistic individuals' needs. This means believing what the autistic person says without requiring proof from the victim. If proof is required administratively, the burden should not fall on the autistic alleged victim. The potential bully should be asked to provide proof they did not engage in such behavior. The bullying should be stopped immediately. The person who was bullied should receive support and understanding, not be told to change. Any interventions should ensure the victim's safety, not just punish the bully. There should also be follow-up to ensure bullying doesn't continue in more subtle ways.

Building Inclusive Communities

The most effective way to prevent bullying is fostering communities that genuinely value neurodivergent perspectives and ensure everyone feels included. This means educating everyone about autism, having clear rules and sanctions for disability-based bullying as discrimination, leaders who model inclusion and stand against unfair treatment, celebrating successes of people who think differently, and establishing support networks connecting autistic people with allies and advocates.

The Growing Community: From Invisibility to Recognition

The time for treating bullying against autistic people as a minor social problem has passed. The research is clear: we face greater harm from social aggression, and institutions have both legal obligation and moral duty to provide enhanced protection. More importantly, we are not a "small community" with little representation. Our community of autistic individuals is growing exponentially as late-diagnosed individuals—men and women in their 30s, 40s, 50s, and beyond—finally receive recognition and understanding they've sought for decades.

This rise in late diagnoses reveals something important: there isn't a sudden outbreak needing to be stopped or fixed. Instead, we're seeing natural human variation that has always existed but was hidden because individuals had to conceal their true selves to fit in. The significant increase in adult diagnoses, especially women, shows that we only seemed rare because of misunderstanding of autism, inadequate diagnostic tools, and autistic people working extremely hard to blend in with neurotypical expectations.

Current diagnostic understanding shows autism was never as rare as people thought. We're now seeing a population that has always been here, living among us, contributing to communities, raising families, working, and improving the world, all while expending enormous energy to blend in. Each new diagnosis isn't a new case of autism, but someone finally being seen after years or decades of feeling different, struggling with social situations, and working much harder than others to navigate a world designed for different kinds of minds.

Autism is simply another of nature's remarkable survival strategies. Many animals and insects have developed camouflaging methods so effective that even scientists struggle to detect them. Leaf insects look so much like leaves that people didn't know about them for hundreds of years. Stick insects can remain motionless for hours, resembling twigs or branches. The leafy sea dragon has appendages resembling seaweed, and people once thought it was mythical because it could hide so well.

Even more remarkably, groups of animals scientists thought were identical have turned out to be different species living together, each with unique traits hidden by outward similarity. Just as these camouflaged creatures have always been present in their ecosystems—contributing to pollination, serving as links in food chains, and maintaining ecological balance—autistic individuals have always been integral parts of human society, their contributions often unrecognized because their differences remained carefully concealed beneath protective masking behaviors.

The Call to Action: Protecting the Already Wounded

Mikayla Raines' husband said, "To those of you who contributed to her pain, I wish you could understand the depth of what she felt. I wish you could comprehend what I feel." His words illustrate the devastating reality that bullying against autistic individuals is not simply cruel—it can have fatal consequences.

Every teacher who ignores an autistic student's concerns about bullying, every manager who allows workplace harassment of neurodivergent employees, and every community member who remains silent when witnessing unfair treatment of disabled people bears responsibility for the serious harm that results.

We are not asking for special treatment—we are demanding equal protection under the law and basic human dignity. When someone enters a fight already wounded, they deserve additional support, not blame for their vulnerability.

Mikayla Raines will not be the last autistic individual to reach that tragic conclusion unless we act. Her death should serve as a wake-up call that the stakes are life and death, and that our response must match the urgency of the crisis.

For schools and organizations, this means recognizing that autistic people are more vulnerable to bullying harm. They need policies and procedures focused on autistic individuals' needs and staff training to recognize and stop autism-targeted bullying. These institutions should ensure their actions protect victims, not just punish bullies. They should also establish systems to help autistic people recover from bullying-related harm.

For communities, this means learning about autism and neurodiversity, speaking out against ableist language and behavior, supporting autistic individuals and families, advocating for inclusive practices, and understanding that protecting neurodivergent members benefits everyone.

For autistic individuals, this means knowing you deserve protection and support. Bullying against you is not your fault. Seek help from trusted adults and professionals. Connect with other autistic individuals and advocates. Remember that your life has value and meaning.

The invisible wounds of bullying against autistic individuals are real, documented, and deadly. But they are not inevitable. With proper recognition, intervention, and prevention, we can create a world where neurodivergent individuals are protected, valued, and allowed to thrive.

We must make a clear choice: either continue allowing autistic individuals to be harmed by social aggression, or actively take steps to protect their humanity and well-being. This requires immediate action from all of us—educators, employers, community members, and leaders—to ensure protection, support, and inclusion for those who are most vulnerable. Our actions now determine their future.

The tragic irony is that sometimes, when the world demands we silence ourselves completely—our voices, our truth, even our bodily reality—the only escape from that suffocating muteness feels permanent. Society has taught us that our silence serves everyone better than our authentic voices—a lesson so thoroughly internalized that some neurodivergent women choose eternal silence over a lifetime of being told their voices, their experiences, and even their physical injuries don't matter.

***

This chapter is dedicated to Mikayla Raines and every autistic individual who has suffered in silence, every family who has watched their loved one be systematically destroyed by social aggression, and every life lost to bullying-related suicide. Your pain is real, your wounds are valid, and your lives matter.

To honor Mikaela's memory and support her mission, go to SaveAFox, 12245 175th St WLakeville, MN 55044, USA, her 501(c)(3) nonprofit domestic fox sanctuary. All donations are tax deductible.

- *Shop her website at* https://www.saveafox.org/donate
- *Sponsor a Fox at* https://www.saveafox.org/fox-sponsor-agreement
- *Donate at* https://www.saveafox.org/donate
- Venmo: @saveafox
- PayPal: @saveafox
- GoFundMe: https://gofund.me/372cbb6d

***

RELATIONSHIPS, REJECTION, AND RESILIENCE

At thirteen, a psychologist specializing in high-potential detection conducted an exhaustive intelligence assessment of my abilities and informed my mother that I had an IQ comparable to that of a candidate in the Mensa organization. My mother was beaming with pride while I sat in that sterile office feeling like a specimen under a microscope, wondering why being high-potential felt more like a curse than a blessing. The adults spoke about me as if I weren't there, discussing my "potential," my unusually well-balanced intellectual abilities, and my "behavioral concerns" in the same breath. What none of us understood then was that I also had high cognitive abilities. Therefore, my brilliant mind was housed in a nervous system that experienced the world like a live wire. Every sound was amplified, every texture felt like sandpaper against my skin, every social interaction a complex puzzle I couldn't solve, no matter how high my IQ tested.

***

A groundbreaking study reveals a deeply troubling paradox: exceptional cognitive ability, traditionally viewed as a protective factor, actually amplifies suicide risk among autistic individuals to devastating levels. Casten et al. (2022) analyzed over 3,000 participants across two independent samples and discovered that autistic individuals with IQs of 120 or higher were nearly six times more likely to experience suicidal ideation compared to their neurotypical peers with similar cognitive abilities. The research demonstrated that autistic children with suicidal thoughts possessed significantly higher cognitive abilities than those without such thoughts, and remarkably, genetic analyses revealed that polygenic scores for cognitive performance and educational attainment were directly associated with increased suicidal ideation—a pattern that extended even to the parents of autistic youth.

These finding shatter conventional assumptions about giftedness as a buffer against mental health struggles and exposes a hidden crisis within the twice-exceptional community, where the very cognitive strengths that should open doors instead become sources of profound internal conflict, highlighting an urgent need for targeted interventions and support systems specifically designed for high-ability autistic individuals who face this unique and life-threatening vulnerability.

This mix of presenting both exceptional intelligence and cognitive abilities, commonly referred as Twice Exceptional Learners, makes it particularly challenging for girls to socially function the way their gender is expected to. Gould and Ashton-Smith (2011) found that smart autistic girls often seem to hide their autism traits despite their sensory overload, which means they are often diagnosed late or not at all, and ultimately struggle in silence.

Research consistently demonstrates that twice-exceptional girls face a devastating double invisibility in our educational system, where gender bias compounds the already complex challenge of identifying students who are both gifted and learning disabled. These academically capable twice exceptional students may be labeled as "unmotivated" or "lazy" when their academic work is far below their perceived ability. Since girls are diagnosed as gifted far less frequently than their male counterparts, with cultural inclinations to "write off girls' academic strengths as mere hard work" rather than recognizing their true intellectual abilities (Colorado Department of Education, n.d.). This systematic underidentification is further exacerbated by research showing that boys were 1.19 times more likely than girls to be identified as gifted and included in gifted programs, while twice-exceptional students overall represent one of the most underserved populations in schools (Peterson, 2013).

The tragic consequence is that bright girls with learning differences languish in educational limbo, their intellectual gifts masked by undiagnosed disabilities, leading to years of academic frustration, damaged self-esteem, and lost potential. Without proper identification and support, these girls may never receive the accommodations they need to succeed, instead carrying the burden of being perceived as simply not trying hard enough—a mischaracterization that can follow them throughout their educational journey and beyond.

The Language I Didn't Have

Before I knew about autism, before I understood that my brain was wired differently, I collected rejections like some people collect stamps. Each one was carefully classified, examined for meaning and context, and stored away as evidence of my fundamental wrongness.

I remember being eight years old at my very first and last birthday party, which my stepmother had kindly organized at my grandparents' place. I watched the other girls play a game where they whispered secrets and giggled. I approached their circle, desperate to join in, and asked directly, "What are you talking about? Can I play?" The immediate silence that followed was deafening. One girl looked at me with a mixture of pity and annoyance and said, "You don't get it, do you? We're not playing anything." I stood there, genuinely confused, watching as they moved their circle slightly away from me. I was excluded from my own birthday party by the girls I was hoping to finally connect with outside of recess. Clearly, the school context was not an issue; I was.

Research consistently documents how autistic girls experience a particularly insidious form of chronic peer rejection that compounds over time, leaving them feeling fundamentally disconnected from their peer groups. Dean et al. (2014) conducted a landmark study comparing the peer relationships of elementary school children and found that autistic girls "seemed to be overlooked, rather than rejected" and "appeared to be ignored or overlooked" rather than being overtly excluded like autistic boys. This pattern of social invisibility is particularly damaging because girls with autism "were less likely to be listed as a friend, as a member of a group, or as a non-preferred friend," leaving them "neither accepted nor rejected" but instead systematically excluded from the social radar (Dean et al., 2014). The chronic nature of this rejection creates lasting neurological impacts, as demonstrated by Will et al. (2016), who found that adolescents with "a history of chronic peer rejection showed higher activity in brain regions previously linked to the detection of, and the distress caused by, social exclusion". This invisible exclusion is particularly devastating for autistic girls because, unlike boys who are overtly rejected, girls remain trapped in a liminal social space where their difficulties go unrecognized while their fundamental need for connection remains unmet, leading to feelings of profound otherness and social alienation that persist throughout their school years.

"You're so weird" or "sorry, we already have enough players" became the soundtrack of my childhood. Teachers called me "desperate for attention" with "a bad temper" when I had meltdowns that looked like tantrums but felt like my nervous system was short-circuiting. Other children sensed my difference like animals sense an approaching storm—instinctively moving away from something they couldn't name but knew didn't belong.

In my teenage years, the feedback became more sophisticated but no less cutting. Each comment landed like a small knife, precise and sharp, carving away at my sense of self. I developed a particular insidious stress in social situations where my natural communication style and interests were consistently dismissed or pathologized. I was not feminine enough for enjoying and repeating jokes deemed inappropriate for a "proper girl." I did not enjoy girls typical activities such as shopping, or discussing pointless gossips in loud groups of teenage girls suddenly bursting in unbearable loud laughter. For most of us, girls and women, this contributes to higher rates of anxiety, depression, and self-harm in autistic teenage girls compared to their male counterparts (Martini et al., 2025).

I learned that my natural way of being, my direct communication, my passionate interests, and my need for routine and predictability, were fundamentally unacceptable. The pattern repeated itself in friendships, at work, even within my own family. I would give everything—my time, energy, attention, care—only to find myself on the outside looking in, watching as others formed the effortless and lasting connections that I craved but could not develop, no matter how hard I tried.

The Perfect Storm of Trauma

The rejections weren't just social inconveniences—they were happening against a backdrop of trauma that made every dismissal feel existential. The sexual abuse I endured as a child had already taught me that my body wasn't safe, that my needs or safety didn't matter. The physical abuse reinforced that I was powerless, that speaking up would only bring more pain.

My mother would often slap me for "looking furious" when I was trying as hard as I could to look her in the eye and show her the respect she expected. What she called defiance and anger were the intense focus I was trying to convey through my gaze, as I looked directly into her eyes. The physical pain of the slap was nothing compared to the confusion of being punished for trying to do exactly as she asked. In fact, autistic individuals experience significantly higher rates of trauma and abuse compared to the general population.

Cazalis et al. (2022) conducted an online survey of 225 autistic women in France and found extremely high rates of sexual victimization: 88.4% reported experiencing sexual violence when assessed through standardized questionnaires, compared to 68.9% through open-ended questions. Two thirds of victims (68%) were 18 or under when first assaulted, with over half being 15 or younger, and 75% experienced multiple incidents of sexual violence. The study revealed that younger age at first assault significantly increased risk of revictimization, and sexual violence was strongly associated with PTSD and other mental health consequences. Only one third of victims reported the assault, and among those who did, 75% received no meaningful response or support. Based on my experience, I can only confirm every information in this study. It's actually baffling: each milestone seems as if the study was based on my personal life events.

Because I didn't know about autism, I didn't understand my meltdowns, my need for things to stay the same, or my need for routines. People saw these reactions as problems. I wasn't a child with autism trying to cope in a hard world— I was called "difficult," or "manipulative." My shutdowns were my body's way of protecting myself when things became too much. But adults thought I was just "shutting down to avoid responsibility."

The bullying at school felt like a natural extension of what was happening at home. Other children seemed to sense my vulnerability, my differentness, like predators scenting wounded prey. Cazalis et al. (2022) found that "Autistic children were 7.77 times more likely than non-autistic children to have been bullied ($p < 0.001$)", with autistic girls experiencing more relational and overall aggression in mainstream classroom than autistic boys (Sedgewick et al. in 2019).

During particularly overwhelming periods, I would go through episodes of mutism—my throat closing up, words simply disappearing as my system shut down to protect itself. Adults interpreted this as defiance or manipulation, adding punishment to my already overwhelmed nervous system. Research shows that selective mutism (SM) and autism are closely connected and often overlap. Current diagnostic tools struggle to tell the difference between these two conditions because they share many similar traits (Klein, 2019 and Steffenburg, 2018). Studies have found that 63-80% of children first diagnosed with selective mutism also meet the criteria for autism, suggesting that many autism cases are being missed (Muris, 2021). Even in typical children, those with more autistic traits tend to have more selective mutism traits, and there appears to be a genetic link between the two conditions (Stein, 2011). Researchers now view autism, social anxiety, and selective mutism as "allied conditions" that frequently occur together, which explains why their symptoms can be hard to distinguish from each other (Muris, 2021). This research suggests that when a child has selective mutism, it may be worth exploring whether they also have autism.

The Mother's Awakening

Everything began to shift when my sons received their autism diagnoses. Watching them struggle with the same overwhelming sensory experiences, the same social confusion, the same intense interests and need for routine, was like looking into a mirror I'd never been offered before. Except, I thought it was normal since my only reference was my experience, until a preschool teacher, and another teacher suggested my oldest got tested.

I was sitting in my oldest son's Individualized Education Program (IEP) meeting when the autism specialist described his "intense focus on special interests that interfere with social engagement," such as running to the window daily to watch the garbage truck pickup the school trash, or taking never-ending bathroom breaks to flush the toilet over and over again. As she spoke, I flashed back to my own childhood obsession with words or geology. My teachers had called it "antisocial behavior" when I preferred researching during recess instead of playing with other children who would not play with me anyway. Suddenly, I realized that what they had pathologized in me was now being recognized as a core autism trait in my son.

As I advocated for my children, learned about their needs, and celebrated their unique perspectives, I began to recognize myself in every description, every characteristic, every struggle. I finally had a voice to explain those behaviors and refuse the demand to conform, for my children and me. The therapists spoke about autism in boys, but I heard my own childhood echoing in their words. The phenomenon of maternal self-recognition during their children's autism diagnosis process is common and often leads to late diagnosis. The exact same process happened with my oldest son's ASD, and later ADHD diagnosis, mine following shortly after. Sometimes, I wonder if I had neurodivergent girls instead of boys, would they have ever been diagnosed, and would I ever have found out I had both Autism and ADHD? Probably not. Thank God for gifting me with wonderful boys presenting more classic signs of Autism and ADHD than I!

When I finally received my own diagnosis at thirty-one, it wasn't just a medical appointment—it was an archaeological search of my entire life. Every rejection, every misunderstanding, every time I felt like an alien trying to pass as human suddenly had context, and made sense. Late-diagnosed autistic women found that receiving a diagnosis in adulthood often triggers a complete reframing of one's life narrative. Participants described feeling "finally understood" and experiencing both grief for their unrecognized struggles and relief at having an explanation for their differences. Ultimately, my diagnosis led me to seek psychological help to reframe my identity, define my aspirations and goals, get a divorce, finish my education, and create an entirely new life better adjusted to my neurological differences. Dr. Gray Atherton emphasizes that receiving a late diagnosis matters and assures viewers that, although a late diagnosis may be complex and confusing, the identity and understanding that come with it can have a significant positive impact on personal acceptance.

The ADHD diagnosis at forty-two added another layer of understanding. Studies "show that between 30 and 50% of individuals with ASD manifest ADHD symptoms (particularly at pre-school age), and similarly, estimates suggest two-thirds of individuals with ADHD show features of ASD (Davis and Kollins, 2012). Having both autism and ADHD feels like having a brain that craves routine and predictability while simultaneously struggling to maintain focus and consistency. It's like being a perfectionist who struggles with organization, someone who craves structure but gets overwhelmed by too much of it.

Rewriting the Story

With diagnosis came the radical act of self-compassion, a completely foreign concept to me. I began to reframe my history not as a series of personal failures, but as the journey of a neurodivergent person trying to survive in a world that didn't understand her needs.

I found old papers from high school, college, and my first pregnancy, where I'd written the same aspirational to-do lists: Building lasting friendships, developing structured routines and systems to organize my finances, my life, my children's lives, etc. Reading those comments post-diagnosis, I no longer saw a broken teenager or woman, but an undiagnosed autistic girl desperately trying to understand why the world felt so difficult to navigate. I was never broken. I was just autistic in a world that didn't recognize autism in girls.

The meltdowns weren't personal failings—they were my body's way of reacting to too much happening around me. The social struggles didn't mean I wasn't good enough—they happened because I didn't have the same social guidebook that everyone else seemed to get. The strong interests that others called "obsessive" were actually things that made me happy and knowledgeable.

As a child, I would embark on very strong friendships but couldn't understand when they were exploitative. I remember one friendship where we competed for grades. She would submit drawings very similar to mine after reaching into my backpack during English class when we were separated into different groups. I started discreetly taking my notebooks with me, her copying stopped, and shortly after, our friendship ended. Similarly, in middle school, another girl would call me every Wednesday evening before our Thursday literature assignments were due, essentially having me dictate her entire essay over the phone. When I stopped answering her calls, that friendship also fizzled.

These experiences taught me that my eagerness to connect made me vulnerable to exploitation. First, we are mocked, bullied, and cruelly marginalized. Once children mature enough to stop those practices, we become easy prey for "friendships with interests" that we tolerate because we are so eager to please and connect.

Wilson et al.(2023) studied the impact of autism diagnosis on self-concept in late-diagnosed women, finding significant improvements in self-compassion and reduced self-criticism following diagnosis. Late-diagnosed autistic women often experience a "diagnostic relief," reducing self-blame to replace it with self-understanding that can be therapeutic in itself.

The Revolutionary Act of Social Energy Management

For the first time in my life, I began treating my social energy like the finite resource it is. When someone wanted to engage in small talk about the weather, I cut it short to save my social energy for conversations that mattered to me. It may sound blunt to neurotypical ears, but it's honest, strategic, and paramount for me to have the energy to be present with my family members at night.

A colleague once asked if I wanted to grab coffee to "catch up"—translation: engage in 45 minutes of surface-level conversation about weekend plans and weather patterns. My old self would have accepted and spent the next three days recovering from the social drain. My post-diagnosis self declined without any specific reason other than that I needed to rest.

I started explaining my social energy management using a fitness analogy that neurotypicals could understand. If you have CrossFit training at 6 p.m. every day—something that matters to you—would you go on an impromptu run at noon because a friend suggested it or would you save your energy for

CrossFit? Social energy works similarly for individuals with autism.

Social energy depletion in autistic individuals happens much faster than in the neurotypical population, especially without accommodations because of the extra resources we use to treat the extra information our brain does not filter out or analyze to allow socialization. Forced social interactions that don't align with personal interests or values create significantly more fatigue than chosen social engagement around meaningful topics. Once diagnosed, we usually develop more assertive boundary-setting skills to defend our social energy resources and use them with whomever we want, improving our social anxiety. I personally no longer care about cutting small talks pretty abruptly if I'm running out of social energy and know I have to save my sanity for an upcoming meeting.

Some relationships didn't survive this new authenticity. People who had grown comfortable with my masked self weren't prepared for the real me—the one who needed advance notice of plans, who had strong reactions to unexpected changes, who couldn't pretend to enjoy small talk when I was desperate to dive deep into meaningful conversation. Reducing masking behaviors, while beneficial for mental health, can initially strain existing relationships built on masked presentations. At the end of the day, do those relationships based on performance even matter? I personally don't think so. If I have to "put on a show" to entertain you, then I am expecting you to return me the favor every other day. How does that sound?

But the relationships that did survive became deeper, richer, and more genuine. I attracted other neurodivergent individuals who understood my way of being, who didn't see my intensity as too much or my need for clarity as overthinking. I also attracted more mature and older friends who were at a point in their lives where they had grown tired of pretending and conforming, just as I had.

I stopped apologizing for my need to rock, fidget, or move. In meetings, I brought carefully selected fidget tools. At home, I allowed myself to pace when thinking. I learned to say "I need advance notice for plan changes," without apologizing. I also stopped answering phone calls. They drain me because of the hyperfocus required to compensate for the lack of visual cues. I removed 90% of my phone's notifications and decided to check my emails, messages, and missed calls a few times a day, only when I feel like it. Instead of apologizing for my directness, missed calls, and delayed answers, I began framing it as a matter of clarity. "I want to be clear about my communication style" became my standard opening phrase, replacing "Sorry if this sounds demanding, but..." I also realized that declining a call really is an option, and it is just as valid as answering. In fact, it's a great way to disengage from a potential sneaky attack or useless tensions, such as group text chains in which members sometimes use passive-aggressive tactics or a hint of public shaming to pressure others into doing something. My old self would have used elaborate replies to defend my position, restore my truth, and justify myself to an entire group. My new, confident self no longer bothers answering. If the behavior persists, I enjoy hitting the block button and calling it a day. All those reactions considered "normal" for most only became acceptable for me after a proper diagnosis and the understanding that I was not the problem complicating everyone's lives.

I also started requesting specific seating in restaurants (in comfortable corners, further away from the source of noise), bringing noise-canceling headphones to public spaces, and choosing clothing based on texture comfort rather than fashion trends. Learning that I could say "no" to social events was revolutionary. For decades, I forced myself into situations that left me drained for days, thinking this was just the price of being social. That time is over, and my quality of life has grown exponentially.

The Strength Born from Struggle

Looking back now, I can see that those thirty-one years of rejection, while painful, weren't wasted. They taught me resilience in ways that acceptance never could have. They sharpened my observation skills—I can read tiny facial expressions and body language as well as someone who once needed these skills to get by. Long-term adversity built skills and resilience that now shape my empathy and understanding of others. But I only benefit from them because I made it out alive and, paradoxically, got a proper late diagnosis early enough. Not everyone has this chance. At a recent work meeting, I noticed a subtle change in a colleague's facial expression and the way she sat when we discussed a project deadline. While others listened and agreed, I saw her distress and quietly asked if she needed help. She later thanked me, saying she'd been struggling but felt unable to say so. My habit of always watching others' emotions for my own safety had turned into a strength for helping others.

Research indicates that empathy in autistic women presents a complex profile that challenges common misconceptions about autism and emotional understanding. We demonstrate what researchers call "hyper-empathy," experiencing intense emotional resonance with others despite potential cognitive difficulties in emotion recognition. This emotional intensity can create both meaningful social connections and overwhelming experiences.

A key characteristic observed is delayed emotional processing, where responses may appear temporally misaligned with social situations. Studies suggest that autistic women typically develop more sophisticated social awareness and communication abilities compared to autistic men, enabling more complex social engagement patterns.

However, these strengths coexist with significant vulnerabilities. The pressure to camouflage autistic traits, combined with heightened empathetic responses, contributes to elevated mental health risks and often delays proper diagnosis and support access.

I developed exceptional skills in reading emotional states and body language, particularly in my childhood and teenage years when I experienced chronic social difficulties. This "compensatory hypervigilance" can become a significant strength in understanding others' emotional needs, helping us to develop heightened affective empathy, sometimes to an overwhelming degree.

My ability to care for others became a strength. I could sense when others were hurting without feeling the need to fix things. I became comfortable with emotions that unsettled others, and saw the person behind their actions because I once longed for that understanding. My way of caring doesn't follow conventional empathy—I don't always mirror feelings or offer standard comfort. Instead, I give my genuine, impartial help and understanding of complex topics.

The Ripple Effect

Understanding my own differences didn't just change how I saw myself—it changed how I raised my sons. Instead of viewing their autistic traits as problems, I celebrated them as natural differences. During meltdowns, I recognized overwhelm rather than misbehavior; and when they focused intently, I saw passion instead of obsession. Evidence from Crane et al. (2021) indicates that autistic parents of autistic children demonstrate superior understanding and acceptance of their children's needs compared to previous research with neurotypical parents, with their shared neurotype fostering natural empathy and more positive approaches to discussing autism within the family.

As an autistic mother of autistic children, I have experienced this fact firsthand, facing some of our neurotypical family members making a point in pushing masking tendencies and "conformity" in the name of "social integration and acceptance" without wondering about my children's mental health and autistic reality. I had to become their advocate in a world that expects everyone to be the same, their supporter in school meetings, and their safe haven when life felt overwhelming and their special interests were kept away from them. When my oldest son's teacher said he was "disrupting class" by tapping his pencil, I could explain that he wasn't being defiant but needed to do this to help himself focus. Because I understood what he was doing, I could ask for the help he needed: we switched his hard pencil to a soft, quiet material so he could keep self-regulating in silence, instead of asking him to stop.

"My late diagnosis opened doors to a new community. Online forums, support groups, and friendships with other late-diagnosed autistic adults revealed that my experience wasn't unique. I found peace watching videos of people like Tim Burton or Elon Musk, or documentaries about figures like Nikola Tesla or Albert Einstein, whom I always recognize as sharing traits with me. Whether formally diagnosed or not, I identified with their behaviors, words, and intellectual satisfaction.

Research by Shea et al. (2024) demonstrated that autistic-delivered peer support programs improve community functioning and reduce social isolation, with participants showing marked improvements in social functioning and increased engagement with mental health services after three months.

The Intersection of Trauma and Autism

Learning the difference between my reactions to trauma and my natural autistic way of thinking became very important for my healing. Some of my constant alertness comes from trauma—the habit of watching for danger in others' actions to keep myself safe. But some of it comes from autism—my natural sensitivity to changes around me, people's faces, and how people interact.

I become very alert every time someone acts in a passive-aggressive way. This isn't just feeling awkward—it's my whole body reacting to past trauma. As a child, or later in life, in abusive relationships, the people who hurt me often came home in unpredictable moods, which made me feel I had to be on guard. I learned to be like a human weather sensor, trying to notice every tone of voice, every tiny facial change, every small action to avoid making their moods worse.

My heightened alertness became so acute that I could detect mood changes in the subtlest behaviors—how someone walked, closed a car door, or hesitated before responding. Because of this sensitivity, I remove anyone who displays passive-aggressive behavior from my life, whether in work settings, friendships, or other relationships. I even left an excellent job after just two months when I recognized warning signs in a collaborator I was meant to work closely with. While I regretted losing the company, the benefits, and my other colleagues, I wouldn't change that decision if I had to make it again.

Human toxicity affects autistic individuals more intensely because our hyperanalytical minds are constantly working to decode our environment. Toxic individuals maintain control by sending mixed messages designed to make their victims doubt their instincts, feelings, boundaries, standards, and emotions—a vulnerability we naturally have and further develop with the negative feedback following our instinctive reactions.

In a recent study (Attwood, T., & Garnett, M. (2024), Attwood et al. describes how the high levels of stress and anxiety experienced by autistic individuals can make them particularly sensitive and reactive to traumatic events, causing hypervigilance, low resilience and amplification of the depth of emotional response. Rumball et al. (2020) found that autistic individuals with trauma histories show heightened physiological responses to specific triggers, particularly those involving unpredictable social dynamics.

The trauma part means I get triggered by sudden mood changes, which bring up feelings of fear and helplessness, and remind my body of past abuse. The autistic part means I am sensitive to changes in routine, my surroundings, or how people act. I notice when things don't match up, I find it hard to rely on words and tend to pay closer attention to behavioral trends, body language, tone, consistency and cues to decode an individual's mood.

Research demonstrates that autistic trauma survivors who implement protective strategies and boundaries around triggering behaviors can experience significant improvements in anxiety and overall functioning. Autistic individuals have more reactive nervous systems and less flexibility in managing stressors (Beauchaine et al., 2013; Fenning et al., 2019), making boundaries around triggering behaviors particularly crucial for nervous system regulation. The autistic nervous system's reduced flexibility hampers the ability to cope with acute stressors and contributes to increased vulnerability following trauma (Thapa & Alvares, 2019). My boundary regarding passive-aggressive behavior isn't negotiable because my nervous system's response is involuntary, reflecting the documented reality that autistic nervous systems are less flexible, making it harder to return to baseline once triggered.

Trauma Response and the Emergence of Imaginary Companions

The painful loneliness of middle school grew into what felt like depression in eighth grade. That was when I started making up imaginary friends—something that research shows is both common and helpful for people with autism.

Davis et al. (2023) found that nearly half (almost 50%) of autistic children in the study had imaginary companions, and those with imaginary friends demonstrated significantly higher theory of mind and social skills scores compared to their autistic peers without imaginary friends, regardless of their communication abilities. My imaginary companions became essential to my survival. In the middle of the night, I would sneak out of bed to write, pouring out my pain while my imaginary friends offered reassurance and wisdom.

These late night writing sessions weren't just escapes or signs of detachment, but ways to cope with challenges. They gave me the social understanding and support I couldn't find in real life and helped me develop skills for building friendships later in life. My imaginary friends weren't evidence of something wrong—they showed my mind's ability to create the caring environment I lacked. That need to create safe, understandable worlds didn't go away—it changed. What used to be imaginary friends turned into online characters, avatars, and groups. Where others saw make-believe, I found something useful. And finally, I wasn't scolded for making things up—I was respected for it. Thanks to the Internet, my world slowly began to open up.

The Gift of Authentic Connection

The biggest change has been learning to believe that a real connection is possible. When I stopped trying to be what I thought others wanted and started being my true self, I found that the right people—my people—were attracted to the very things I'd spent years trying to hide. At a recent social gathering, instead of masking through forced small talk, I engaged naturally and shared my personal journey when someone mentioned struggling with their mental health. To my surprise, this sparked an animated conversation with others who shared similar experiences.

My strong feelings, passion, honesty, and deep loyalty—these aren't flaws to fix, but valuable qualities. They make me a good friend, a devoted supporter, a loving mother, and a valued part of any community that truly knows me.

Crompton et al. (2020) found that when autistic individuals interact with other autistic individuals, communication effectiveness and rapport are significantly higher than in interactions with individuals of mixed neurotype. This "double empathy" research suggests that communication difficulties may be bidirectional rather than solely an autistic deficit. Specifically, the information transfer study demonstrated that autistic people recall information shared by autistic peers as effectively as non-autistic people recall information shared by non-autistic peers, but information sharing is significantly poorer in chains of mixed neurotypes.

The relationships I have now are built on honesty rather than pretense. My friends and family understand my autistic meltdowns, are aware and willing to accommodate my sensory needs, and value my unique perspective based on who I really am.

Recognizing Our Resilience

The journey from rejection to strength isn't about becoming someone new—it's about discovering who we've always been beneath the layers of hiding and self-doubt. It's about seeing that our way of experiencing the world, even if it's different, is real and important. As late-diagnosed autistic women, we often experience "narrative reconstruction" following diagnosis—a process of reinterpreting past social failures through the lens of neurological difference rather than personal inadequacy. When I revisit past rejections, I see that many weren't about me being "wrong" but about fundamental incompatibilities in communication styles and social needs.

Tierney et al. (2016) documented common coping strategies in undiagnosed autistic females, including people-pleasing, perfectionism, social withdrawal, and intellectual compensation. While these strategies helped survival in hostile environments, they come at a significant psychological cost. I developed a set of strategies to cope: watching others closely to learn behavior, being constantly aware of others' moods, striving for perfection, and people-pleasing, all consistent with the masking and social coping behaviors. Autistic females often describe "wearing a mask" or taking on a certain "persona" in social situations, and many described going to great lengths to avoid conflict, feeling the need to "please, appease and apologize" to feel accepted.

My safest relationships have been with people who appreciate my directness rather than finding it rude, who get excited when I share my special interests rather than looking bored, and who give me space to process without taking my need for time personally. In that sense, friendships with men are often easier.

A Sedgewick et al. (2019) study also found that although autistic women's relationship experiences shared many similarities with neurotypical women, their difficulties with social inference created heightened vulnerability to negative social situations, particularly in intimate contexts, highlighting the need for targeted safety training to support their transition to fulfilling adult relationships.

I started seeing my strengths: "overly sensitive" became "very aware," "rigid" became steady and dependable, "obsessions" became deep knowledge and focus, and my "blunt" comments reflected honesty. Russell et al. (2019) identified autism strengths, including enhanced pattern recognition, attention to detail, systematic thinking, and focus. The study also found that in interviews with 28 autistic adults, the ability to hyperfocus, attention to detail, good memory, and creativity were the most frequently described traits, along with specific qualities relating to social interaction such as honesty, loyalty, and empathy.

Long-term studies by Cage et al. (2018) demonstrated that autism acceptance from external sources and personal acceptance significantly predicted lower depression scores. Feeling accepted as an autistic person could indeed act as a protective factor against depression and mental health difficulties. Resilience isn't a place you reach—it's something you practice every day. It means being kind to yourself instead of only criticizing, finding community instead of being alone, and having words for your experiences instead of just confusion.

Today, if rejection occurs, I view it in a new light. Not everyone will understand or value different ways of being, and that doesn't mean I'm not worthy. Some people look for easy, shallow connections to collect like marbles. I am designed for fewer, deeper, and real ones. Therefore, we're not a good fit, and that's okay. Post-diagnostic adjustment involves not only understanding autism but also actively reconstructing one's narrative and relationships to align with an authentic neurodivergent identity (Bargiela et al., 2016). Focusing on authentic relationships not only brings lasting fulfillment and self-acceptance but is also the only way for us to engage in a social life that supports our mental health.

DIGITAL BELONGING: ONLINE FREEDOM AND CONNECTION

The internet didn't make me less social—it taught me how to be social in ways that actually worked for my brain.

Introduction: From Survival to Thriving

3 a.m. While my neurotypical peers slept soundly after their evening social gatherings, I found myself fully engaged in a collaborative project with teammates across three time zones. For the first time in my life, my natural circadian rhythms, my need for detailed communication, and my intense focus were assets rather than obstacles. This wasn't insomnia or social avoidance—this was finally finding my people and my pace.

I was 31 when I received my autism diagnosis, just months after my oldest son was diagnosed. When I turned 42, I received an ADHD diagnosis, again shortly after my son's diagnosis. Yet, long before any formal labels, the internet had quietly become the place where I finally made sense.

While peers enjoyed playground play and, later, office water cooler conversations, I found my most meaningful connections in forum discussions, online learning communities, and endless online research. What others called "hiding behind a screen" felt like finding my voice and removing the exhausting mask I wore in physical spaces. The digital world was not an escape from reality—it became a training ground for understanding others and myself, as well as for healing. Slowly, it allowed me to push away the debilitating fear of rejection that had defined my offline interactions. I was able to resume my studies, complete my education, grow a business, and find my place and voice in the world.

Throughout this chapter, I'll refer to "AuDHD," a term used in neurodivergent communities to describe individuals who are both autistic and have ADHD—a co-occurrence that affects approximately 40% of autistic individuals (Rong et al., 2021). This dual presentation creates unique challenges and strengths that are particularly relevant to understanding digital engagement patterns.

Google became my go-to source for navigating social mysteries—everything from interpreting body language to understanding the unspoken rules of splitting a restaurant bill. The pervasive myth that online engagement is inherently isolating or unhealthy for autistic individuals demands critical examination.

For people like us, online spaces serve as crucial developmental environments, providing safety, understanding, and genuine connections when traditional spaces consistently fall short. This reality has profound implications for how we approach digital safety, inclusion, and accommodation. To parents of autistic children, I want to emphasize that online engagement doesn't detract from real-life relationships and activities—it enhances them and often makes them possible.

To understand this digital transformation, consider that autistic people typically employ three adaptive strategies: compensation (learning new approaches to handle social situations, such as developing scripts for online forum interactions), masking (concealing autistic traits to appear more neurotypical, like forcing excitement during video calls), and assimilation (fundamentally altering oneself to fit in, such as suppressing special interests to seem "normal"). Digital environments transform how these strategies operate, often eliminating the need for masking or harmful assimilation while enhancing the effectiveness of positive compensation strategies.

Digital Social Development: Reframing Virtual Interaction

Beyond Survival: From Coping to Skill Building

A persistent concern about online engagement centers on whether social skills developed in digital spaces transfer to face-to-face interactions. This question reveals a fundamental misunderstanding of what constitutes social competence and how various social contexts interconnect. Recent research by Hassrick et al. (2021) provides compelling evidence that challenges these assumptions.

Their systematic review of 32 studies examining how autistic people use information and communication technology revealed that online communication offers significant advantages: reduced stress through asynchronous messaging that allows extended processing time, increased control and calmness during interactions, and opportunities for positive identity formation through autistic community connections. Critically, participants reported that online communities served as learning environments for developing effective social strategies—not temporary coping mechanisms, but genuine skill-building opportunities.

Economic empowerment

Digital work environments don't merely accommodate autistic individuals—they unleash capabilities that traditional workplaces systematically suppress or ignore entirely.

Research demonstrates that autistic employees frequently outperform neurotypical colleagues by significant margins in roles requiring sustained attention, pattern recognition, and quality control, with productivity gains ranging around 30%. Indeed, Australia's Department of Human Services (DHS) saw a 30% increase in productivity in teams that integrated neurodivergent talent in software-testing roles. A study published in Harvard Business Review has also reported that teams with neurodivergent professionals in some roles can be 30% more productive than those without neurodivergent professionals. Regarding participants in JPMorgan Chase's "Autism at Work initiative," a report found that these professionals "made fewer errors and were 90% to 140% more productive than neurotypical employees" (Price, 2022).

My 17-year career in localization quality control exemplifies this transformation. Despite having zero industry knowledge or specialized training, I applied online for an entry-level position and was invited to take an assessment two hours away. Not only did I pass—I exceeded every benchmark. The results were so exceptional that they brought me back for additional testing, convinced there had been an error. There hadn't been. Within weeks, I was redirected from the entry-level role to quality control management, overseeing translation teams for Fortune 500 companies.

What neurotypical colleagues found mentally exhausting —scanning dense technical documents for subtle errors, inconsistencies, and pattern deviations—felt effortless to me. Tasks allocated 40 hours of work time typically required just one to two hours of my focused attention. This efficiency wasn't the result of cutting corners or superficial review; my error detection rates consistently outperformed industry standards. Soon, I was managing multiple concurrent positions, each building on capabilities that had been invisible or problematic in every traditional workplace I'd previously encountered.

This represents far more than economic empowerment—it's a fundamental paradigm shift from viewing autism as a disability requiring accommodation to recognizing it as a cognitive architecture offering distinct professional advantages in an increasingly digital economy.

The Double-Edged Digital Sword

However, Hassrick et al. (2021) also identified significant risks: greater vulnerability to cyberbullying and deception, tendencies toward over-disclosure of personal information, and increased likelihood of problematic internet use compared to non-autistic peers. These findings underscore the importance of what researchers termed "social naivety"— autistic individuals must maintain awareness of their increased vulnerability and actively seek clarification when confused during online interactions.

Platform-Specific Considerations

Different digital platforms serve distinct social and developmental needs for autistic individuals. Structured environments like specialized forums and professional networks (LinkedIn, GitHub) provide optimal conditions for skill development, while visual platforms (Instagram, TikTok) may increase masking behaviors and social comparison stress. Understanding these platform-specific dynamics is crucial for parents, educators, and autistic individuals themselves when making decisions about digital engagement.

The research particularly highlighted how feelings of belonging to online communities correlated positively with self-esteem. A participant highlighted the importance of seeing others sharing their experiences to improve self-perception while another participant emphasized how social media provided crucial insight into representation, especially for women (Skafle et al., 2024). Like any other community, tensions and discord also hindered community building with key topics regarding "proper" language use. One participant described feeling deterred by the highly critical debates within some social media groups: "For example, when in some of these groups there's a young mother who says, 'Hi, my daughter was just diagnosed, and now that I understand she has autism, I'm wondering . . .' And then the first thing that comes up is criticism such as 'don't say that she has autism, you have to say autistic,' and then you wind up being afraid of saying something wrong. You become afraid of using the wrong words" (Skafle et al., 2024). I also felt alienated by such harsh discussions within the community, particularly concerning the use of language (identity-first vs. person-first language) and debates over controversial interventions like Applied Behavior Analysis (ABA) and Early Intensive Behavioural Intervention (EIBI). At that time, I was still learning about myself and autism, and trully did not need an additional layer of controversy and opacity keeping me away from the vital answers and support I needed within the very group of people that was excluded by most other communities. How ironic! Participants found that unlike traditional social situations that consistently exhausted them, online spaces allowed them to build skills that fostered genuine growth rather than merely survival.

Neurocognitive Benefits of Digital Communication

Text-based communication offers distinct neurological advantages for autistic individuals. The same systematic review found that digital interaction provides greater control over social engagement and increased feelings of calm during communication. This aligns with neuroimaging studies showing that autistic individuals process language and logic through different neural pathways, often with enhanced efficiency in text-based formats compared to verbal processing (Anderson et al., 2022).

Digital Accessibility Tools

Modern digital accessibility features—including customizable text size, reading speed controls, noise-canceling options, captions for videos and visual scheduling tools—create personalized communication environments that accommodate diverse sensory and processing needs. These tools don't just level the playing field; they often reveal capabilities that standard communication methods obscure. For instance, autistic individuals frequently demonstrate superior written communication skills when freed from the cognitive load of simultaneous speech processing and nonverbal cue interpretation (Noureddine, 2024).

For me, digital communication eliminates the complex timing challenges inherent in group conversations. I can send messages when thoughts crystallize without worrying about interruption patterns or seeming rude. This fundamental shift from reactive to proactive communication has been transformational—so much so that I've largely discontinued participation in group voice discussions, not from social avoidance, but from recognizing a more effective communication medium for my cognitive style.

The Neuroscience of Digital Comfort: Understanding the Autistic Brain Online

Cognitive Load Theory and Digital Processing

The superior performance of many autistic individuals in digital environments finds its explanation in cognitive load theory. Research indicates that autistic brains process information with exceptional attention to detail but may experience challenges integrating these details into broader contextual frameworks (Mottron et al., 2006). This processing style creates both remarkable strengths and significant challenges in traditional social environments.

Contemporary research has moved beyond the deficit-focused "theory of mind" model originally proposed by Baron-Cohen et al. (1985), which suggested that autistic people struggle to understand others' mental states. Modern frameworks, particularly Damian Milton's "double empathy problem" (Milton, 2012), propose that communication difficulties arise from mutual misunderstanding between neurotypical and autistic individuals who process social information through fundamentally different cognitive pathways.

Recent neuroimaging studies reveal that autistic brains show enhanced connectivity in certain regions associated with pattern recognition and systematic processing, while showing different activation patterns in areas traditionally associated with social cognition (Thompson et al., 2023). Importantly, these differences don't represent deficits but rather alternative neural strategies that may be better suited to certain environments—particularly digital ones that emphasize structured, detailed communication over rapid nonverbal processing.

Digital environments significantly reduce what researchers call "social cognitive load"—the mental resources required to simultaneously process verbal content, facial expressions, tone variations, body language, and contextual social rules. During my university experience, positioning myself in a corner wearing a hoodie, strategically facing away from the crowd (like joining online sessions with cameras disabled), allowed me to focus entirely on the content without the exhausting work of managing eye contact or controlling fidgety behaviors. My preferred learning position might appear disengaging in traditional classrooms, but the effort to be physically present while mentally engaged represents significant accommodation—one that deserves recognition rather than judgment.

Executive Function and AuDHD Complexity

The co-occurrence of autism and ADHD adds layers of complexity to understanding individual support needs. Recent meta-analysis by Rong et al. (2021) found pooled prevalence rates of ADHD among autistic individuals at 38.5% for current diagnosis and 40.2% for lifetime diagnosis. Additional research indicates that 32.8% of autistic children also meet ADHD criteria (Canals et al., 2024). This dual presentation, commonly referred to as "AuDHD" in neurodivergent communities, involves complex interactions of traits and support needs that differ significantly from either condition alone.

The experience of growing up autistic varies dramatically across generations. While older autistic adults like myself had to discover digital accommodation strategies through trial and error, younger autistic individuals are often digital natives who intuitively leverage these environments for communication and learning. However, this generational divide also means that younger autistic people may lack awareness of the skills they've developed digitally, potentially undervaluing their own competencies when transitioning to traditional settings.

Digital platforms provide an external scaffolding through features that compensate for executive functioning differences. Message histories serve as external memory aids, allowing users to review previous conversations and parents to check the safety and nature of their children's online interactions. Asynchronous communication allows for thoughtful responses, providing processing time without the pressure of time constraints or performance anxiety, a great advantage for those with alexithymia or the difficulty to identify, describe and express their own emotions. Platform-specific interaction guidelines also create clear behavioral expectations, reducing the ambiguity that often characterizes offline social situations. Interest-based community organization facilitates connection around shared passions, eliminat\ing the challenge of generating conversation topics spontaneously.

Virtual Reality and Emerging Technologies

Emerging technologies like virtual reality (VR) and AI-powered communication assistants represent the next frontier in digital accommodation. Early research suggests that VR environments can provide graduated exposure to social situations while maintaining the safety and control that make digital spaces effective. Meanwhile, AI assistants are beginning to offer real-time social cue interpretation and response suggestions, potentially bridging the gap between digital comfort and face-to-face interaction requirements.

The research on the Virtual Reality Enhancement of Social Skills (VRESS) software by Kourtesis et al., 2023 provided several key benefits for the implementation of technological interventions in adults with Autism Spectrum Disorder (ASD). Most importantly, the study offers substantial evidence confirming that immersive VR social skills training is an appropriate, feasible, and highly acceptable service for adults with ASD, with participants reporting very high usability and user experience while experiencing minimal to absent cybersickness. Utilizing ecologically valid social scenarios, the study generated crucial insights into the clinical features of ASD, demonstrating that performance in the VR social scenarios (specifically the number of prompts required) was the best predictor of the participants' ASD functionality level. Furthermore, the findings clarify the significant role of executive functions, establishing that planning ability was the best predictor of social performance in VR, suggesting its deep implication in social skills. These results help guide future clinical software development by suggesting an errorless learning approach should be preferred in VR social training to enhance user acceptability and positive outcomes.

Digital Unmasking: The Liberation of Authentic Expression

Autistic individuals, particularly women and non-binary people, often expend enormous energy on camouflaging, masking, and assimilation—strategies that create significant psychological distress while obscuring authentic identity (Hull et al., 2020). Digital environments provide crucial respite from these exhausting performance demands while enabling the development of genuine communication skills.

The benefits of digital unmasking are not equally accessible across all populations. Autistic individuals who are also racial minorities, LGBTQ+, or from lower socioeconomic backgrounds may face additional barriers to authentic online expression, including platform bias, limited internet access, and intersecting discrimination that persists even in digital spaces. Therefore, additional research specifically examining these intersections should be done to create a truly inclusive digital environment.

In digital spaces, the pressure to maintain appropriate facial expressions, interpret tonal variations, or follow implicit social protocols diminishes significantly. There's no need to suppress stimming behaviors or camouflage intense interests. This reduced pressure allows authentic self-expression while providing opportunities to develop communication skills in supportive, lower-stakes environments. Not to mention, this also allows us to save our limited supply of social energy, improving the quality of our physical social life after work and school, which are no longer draining us.

Rather than simply hiding difficulties, digital environments often reveal capabilities that physical spaces systematically obscure. Creative expression through digital art, avatar customization, or multimedia communication can represent authentic self-presentation more accurately than appearance or in-person behavioral constraints allow. Online, quirky avatars or self-representations are not only no longer discriminated against, but they are valued and encouraged, helping us rebuild our self-esteem and value with authentic expression.

Personal Transformation Through Digital Work

My professional journey exemplifies this transformation potential. After years of struggling in traditional employment or study—office and school environments with harsh fluorescent lighting, overwhelming auditory input, and requiring constant performance of neurotypical social scripts, I discovered remote digital work and study. The change was so dramatic that I maintained perfect attendance for 15 consecutive years (even on days I went through surgeries, connecting right before and after surgical interventions), working seven days a week because it is part of my routine. In my prior employment experiences, it was unprecedented for me to remain beyond my scheduled hours, given the level of fatigue and desire for solitude I consistently felt at the end of each shift.

Specific Professional Outcomes

The transition to digital work didn't just improve my professional stability—it revealed capabilities that traditional workplaces had systematically undervalued. My attention to detail, pattern recognition abilities, and capacity for sustained focus became professional assets, rather than social liabilities, reflecting my natural discipline. Within two months of transitioning to remote work, I had advanced from an entry-level position to a senior position, based purely on performance metrics rather than interpersonal politics or presentation skills.

In digital work environments, traits that had previously attracted criticism became recognized strengths. Meticulous attention to detail, passion for thorough research, pattern recognition abilities, and capacity for sustained concentration were not just valued—they were essential. I successfully applied for entry-level positions and secured quality control editor roles based solely on demonstrated competency rather than interview performance or cultural fit assessments.

The contrast was remarkable. Instead of exhausting energy on masking confusion and performing neurotypical communication styles, I could communicate clearly and passionately about work that genuinely engaged me. Rather than deploying harmful assimilation strategies, I could utilize accommodating approaches that enhanced rather than diminished performance quality. Even video meetings followed predictable structures with defined speaking turns and time limits, allowing preparation and reducing performance anxiety.

Remote Work Research

Studies of remote work effectiveness consistently demonstrate that autistic employees often exceed performance expectations when environmental barriers are removed. Research has also found that employees with autism have dramatically lower turnover rates than neurotypical employees (Griffiths et al., 2020). These findings call into question established views regarding the workplace capabilities of autistic individuals when suitable accommodations are implemented.

This professional transformation provided the foundation for rebuilding not just career stability, but also an entire life trajectory. Before discovering digital work, my history was characterized by repeated false starts: dropping out of educational programs up to six times in a single academic year, resigning from every position during overwhelming meltdowns despite strong performance reviews and advancement opportunities. Desperate for fresh beginnings to escape the shame that followed each "failure," I became a relocation expert. Each time, I fled further and further away from my embarrassment with increasingly dramatic geographical relocations: changing schools, leaving Paris, then its department, its region, leaving North to go South, eventually emigrating to the United States entirely, then to the West Coast as if the Atlantic Ocean between France and the East Coast of the United States were not enough. Starting over became a way of life, and my painful disappointment grew heavier with each relocation as I felt increasingly unrooted.

Digital work enabled exactly the fresh start I desperately needed while providing the skills and confidence necessary for eventually rebuilding successful offline relationships and activities. In appropriate environmental conditions, I wasn't broken or deficient—I was thriving. Without digital work serving as a lifeline during my most vulnerable years, I genuinely believe I would not be here to share this story. In fact, my starting point, finally settling in the same place, is perfectly aligned with the beginning of my online employment.

Special Interests as Social Connectors

Recent research challenges the pathological framing of autistic special interests, instead recognizing them as vehicles for social connection and personal development (Grove et al., 2018). Digital platforms excel at connecting individuals around shared interests, facilitating meaningful relationships based on genuine mutual engagement rather than social performance.

Online Advocacy and Representation

Digital platforms have revolutionized autistic self-advocacy and representation. Social media campaigns like #ActuallyAutistic hashtag have enabled autistic individuals to challenge misconceptions, share authentic experiences, and influence policy discussions in ways that traditional advocacy organizations—often led by non-autistic individuals—could never achieve. This shift from being subjects of research and intervention to being agents of change represents a fundamental transformation in autism discourse. Who better than us could tell our experience?

Online communities organized around specific interests provide natural conversation frameworks that reduce social anxiety while enabling leadership development. When autistic individuals can discuss topics within their expertise areas, communication flows more naturally, social confidence increases, and unique perspectives can emerge as valued contributions rather than social oddities.

The educational contrast between my traditional schooling and my sons' digital learning journey illustrates the transformative potential of accommodating rather than fighting neurological differences. While I struggled through classrooms where sensory overload made information retention nearly impossible—spending evenings until 11 p.m. attempting to relearn material missed during overwhelming school days—my children thrived in environments designed around their learning styles rather than against them.

Educational Research Outcomes

The study, *"It just fits my needs better": Autistic students and parents' experiences of learning from home during the early phase of the COVID-19 pandemic*, found that while the initial transition to remote learning was extremely challenging and parents felt poorly supported by schools, many autistic children subsequently flourished both personally and educationally (Heyworth et al., 2021). This flourishing was less surprising than it first appeared, given that the home environment mitigated many inherent barriers of conventional schooling, such as sensory overwhelm and complex social demands. The positive experiences were attributed to three key ingredients provided by the home context: People (connected, trusting relationships, typically with parents, who provided personalized support and prioritized mental health), Place (the sensory and social safety of home, which reduced demands and distractions), and Time (flexibility to pace and structure learning according to individual needs, which fostered autonomy and allowed for necessary decompression). These findings emphasize that institutional educational settings should prioritize trusting student-teacher relationships, improve the physical learning environment to reduce sensory and social stress, and allow for greater flexibility in the school day to foster autonomy. Notably, these improvements persist when students return to traditional settings, suggesting that digital learning provides foundational skills rather than temporary accommodations.

My academic experience was characterized by frustration despite intellectual capability, social isolation during unstructured periods, and gradual loss of extracurricular activities that had provided rare positive social experiences. The exhausting cycle—struggling to concentrate in overstimulating environments, requiring extensive makeup work at home, falling progressively behind socially and emotionally—felt interminable and demoralizing.

My sons experienced something entirely different. Home-based learning eliminated sensory barriers that had derailed my education, while structured tennis training provided social interaction built around shared goals, a structured athletic environment, and mutual respect. They maintained reasonable sleep schedules, experienced daily accomplishment rather than defeat, learned a growth mindset at school while reinforcing it on the tennis court, and awakened refreshed rather than dreading another day of struggle. Their academic performance soared not because material was simplified, but because delivery methods finally matched their information processing styles.

The ultimate test came when my younger son chose to return to traditional public high school after three years of online learning. His transition was remarkably smooth —he immediately formed friendships, excelled academically, and confidently participated in clubs and activities. Most importantly, he approached his autism diagnosis as simply one aspect of his identity, advocating for quiet spaces when overwhelmed and making social choices based on personal needs rather than external pressure.

Those three years of digital learning had provided something I never had the opportunity to develop: a deep understanding of his learning style, clear personal boundaries, and unshakable confidence in his intellectual abilities. He learned to appreciate how his autistic mind operated rather than viewing it as something to conceal or overcome. The structured, low-pressure online environment enabled him to develop genuine social competence and self-advocacy skills that transferred seamlessly to traditional settings when he felt ready. He possessed confidence, self-worth, and self-esteem that I did not develop until my late thirties.

Addressing Digital Challenges and Concerns

Cyberbullying and Online Safety

While digital environments offer significant advantages for autistic individuals, they also present unique vulnerabilities. Research consistently shows that autistic people experience higher rates of cyberbullying and online exploitation (Nixon, 2014). The same traits that make us excellent at pattern recognition and detail-oriented work can also make us vulnerable to manipulation and social deception.

Digital Literacy and Safety Guidelines

Developing autism-specific digital literacy programs represents a critical need. These programs should address not just technical skills but social navigation strategies, including recognizing manipulation tactics, understanding privacy implications, and developing healthy boundaries around information sharing. Research suggests that autistic individuals benefit from explicit instruction in areas that neurotypical individuals often learn intuitively (Schipul, 2016).

Echo Chambers and Social Isolation

Critics often argue that online communities can create echo chambers that reinforce problematic behaviors or prevent social growth. However, research suggests that this concern, while valid, applies more broadly to internet usage patterns rather than being specific to autistic engagement (Pariser, 2011).

Healthy Digital Boundaries

Establishing healthy digital boundaries requires particular attention for autistic individuals, who may struggle with executive function and time management. Structured approaches—including scheduled online and offline time, diverse digital community participation, and regular self-assessment of digital habits—can maximize benefits while minimizing risks. The goal isn't to limit digital engagement but to ensure it remains enriching and safe rather than compulsive.

The Quality vs. Quantity Debate

Some researchers question whether online relationships can provide the depth and emotional support of face-to-face connections. However, this perspective often reflects neurotypical assumptions about what constitutes meaningful social interaction. For many autistic individuals, the reduced cognitive load of digital communication enables deeper, more authentic connections than would be possible in traditional social contexts. It's not always the case, especially when interacting with acquaintances, strangers, or anyone in contexts that require us to mask and assimilate.

Implications and Future Directions

Policy and Educational Recommendations

The research presented here has significant implications for educational policy, workplace accommodation, and digital accessibility standards. Educational institutions should recognize digital learning as a legitimate accommodation rather than a lesser alternative. Employers should understand that remote work arrangements often reveal rather than conceal autistic capabilities.

Specific Policy Recommendations

Concrete policy recommendations include:
- Recognizing digital learning accommodations as equivalent to other disability services
- Requiring employers to consider remote work as a reasonable accommodation and not as a "favors"
- Developing autism-specific digital safety curricula
- Funding research into VR and AI-assisted communication tools
- Ensuring digital accessibility features are available across all major platforms

Technology Development Priorities

Future technology development should prioritize features that enhance rather than replace human connection. This includes

AI-powered social cue interpretation tools, customizable sensory interfaces, and platforms designed specifically for neurodivergent communication styles.

International Perspectives

Research on autism and digital engagement remains heavily concentrated in Western, English-speaking populations. To encompass diverse cultural contexts, languages, and socioeconomic conditions, expanding research is crucial for creating truly inclusive digital environments.

Critical gaps remain in our understanding of autism and digital engagement. Research priorities should include longitudinal studies on digital-to-physical skill transfer, investigations of platform-specific effects, examinations of intersectional identities within digital autism communities, and the development of autism-specific digital wellness metrics.

Toward Digital Inclusion and Understanding

The evidence is clear: digital environments are not escape mechanisms or inferior substitutes for "real" social interaction. For many autistic individuals, these environments represent optimal learning and communication settings that reveal capabilities systematically obscured by traditional social contexts. The question is not whether autistic people should engage with digital technology—we already do, and research consistently demonstrates positive outcomes when we're allowed to do so authentically.

The question is whether society will recognize digital engagement as a legitimate form of social development and create policies, educational approaches, and workplace cultures that build upon, rather than undermine, these natural strengths. My personal transformation from repeated academic and professional failures to sustained success illustrates what becomes possible when environments align with rather than fight against neurodivergent information processing styles.

Call to Action

For parents of autistic children: embrace their digital interests as legitimate social and learning opportunities rather than obstacles to overcome. Obviously, implement safety guards with software monitoring their activities and provide them with online safety training.

For educators: recognize that digital engagement often represents accommodation, not avoidance, and digital access is here to stay. Therefore, digital best practices should be included in all curricula.

For employers: recognize that remote work often reveals autistic capabilities that traditional environments obscure. Refrain from constantly "checking" on your remote neurodivergent workers, as you are interrupting their thinking processes, keeping them away from doing their best work, and taking away the benefit of remote accommodations.

For researchers: prioritize autistic voices in research design and interpretation and include intersectional communities.

The Internet didn't make me less social—it taught me how to be social in ways that worked for my brain. This same potential exists for countless other autistic individuals if we have the wisdom to support rather than pathologize their digital engagement. The future of autism acceptance may well depend on our ability to recognize digital spaces as legitimate communities deserving of respect, protection, and continued development.

Future Vision

Imagine educational systems that leverage digital platforms to provide individualized learning experiences, workplaces that measure contribution rather than conformity, and social policies that recognize diverse forms of community participation. This vision isn't utopian—it's achievable through continued research, advocacy, and the courage to challenge assumptions about what constitutes authentic human connection.

**

UNLEARNING SHAME
AND REBUILDING SELF

My transformation began with the realization that I had spent decades punishing, hiding, and apologizing for who I am. The heart of my story is not about a label, but about reclaiming self-acceptance and gaining a deeper understanding of myself.

The Compounding Effect of Late Diagnosis

I received my autism diagnosis at 31. I learned my lifelong struggles weren't personal failings, they were autism. Eleven years later, I was diagnosed with ADHD, finally explaining the trouble I had with planning, organizing, and paying attention since I was a child.

My autism evaluation took months: forms, tests, and questions about my childhood. When I finally heard "autism spectrum disorder," I felt relief—my struggles had a name, an explanation, and a community.

Three days after my autism diagnosis, I wrote: "I keep cycling between relief and grief. Relief because finally, FINALLY, someone understands why I've always felt as if I'm translating the world every second of the day to be able to perform in every single daily activity and interaction. Why parties feel like performance Art. Why I can give presentations to hundreds of people but struggle to engage in small talk with just one coworker? Why certain fabrics make me want to crawl out of my skin. Why I memorize social scripts as if I were learning a foreign language to meet my own family members... But also grief. Grief because of the young girl I used to be, who could have been playing with other children at recess instead of sitting alone every day, convinced she was fundamentally defective. Grief because of the fifteen-year-old girl who had lost trust in everyone, including herself, to the point of depriving herself of food, ending up at barely 80 lbs for 5'9, still feeling too exposed. How many years did I spend trying to blame myself for acting in the world according to my true nature? How many people did I apologize to, or was I asked to apologize to, while I had done nothing wrong? If anything, THEY all owed me an apology! An apology for diminishing me, mocking me, ridiculing me, hurting me, and suffocating me with their subjective standards. Grief slowly turned to anger, resentment, and a rainbow of mixed feelings that took me years to come to peace with."

***

This late recognition is sadly common. The "double empathy problem," identified by researcher Damian Milton, explains that communication difficulties between autistic and non-autistic individuals occur on both sides (Milton, 2012). It's not that autistic people lack empathy or social understanding—it's that there is a basic difference in how people communicate and understand the world.

But society has historically blamed autistic people for this mismatch. When autistic girls don't fit the narrow, male-centric diagnostic criteria developed in the 1940s, they're misdiagnosed with anxiety, depression, eating disorders, or personality disorders. They're told they're "too sensitive," "overthinking everything," or "need to try harder" to fit in.

My own path to getting diagnosed shows this clearly. Before my diagnosis, I was called anxious, depressive, anorexic, bulimic, obsessive, among others. Each diagnosis explained part of what I was going through but essentially missed the real difference in how my brain works that explained everything.

Research by Lai and colleagues (2015) found that women with late diagnoses report higher rates of depression, anxiety, and suicidal ideation compared to those diagnosed earlier. Autism does not inherently causes mental health problems, it is the lack of diagnose and accommodations that leads to a huge psychological toll altering our life trajectory (with dreams, true interests, passions and goals often abandoned or hidden). Soon, we found ourselves in abusive romantic partnerships and friendships instead of finding comfort in healthy connections with like-minded people.

The Grief and Relief of Recognition

I cried after my diagnosis. Not because I was sad, but because I wasn't broken, mean, or unworthy of love, after all. There was a reason. It wasn't my fault.

Earlier clarity would have meant: supports and accommodations, success in my studies, self-understanding instead of shame, strategies that work with my neurology, community, protection from victimization, and fewer traumas. I might have even loved myself enough to pursue relationships I thought I didn't deserve.

Grief quickly sinks in. The later the diagnosis, the longer the grief. The road to rebuilding our sense of self seems to stretch out considerably. Accepting every part of our life under our new, true identity—what we like, want, and are good at—takes time and is similar to detective work, turning back the clock to find the lost clues of our personality behind the masks, the assimilation, before we "muted" ourselves completely to become the shadow of ourselves, the only form in which society tolerated us.

For parents of children who think or act differently, discovering the situation early and with kindness is not just about seeking help. It's about shaping how our child sees themselves. When they understand their differences as simply different ways their brains work rather than personal failures, they gain strength instead of feeling ashamed, and they learn to speak up for themselves instead of blaming themselves. In fact, autistic children who get early, positive support feel better about themselves and have better mental health (Cage et al., 2018).

How Shame Shows Up, Even After Diagnosis

Getting diagnosed didn't magically erase thirty-one years of internalized shame. Years later, I still catch myself in familiar patterns: I apologize when I cannot hear because my brain does not filter background noise. Last month, I found myself saying "sorry" to strangers in a coffee shop when I started rocking slightly while reading. It's a harmless self-regulation strategy, and the couple at the next table hadn't even noticed. My internal shame monitor, though, activated before I could think rationally about the situation.

I still adjust my behavior at work, watching my tone to sound just the right amount of excited. During a recent interview, I practiced answers to demonstrate that I cared without seeming too focused, and to convey that I knew things without coming across as too intense.

I still doubt how I read social situations, wondering if my honest feedback is "too direct" or if my questions sound like criticism. When a friend seems distant, my first thought is "What did I do wrong?" instead of "They might be having a bad day." I can spend twenty minutes going over texts, looking for signs that I was too blunt or asked too many questions. The shame shows up in smaller ways, too. I avoid some autistic groups online because I worry I'm "not autistic enough": I can look people in the eye, I have close friends, and I've done well at work. The same inner voice that once told me I was "too much" now says I'm "not enough" to fully call myself neurodivergent.

Rebuilding began with small, real changes that respected how my brain works, rather than fighting against it. The first boundary I set was about meetings. After my diagnosis, I began requesting agendas in advance and asking that meetings start with a brief overview of expectations. I initially felt skepticism, with coworkers wondering: "Can't you just go with the flow?" But I persisted, explaining that having clear expectations helped me contribute more effectively. Within a month, three other team members had thanked me privately for pushing for this change. "Actually," one colleague said, "I had no idea how much mental energy I was spending trying to figure out what we were supposed to accomplish in these meetings."

I started rocking openly—small movements, such as squeezing a stress ball during phone calls or gently rocking while thinking. The first time I did this during a video call, without saying sorry or just turning off my camera to focus, I felt as if I was breaking a big rule. My heart raced, and I got ready for people to judge me or ask questions. But nothing bad happened. In fact, coworkers said I seemed more focused and clear.

The next milestone was learning to say no without lengthy explanations. "I won't be able to attend the holiday party," instead of giving details about my trouble with noise or how much energy social events take. Now, I simply state what I need, such as asking for written instructions instead of apologizing for wanting things explained clearly. I figured that if people really want to know the motivation behind it, they can always ask me. Most don't.

The first time I left a restaurant because it was too loud, I felt embarrassed. But my friend just said, "No problem, let's find somewhere quieter." That simple acceptance taught me that my needs weren't unreasonable, they were just different. We went next door, had a great time, and I went back home without a migraine.

Most importantly, I began to embrace my autistic traits. My "obsessive" attention to detail? It is why I catch mistakes others miss and why clients trust my work. So, instead of apologizing for being "picky," I started to take pride in my peculiarities.

My "intensity" about my interests? It has helped me come up with new ideas in every job I've had and makes me interesting to talk to. My "sensitivity"? I use it to notice patterns in information, relationships, and how things work that others miss, to sense how teams are feeling even when it is not expressed, to identify what people want that others do not see, and to spot problems before they have a real impact.

Creating Permission for Authenticity

I started writing literal permission slips for myself to be my authentic self. I kept them where I could see them—in my phone and laptop notes, on sticky notes, on my bathroom mirror:

- "I give myself permission to need advance notice about plans."
- "I give myself permission to have intense interests that bring me joy."
- "I give myself permission to communicate directly and honestly."
- "I give myself permission to stim or rock when I need to regulate."
- "I give myself permission to leave social situations when I'm overwhelmed."

For every autistic trait I had been taught as negative, I found three ways it was helpful. My need for routine was not "being stubborn," but a way to create stability that helped me do well, made chores easier, and made sure I did not forget important things. My detailed questions were not "overthinking"—they ensured I understood what was needed, helped prevent mistakes, and demonstrated that I was careful. I began paying attention to which activities drained me and which restored me, honoring these patterns rather than fighting them. I discovered that small talk at networking events exhausts me within minutes, but deep conversations about shared interests can energize me for hours. Now I structure my social interactions accordingly. I avoid large physical events but have more one-on-one coffee meetings with friends who share similar interests or simply accept me for who I am. This journey back to myself is ongoing—but every step I take is one toward embracing a life rooted in authenticity, clarity, and hard-won self-respect.

Reclaiming Body Autonomy: Beyond the Eating Disorder Narrative

I was twenty-eight when a concerned friend pulled me aside after dinner. "I've noticed you barely ate anything tonight. And last week at the restaurant, you just picked at your salad. Are you okay? Are you... struggling with food?" Her question hit me like a physical blow, not because it was unkind, but because it revealed how my carefully managed eating patterns looked from the outside. What she saw as potential disordered eating was my body's sophisticated system for avoiding the crushing fatigue, brain fog, digestive pain, bloating, constipation, or diarrhea that followed most meals. My eating patterns had been the source of public shaming and embarrassment by family members since my childhood. It seemed that wherever I went, people felt entitled to comment on my eating habits, as though they knew better than I did what I should consume.

The Critical Distinction: Sensory Needs vs. Body Image Concerns

The confusion my friend felt reflects widespread misunderstanding in medical and social contexts. Research by William Mandy and Kate Tchanturia (2015) shows that autistic women are often wrongly diagnosed with eating disorders before people realize they are autistic. This happens because the behaviors can initially appear similar, such as having limited food choices, specific eating habits, and a strong focus on food and eating routines. However, the reasons behind these behaviors are fundamentally different. Traditional eating disorders are often rooted in body image concerns and a desire for control or perfection. For autistic people, eating differences come from real neurological and sensory realities that have nothing to do with appearance or weight.

Studies by Kushak and others (2016) found that people with autism often have differences in how their bodies make and use digestive enzymes, which can make it harder to digest some foods. Additionally, our sensory differences impact all our senses, including the nerves in our stomach and gut that send messages about pain, fullness, texture, and temperature to the brain.

Moving Beyond Pathologizing Food Differences

Understanding sensory needs means shifting our questions from "What's wrong with this eating?" to "What's the body asking for?" Rather than pathologizing preferences based on genuine sensory or digestive needs, we need to investigate thoroughly before labeling eating differences as disorders, while creating supportive environments that benefit everyone.

Creating a Sensory Eating Profile

Moving from shame to kindness with myself meant changing how I thought about food and my relationship with hunger. I started keeping a sensory eating journal, tracking not just what I ate but how different foods affected my energy, mood, digestion, and sensory processing.

Creating my own sensory eating profile was key to reclaiming my relationship with food:

- **Safe Food:** Plain Greek yogurt, cooked vegetables or fruits in puree with simple seasonings, lean proteins eaten separately, smoothies, juices, soups, and warm drinks. I prefer raw fruits or vegetables alone for easier digestion. Cereals, bread, quinoa, rice, and pasta work best as standalone meals when seasoned simply. These aren't "diet foods"—they're foods that work with my sensory and digestive needs.

- **Challenging Textures:** Mixed textures, such as granola in yogurt, trigger sensory overload and affect my ability to eat. Honoring these preferences is sensory management, not "picky eating."

- **Environmental Factors:** Quiet spaces and soft lighting support better digestion. Consuming food while stressed or overstimulated can lead to digestive problems, regardless of what I eat.

- **Energy Patterns:** Eating smaller amounts more frequently maintains my energy and attention better than traditional three-meal patterns. This results in roughly five smaller meals daily, with flexibility for social dining when I combine meals and schedule recovery time.

To understand an autistic person's relationship with food, I often compare it to the difference between flying a traditional airplane and piloting a glider. Both reach beautiful destinations, but the experience, controls, and conditions needed for success are completely different. An autistic person's food choices might look "disordered" to someone with typical senses, but they're often precisely calibrated responses to a different sensory and digestive operating system.

From Self-Advocacy to Self-Compassion

Self-advocacy was my first step: learning to ask for what I needed and standing up for my right to support. But I was still just reacting to problems, still thinking of my autism as something to fix. Self-compassion was different. It meant releasing the need to justify my existence or prove my worth. Instead of "I'm so awkward," I started telling myself, "I'm learning to communicate in a neurotypical world, and that's challenging." Instead of "I'm too sensitive," I began thinking, "I process sensory information differently, and that's both a strength and something I need to accommodate." After meltdowns, I was no longer on a "social time out," ashamed, allowing a partner to disparage my natural physical, emotional reactions to their wrongdoing, their lack of care and respect, their manipulation, their insecurities, their substance abuse, their narcissism, their insecurities, gaslighting and cowardice. I started focusing on taking care of myself: drinking water, wearing comfortable clothes, engaging in the familiar activities that made me feel good and happy, and speaking kindly to myself. Most importantly, I learned to enforce the boundaries that would keep me physically, and emotionally safe from future autistic meltdowns. Five years later, I have not experienced a single one. I promised myself that no one is worth an autistic meltdown. This is where I draw the line.

The Accommodations That Transform Lives

I realized the importance of accommodating autistic behaviors rather than trying to eliminate them. Instead of demanding eye contact, I accepted that some people communicate better when looking away. Instead of forcing participation in group activities, I recognized that some individuals contribute more effectively through written work or one-on-one discussions. These seemingly small accommodations are the foundation of lasting inclusion.

The Social Cost of Professional Masking

When I began my current role, my manager assigned me to research emerging trends in our industry. While this might have been routine for someone else, I found purpose in exploring deeply and produced three improvements, including one key insight. However, my manager chose to redo the report because of its format without using my findings. Two years later, she announced she had discovered the key category I had already reported. Realizing that my neurobiological differences wouldn't be acknowledged or accommodated, I decided she wouldn't benefit from them either.

In a world that constantly critiques difference, valuing it provides the singular perspectives actually needed to uncover key insights.

Moving Forward: From Accommodation to Revolution

Rebuilding isn't about becoming someone new—it's about returning to the person I was before the world taught me to be ashamed. From the lonely lunch table at eight, to the panic attacks at sixteen, and the post-work autistic burnouts at twenty-five—each stage showed me what misunderstanding cost me. But every mask I wore was a survival strategy that taught me valuable lessons about resilience, observation, and human behavior.

The work of unlearning shame is ongoing. Some days, you'll catch yourself apologizing for stimming or hiding your interests. That's okay. Healing isn't a linear process, and self-compassion involves patience with your own journey.

Creating Change Beyond the Individual

Research consistently shows that autistic individuals who receive affirmative, identity-positive support demonstrate better mental health outcomes than those who receive interventions focused on appearing "normal" (Cage et al., 2018). The goal isn't to eliminate your autism—it's to create a life where your autism can exist without shame.

As autistic individuals, we can choose one thing each week to do our way. As parents, we can affirm our children's neurodivergent strengths and help them develop positive identities from the start. As professionals, we can examine our practices through the lens of neurodiversity, offering accommodations that create more inclusive environments for everyone.

The journey from living undiagnosed to rebuilding an authentic self requires both individual healing and systemic change. Honoring our differences and pushing for a world that embraces natural human variation is essential. It's about supporting neurodiversity, challenging harmful narratives, and creating spaces where every person can thrive authentically.

**

NEURODIVERGENT THRIVING: HONORING OUR OWN RULES

When Nighttime Becomes Your Most Productive Hour

1 a.m. The house is silent as I sit at the coffee table, on the floor, working on research papers, refining ideas, and allowing myself to enjoy the flow of my creative and thinking process, my laptop lighting the darkness. I recall the first time I discovered this sensory refuge in the middle of the night, when I was around thirteen. I would silently get up, sneak into my step-father's artist studio with a notebook, and write. That special time carved out of my sleep quickly became the secret escape I longed for daily. For years, I was forced into typical schedules, only to feel drained and frustrated, unable to perform at work or enjoy my family and creative side. But research by Mamashli et al. (2023) found that "in quiet conditions, no differences were found between ASD and TD peers." But in noisy conditions, "ASD children seem to have increased recruitment of neural resources, with reduced beta band top-down modulation (required to mitigate the impact of noise on auditory processing)." This confirms what my body always knew: autistic individuals often excel during unconventional hours, when sensory distractions are minimized. Unfortunately, once my parents found out about my nocturnal activities, I was told to prioritize my sleep. I eventually resumed this habit later in life, and it became my guilty pleasure.

Embracing these occasional hours in the middle of the night, between two sleep cycles, has become core to living life on my terms and embracing my natural rhythm. It has also transformed my productivity. I accomplish more between midnight and 6 a.m. than I do in a typical workweek. The way my brain notices patterns, which makes social situations during the day tiring, also enables me to put together complicated research and spot connections that others might not see. During these quiet hours, my mind moves through information easily and naturally, in a way that respects how my brain is wired, instead of fighting it. So, let's just recognize and honor the work rhythm and environment that maximizes our energy and productivity, even if it isn't "traditional."

From Survival Scripts To Life Under My Own Terms

For forty-two years, I lived by what I call "survival scripts"— rules I learned to make myself smaller, quieter, and easier for non-autistic people to accept. These weren't choices I made intentionally, but habits that became a part of me: Don't be too much. Don't be too intense. Avoid discussing your special interests. Don't stim in public. Disregard and hide your needs. The survival scripts showed up in many small ways every day. I would hide my excitement when conversations were about things I knew a lot about. I learned to keep my hands still, even when my body really needed to move to feel better. I made myself maintain eye contact, even when it felt very uncomfortable. The change to living my life under my own terms started with small acts of standing up for myself: wearing noise-canceling headphones in grocery stores, at the theater or even at a noisy restaurant to give myself a sensory break without saying sorry, declining invitations to social events that would leave me feeling off for days, and letting myself focus deeply on projects that truly interested me instead of forcing myself to pay attention to things that really didn't matter to me.

Honoring each additional personal term felt like getting back a part of myself I had lost. Instead of answering right away, I started saying, "Let me think about that and I'll get back to you," to allow myself to feel excited or anxious about a proposal, and figure out a reason to politely decline whatever draining activity or event came my way if needed. Eventually, I grew tired of feeling haunted by the idea of "delivering my excuse" and moved on to provide a respectful and immediate refusal. This allowed me to save my energy for what mattered to me and gain control of my time, my most precious asset. I asked for things in writing after important conversations, knowing that I understood and retained information better when I could read it. I was honest about my energy, clearly saying when I didn't have much left for socializing instead of pushing myself until I was completely worn out. Little by little, I began to conceive the possibility of a future life fully under my own terms.

This gradual process led to a more profound realization: Normalcy is something each of us must define for ourselves. The most revolutionary shift in my life occurred when I decided to apply the consequences of a fact I realized, and any human does, a long time ago: "normalcy" does not exist in itself; it is a subjective concept that is up to each individual to define. Therefore, no one owes anyone normalcy... including us, autistic, hyperactive, neurodivergent individuals. Complying with "standards" to appear "normal" is some kind of illusion of the mind.

Interestingly enough, as obvious as this truth about normalcy is to most of us, we rarely consider its intricacy and logical consequences fully. We continue to state well-intentioned cliches, such as "Every child should have a normal childhood," which ultimately becomes so relative to perspective, culture, environment, personal experience, and social class that the concepts of "normal childhood" or "normal life" are empty and meaningless on their own. There is absolutely no valid reason to shrink ourselves to fit social expectations that are highly subjective and prone to constant change. Because of their inherent subjectivity, apologizing for being authentically autistic not only alters our well-being but is completely nonsensical. Therefore, refusing to mask is not only central to redefining our identity and success on our own terms, but it is also our only valid option. So let's define normalcy for ourselves and stop apologizing for living authentically. Social norms should not dictate our identity or values.

Research by Seers and Hogg (2023) documents this pattern in late-diagnosed autistic women, finding that post-diagnosis, women often experience "identity reconstruction," where childhood survival strategies are consciously replaced with self-advocacy and boundary setting. This process isn't just personal growth—it's revolutionary resistance against internalized systems based on conformity, normalcy, and standard as the price of inclusion, all empty and subjective concepts.

The Architecture of Authentic Routines

My morning routine begins alone, preferably in silence. This isn't a refusal of social interactions or a bad mood when I wake up; it is my gentle way of getting ready for social interactions. Once I leave my bedroom, I am ready to talk, work, or do anything. However, during the 25 minutes preceding this moment, I need to make my bed, get ready in the bathroom, get dressed, and brush my hair in silence, allowing myself to organize my day's priorities and goals, and detail processes and potential schedule details. Once done, I am ready to take my children to school. The key element is not talking to anyone yet, allowing space for internal planning and decision-making, and avoiding decision fatigue later in the day without the cognitive load of social interaction. Once everyone's at school, my drive to the same Starbucks feels like another quiet time to think. I order the same drink and pastry every time, so I don't have to make extra decisions and can save my mental energy for being creative. I sit at what regulars call "my table," see the same people who work remotely and respect different ways of working, put on my noise-canceling headphones, and start work. This shows the difference between being too strict and having helpful routines. Being too strict often stems from fear and keeps you stuck; routines, on the other hand, support my focus, reduce anxiety, conserve mental energy, and help me get things done. My routine isn't about controlling everything, but about setting things up so that my brain works at its best. Healthy routines can support well-being without becoming restrictive; find balance that boosts, not hinders, your strengths.

Business Models Designed Around Hyperfocus

Instead of apologizing for not being able to focus on boring tasks, I developed a way to utilize my ability to focus deeply for extended periods. When I research on topics that interest me, I can work 8-10 hours in a row and get done in a day what might take other weeks.

Research by Ashinoff and Abu-Akel (2021) distinguishes between beneficial and problematic hyperfocus. Productive flow states involve intense concentration, leading to high-quality output without compromising physical well-being. In contrast, problematic hyperfocus involves losing awareness of basic needs, such as food, water, or taking bathroom breaks. With this in mind, to maintain a flow state productive, before starting any task requiring hyperfocus, gather snacks and water within reach, wear comfortable clothing, set up optimal lighting and headphones, put the phone on silent or airplane mode and inform your family or coworkers of the session duration. During extended focus, set timers for movement breaks every 2 hours, keep fidget tools within easy reach and maintain boundary protection (closed door, "Do Not Disturb" sign). Once done, save and organize your work, plan out your next session before transitioning to normal activities.

The Science of Thriving Differently

Having both autism and ADHD creates what I call "cognitive weather patterns" or natural changes in my ability to pay attention and my energy level. On some days, my brain feels very focused and can solve complex problems. On other days, my attention jumps quickly between multiple projects. In addition to that cognitive pattern, my ADHD impacts tremendously my focus: in an amazing way when it comes to my genuine interests, in a challenging way with topics I have no or little interest in. So my focus is mostly based on what interests me, not just what is important. I can't just choose to focus because something matters—my brain needs real interest, something new, or excitement to pay attention for a long time.

Research by Sokolova et al. (2017) found that autism and ADHD co-occur in 22-83% of cases, particularly in females. This combination creates challenges around emotional regulation and executive functioning, but also distinctive strengths in pattern recognition and creative problem-solving when conditions are right.

Csikszentmihalyi's flow state research describes "being completely involved in an activity for its own sake,"Biscontini, T. (2024), losing track of time while experiencing optimal performance. For neurodivergent individuals, this state can be both more accessible due to their natural hyperfocus abilities and more necessary due to higher baseline stress levels that require regulation through deeply absorbing activities. But the key to reach sustained focus is a genuine interest. In that regard, school becomes quickly a challenge with its plethora of topics that fail to catch our interest.

I remember particularly vividly, school year after school year, the mandatory novels I had no interest in. I would find myself reading them out loud to my mother attempting to keep me focused while my mind was thinking about something else. I had no recollection of what I had just perfectly read, and would end up spending hours reading over and over again the same chapter. It was like my brain was scanning the page, but could not print it. I was unable to retain anything, and naturally being blamed for my "lack of effort" or "laziness." I truly was not. If anything, I might have read those novels ten times more than my classmates to barely retain the name of a couple of key characters and some of the elements of the plot. In contrast, I devoured any non-fiction related to my special interests, usually multiple at the same time, sustaining my focus even waiting for the subway during peak hours.

Living by Design, Not Default

Moving from survival to a meaningful life required letting go of others' expectations and embracing authenticity. Living on my terms isn't just liberating—it's essential to my well-being and growth. Authenticity isn't just a personal change, it is about creating ways of living and working that fit all kinds of brains. When I follow my natural rhythms, set up routines that help me instead of just trying to control things, and do work that uses my real strengths instead of forcing myself to focus where it doesn't come naturally, my creativity and problem-solving skills grow exponentially. Over the years, observing the same pattern with my neurodivergent children, the natural question that came to me was: What if we stopped trying to force square pegs into round holes and instead designed systems that work with human diversity rather than against it? The challenge is not that we are too much for the world, but that the world has yet to be designed with us in mind.

The Neurodivergent Flow Formula

Achieving flow states consistently requires understanding the specific conditions that enable my neurodivergent brain to access its optimal functioning. Tasks must connect to my special interests or core values to engage my natural motivation systems, because external pressure or obligation alone isn't sufficient to activate the neurochemical cascade that enables sustained attention. When work aligns with my genuine interests, the effort feels effortless, and time becomes irrelevant in the most productive way possible.

Sensory optimization becomes crucial because my environment must support rather than overwhelm my nervous system for flow to occur. This means controlling lighting to avoid the harsh fluorescent bulbs that trigger instant overwhelm, managing sound through noise-canceling headphones or carefully chosen background music, and ensuring physical comfort through appropriate seating, temperature, and clothing choices. What might seem like minor environmental details to neurotypical individuals can mean the difference between accessible flow and impossible concentration for my sensory-sensitive system.

Autonomy preservation is essential because micromanagement or rigid external control disrupts my natural flow state faster than almost any other factor. My brain requires the freedom to approach tasks in whatever order feels most natural, to take breaks when my attention naturally cycles, and to follow interesting tangents that often lead to breakthrough insights. When I feel controlled or monitored, my nervous system shifts into a hypervigilant state that makes the relaxed awareness necessary for flow impossible to achieve.

The skill-challenge balance must be carefully calibrated so

tasks are complex enough to engage my pattern recognition abilities and need for intellectual stimulation without becoming so overwhelming that they trigger executive dysfunction or anxiety. My brain craves complexity and novelty, but there's a narrow window where challenges feel exciting rather than paralyzing. Finding this sweet spot requires ongoing experimentation and honest self-assessment about my current capacity and energy levels.

Purpose clarity helps me understand how my work contributes to larger goals, providing the meaning-making that sustains my motivation through difficult or tedious portions of projects. When I can connect current tasks to bigger-picture outcomes that align with my values —particularly around supporting other neurodivergent individuals or advancing understanding of autism—even administrative work becomes more engaging because it serves a purpose I care deeply about.

Non-Linear Productivity and Interest-Based Nervous Systems

My ADHD brain's interest-based nervous system means that traditional productivity advice often backfires spectacularly, creating more struggle rather than improved performance. Strategies like "just focus," "make a schedule and stick to it," or "do the important things first" assume a neurotypical attention system that can respond to rational priorities and external motivation. My brain requires a completely different approach that honors its need for genuine engagement rather than fighting against its natural operating system.

Studies document that ADHD individuals often experience "inconsistent attention" rather than a true attention deficit, meaning the ability to hyperfocus on interesting tasks while struggling with mundane ones reflects different dopamine regulation patterns rather than a general inability to concentrate. This inconsistency isn't a flaw to be overcome but a feature to be understood and accommodated through strategic task design and environmental optimization.

I practice energy mapping by tracking when my focus is naturally highest throughout different times of day and seasons, allowing me to schedule demanding work during peak performance windows rather than forcing productivity during low-energy periods. This tracking revealed patterns I never would have noticed otherwise, like how my creative thinking peaks and drops during certain hours, how my analytical abilities fluctuate, and how much more sleep I need in comparison to most individuals.

Interest cycling involves rotating between three to four projects simultaneously to maintain the novelty that my ADHD brain requires for sustained engagement. Rather than seeing this as scattered or undisciplined, I've learned to view it as a sophisticated attention management strategy that prevents the boredom that kills motivation for interest-based nervous systems. When I feel my attention beginning to wane on one project, I switch to another rather than forcing continued focus, often returning to the original project with renewed energy and fresh perspectives.

I create urgency strategically by using deadlines and time constraints to activate my natural ADHD motivation systems, since my brain often requires external pressure to initiate tasks that don't provide immediate interest or reward. This isn't procrastination in the traditional sense but rather working with my brain's natural activation patterns. I've learned to distinguish between productive urgency that energizes and motivates and destructive panic that overwhelms and paralyzes. I even tell my family and friends about important deadlines for accountability.

Passion alignment ensures that all major projects

connect to my core values and interests, providing the intrinsic motivation necessary for sustained engagement with complex, long-term work. When projects align with my genuine passions—particularly around neurodiversity advocacy and supporting other late-diagnosed women and individuals—the work feels energizing rather than depleting, even during challenging phases. This alignment also provides resilience during difficult periods, because the deeper purpose sustains motivation when surface-level interest fluctuates.

Recovery integration builds in adequate downtime between intensive focus sessions, recognizing that my neurodivergent brain requires more recovery time than neurotypical productivity models typically account for. Not only do I sleep 8 to 9 hours each night, but I also nap every single day between my two main productive periods. This isn't laziness but neurological necessity—my brain processes information more intensively during focused work, requiring proportionally more rest to integrate new learning and reset for the next productive cycle.

Sensory Regulation as Performance Enhancement

What others call "sensory disorder," I've learned to reframe as "sensory hypersensitivities that require strategic management." This shift in perspective has been revolutionary, moving from seeing my heightened sensory awareness as a limitation to recognizing it as an extraordinary capacity for detecting subtle environmental changes, emotional atmospheres, and quality variations that others miss entirely. My ability to notice when something is slightly off in a room, a conversation, or a system often provides valuable information that leads to important discoveries or prevents problems before they escalate.

My sensory sensitivity makes me an exceptional researcher because I notice inconsistencies in data, contradictions in arguments, and gaps in logic that might escape others who aren't processing information with the same intensity. In advocacy work, my sensitivity to emotional undertones helps me understand when someone is struggling even if they can't articulate it directly, allowing me to provide support that addresses real needs rather than surface presentations. In friendships, my awareness of subtle changes in tone, energy, or behavior helps me respond to loved ones with precision and care.

However, these hypersensitivities require strategic management to remain assets rather than becoming overwhelming liabilities. Noise-canceling headphones have become essential equipment for both focus and nervous system regulation, allowing me to control my auditory environment in ways that support rather than overwhelm my processing capacity. I wear them not just in obviously loud environments but also in spaces with subtle but persistent background noise that would gradually erode my cognitive resources throughout the day.

My sunglasses and headphones haven't left my side since the age of sixteen, serving as crucial protection against visual and auditory overwhelm that can trigger sensory overload, violent migraines and make any other task impossible. I use them everywhere from movie theaters during those overwhelming IMAX experiences where volume levels and screen brightness feel unbearable, to grocery stores with harsh fluorescent lighting, outdoor events where natural light intensity exceeds my comfortable range, even sometimes when it's raining. Rather than suffering through visual and auditory discomfort, I've learned to proactively manage my environment.

I maintain specific texture preferences in fabrics and materials, choosing clothing and furniture based on how they feel against my skin rather than following fashion trends that might create sensory distress throughout the day. Soft, natural fabrics without scratchy seams or labels have become non-negotiable because comfortable clothing allows me to focus on more important things than managing constant tactile irritation. This isn't vanity or pickiness—it's recognizing that sensory comfort directly impacts cognitive performance.

Lighting control through adjustable lamps and bulbs allows me to match my visual environment to my energy levels and task requirements, recognizing that harsh fluorescent lighting can trigger overwhelm while warm, dimmed lighting supports concentration and emotional regulation. I've installed smart bulbs throughout my workspace that can adjust color temperature and intensity throughout the day, supporting my natural circadian rhythms and varying sensory needs.

Temperature regulation through layering systems and environmental controls helps me maintain optimal comfort, since my autistic nervous system is highly sensitive to temperature fluctuations that others might not even notice. I've learned that being too hot or too cold creates a constant background stress that depletes cognitive resources and makes everything else more difficult. Rather than toughing it out, I prioritize thermal comfort as essential for optimal functioning.

Movement integration includes fidget tools strategically placed throughout my environment, a standing desk that allows me to alternate between sitting and standing based on my body's needs, and permission to pace during thinking because my brain often processes information better when my body is in motion. Turns out both my sons are also adept at walking around the house, sometimes following specific movement patterns, to think. This isn't restlessness or inability to sit still—it's how our brains integrate complex information and regulate our nervous systems naturally.

My Personal Rulebook: A Framework for Neurodivergent

Thriving

Understanding My Optimal Performance Windows

My peak focus occurs between 10 p.m. and 3 a.m., when the world is quiet and sensory distractions are minimized, allowing my autistic brain to engage in sustained concentration without competing stimuli from traffic, conversations, or the general bustle of daytime activity. During these hours, my hyperfocus abilities reach their full potential, and I can tackle complex research, writing, or problem-solving tasks that would be impossible during the sensory chaos of typical business hours.

Creative synthesis happens best in early morning hours between 6 a.m. and 8 a.m. after adequate sleep, when my mind is fresh and able to make novel connections between ideas without the cognitive fatigue that accumulates throughout the day. This is when breakthrough insights often emerge, when disparate concepts suddenly click together into coherent frameworks, and when my pattern recognition abilities are most acute. The key is protecting this window from administrative tasks or routine activities that don't require creative thinking.

Structured administrative work requires the support of mid-morning hours from 9 a.m. to 11 a.m., bolstered by caffeine and specific types of background music that help maintain attention on tasks that are necessary but not inherently interesting to my interest-based nervous system. I've learned that trying to force administrative work during my creative peak hours wastes precious cognitive resources, while attempting it during low-energy periods leads to mistakes and frustration.

Administrative tasks that require minimal intellectual focus but sustained attention get scheduled during what I call "TV time"—working on routine tasks while watching familiar shows or documentaries. This may sound counterintuitive, but the background entertainment keeps my brain sufficiently interested to remain present and focused on otherwise mind-numbing work like data entry, filing, or routine correspondence. The show prevents my mind from wandering into more interesting territories while providing just enough stimulation to maintain engagement with boring but necessary tasks.

Social interactions are most successful in the early morning when I'm sufficiently regulated to engage with others and my social energy is at its peak, but before the day's demands have depleted my capacity for the complex cognitive work that social interaction requires for autistic individuals. I've learned to distinguish between interactions that energize me because they involve genuine connection around shared interests or authentic interactions with true friends versus those that drain me because they require sustained masking or small talk performance.

End-of-day social interactions work well only with friends and family who know me well enough to understand if I need to decline at the last minute, and with whom I don't need to engage in masking, small talk, or other socially demanding behaviors that would drain my already depleted reserves. If I must attend a social event with acquaintances or professional contacts, I plan the entire day around conserving social energy, often working from home, taking a nap, and keeping the day "socially light" to save my resources for the evening demand.

Creating Environmental Conditions for Success

Sound control requires either complete silence for maximum concentration during hyperfocus sessions or specific types of background music that enhance rather than distract from cognitive processing. I've discovered that certain instrumental music with consistent patterns actually supports my focus by providing a predictable auditory landscape that masks potentially distracting environmental sounds without demanding linguistic processing that would compete with my thinking.

Lighting preferences center on natural light whenever possible, with warm artificial light as an alternative to the harsh fluorescent lighting that can trigger sensory overwhelm and make concentration impossible. I've learned to be proactive about lighting needs, carrying small lamps to conferences or requesting specific seating in restaurants to avoid the visual assault of poor lighting that can derail my entire evening.

Spatial organization involves maintaining clutter-free environments with personal comfort items nearby, creating predictable visual fields that support rather than stress my processing systems. My workspace includes carefully chosen objects that provide comfort and grounding—fidget tools, photos of my children, plants that add life without demanding maintenance, and books related to my special interests that remind me of my deeper purposes.

Temperature control at slightly cool settings between 68 and 70 degrees Fahrenheit allows me to add comfortable layers as needed rather than dealing with the cognitive drain of being too warm. I've learned that thermal comfort directly impacts my ability to think clearly, and I no longer apologize for needing different temperature settings than others might prefer.

Accessibility requires all necessary tools and resources within easy reach to minimize interruptions to flow states and reduce the executive function demands that come with having to search for or retrieve needed items during focused work. This means keeping water, snacks, writing materials, charging cables, and other essentials in designated places that don't require thought or decision-making to access.

Recognizing My Social Rhythms and Needs

Deep conversations thrive in one-on-one settings that are scheduled in advance and time-limited, allowing me to prepare mentally for the social and emotional energy required while ensuring that interactions don't extend beyond my capacity in ways that would leave me dysregulated for days afterward. These conversations are often the most meaningful and energizing social experiences because they allow for authentic connection without the performance demands of group dynamics.

Group interactions work best with small groups of three to four people maximum, kept to short durations, and centered around shared interests that provide natural conversation structure and reduce the ambiguity that makes social situations cognitively demanding for autistic individuals. When conversations have clear frameworks based on topics I'm genuinely interested in, the social interaction becomes energizing rather than depleting.

Professional meetings require agendas provided in advance with specific outcomes identified, giving my autistic brain the framework needed to participate effectively without the anxiety that comes from unpredictable social and professional demands. I've learned to advocate for this accommodation by explaining that preparation helps me contribute more meaningfully rather than simply making the meeting easier for me personally.

The reality is that most meetings could be replaced with more efficient communication methods like emails or shared documents, but traditional workplace culture often uses meetings to satisfy management's need to feel in control of remote or autonomous workers rather than serving genuine collaborative purposes. My neurodivergent brain recognizes this inefficiency clearly, which sometimes leads to frustration with systems that prioritize appearances over actual productivity.

Social recovery involves 24 to 48 hours of minimal social demand after intense interactions, recognizing that my nervous system requires more downtime than neurotypical social models typically account for. This isn't antisocial behavior but necessary recovery time that allows me to process social experiences, restore my energy reserves, and return to social situations as my authentic self rather than a depleted version struggling to maintain basic politeness.

Communication preferences emphasize written follow-up for important decisions or complex topics, allowing me to process information thoroughly and respond thoughtfully rather than feeling pressured to provide immediate reactions that may not reflect my best thinking. I've learned to request this accommodation by explaining that written communication helps me contribute more meaningfully to important discussions.

Red Flags for Burnout Prevention

Physical warning signs include increased sensory sensitivity where previously tolerable sounds, textures, or lighting become overwhelming and impossible to ignore. This escalation in sensory reactivity often serves as an early warning system that my nervous system is becoming overtaxed and needs immediate attention and care. Disrupted sleep patterns that don't respond to my usual regulation strategies signal that stress levels have exceeded my system's capacity to maintain basic self-regulation.

Frequent illness, headaches, nausea, and digestive issues often accompany burnout as my immune system becomes compromised by chronic stress and the constant effort of functioning in environments that don't naturally support my neurodivergent needs. These physical symptoms aren't separate from my neurological experience, but direct manifestations of my nervous system overwhelm.

Emotional indicators manifest as unexplained irritability where small annoyances trigger disproportionate emotional reactions, signaling that my usual emotional regulation strategies are no longer sufficient for my current stress load. Emotional numbness where I lose access to my usual range of feelings often follows periods of emotional overwhelm, as my system attempts to protect itself by shutting down feeling capacity entirely.

Increased anxiety that doesn't correspond to external circumstances suggests that my nervous system is operating in a state of hypervigilance that has become disconnected from actual environmental threats. This background anxiety makes everything feel more difficult and depletes energy reserves that would normally be available for daily functioning.

Cognitive symptoms involve difficulty concentrating even on preferred activities that usually capture my interest effortlessly, indicating that cognitive resources are being diverted to managing stress rather than engaging with meaningful work. Persistent forgetfulness about important tasks or commitments signals that executive functioning systems are becoming overloaded and failing to maintain their usual organizational capacity.

Executive dysfunction where previously manageable routines become impossible to maintain represents a significant red flag because it indicates that the basic scaffolding supporting my daily functioning is beginning to collapse under stress. When I can't manage simple tasks like meal preparation or basic hygiene, it's time for immediate intervention and support.

Social changes include avoiding previously enjoyed interactions because the energy required for social engagement exceeds my current capacity. Increased masking that feels more effortful than usual signals that my authentic self is becoming less accessible, requiring more conscious effort to present socially acceptable versions of myself. Withdrawal from communities that typically provide support, and connection indicates that even positive relationships feel too demanding for my depleted system.

Behavioral shifts involve abandoning self-care routines I normally maintain without effort, suggesting that the cognitive resources required for basic self-maintenance are being redirected toward just surviving immediate demands. Increased stimming as my nervous system seeks regulation through movement and sensory input can indicate overwhelm, though it's important to distinguish between regulatory stimming and distress stimming.

Green Flags for Optimal Functioning

Engagement indicators include easily entering flow states during preferred activities without the effortful preparation that might be required during more challenging periods. When my system is functioning optimally, hyperfocus becomes accessible and enjoyable rather than something I have to work to achieve. Sustained interest in projects without forcing attention suggests that my natural curiosity and motivation systems are operating effectively.

Natural curiosity about learning and growth opportunities indicates that I have sufficient cognitive and emotional resources to engage with new ideas and challenges rather than just maintaining existing functioning. When I'm thriving, I actively seek out new learning experiences related to my interests rather than feeling overwhelmed by the prospect of additional cognitive demands.

Regulation signs involve stable mood with appropriate emotional responses to situations, indicating that my emotional regulation systems are functioning effectively and I have access to the full range of my emotional experience. Good sleep quality with natural sleep-wake cycles suggests that my nervous system is successfully managing the transition between waking and sleeping states without excessive intervention.

Physical energy that supports daily activities without requiring extraordinary effort or careful resource management indicates that my system is operating efficiently and isn't diverting excessive energy toward managing stress or environmental demands. When I'm thriving, basic self-care and daily tasks feel manageable rather than overwhelming.

Connection markers include enjoying social interactions rather than enduring them, which suggests that I have sufficient social energy to engage authentically rather than simply performing socially acceptable behaviors. Feeling understood by others in meaningful relationships indicates that my authentic self is accessible and that others can connect with who I really am rather than my masked presentation.

Contributing authentically to communities and causes I care about suggests that I have energy and resources beyond basic survival needs, allowing me to engage with purposes larger than immediate self-maintenance. This contribution feels energizing rather than depleting when my system is functioning optimally.

In other terms, when honoring my own rules and meeting my neurodivergent needs, I thrive at every single level of my life. And so should anyone.

***

RETHINKING AUTISM NARRATIVES

The Single Story Problem: Ignoring The Complexity And Diversity Factors

The story most people know about autism starts in 1943 with Leo Kanner's notes on eleven children he said had "autistic disturbances of affective contact." Around the same time, Hans Asperger was writing about what he called "autistic psychopathy" in children. These early medical descriptions set up a way of thinking that focused on illness, problems, and the idea that autism mostly affected white, middle-class boys. We learned from history that single stories become dangerous when they erase the complexity and diversity of lived experiences, and Autism is no exception.

The media amplified these narrow stories, sometimes in harmful ways. From "Rain Man" to "Atypical," autism in movies and TV has mostly shown white men who are awkward but very smart, making it seem like autism is either a special gift or a sad story. In reality, this idea of the "savant" only fits less than 10% of autistic people, but it shapes how most people think about autism and creates unrealistic expectations, giving the impression that autism always looks the same.

The way we diagnose autism is still based on how it often appears in boys, which means girls and people from different backgrounds are often missed. The words we use—like "deficits in social communication," "restricted behaviors," and "impairments"—focus on what we are said to be missing instead of seeing that our brains just work differently.

Framework: Understanding the Paradigm Shift

The neurodiversity movement, initiated by sociologist Judy Singer in 1999, presents a distinct perspective on autism. Instead of seeing autism as a problem that needs to be fixed, neurodiversity sees autism as a natural difference in how people's brains work—one of the many ways humans can be, which helps us all be stronger and more creative. The social model of disability distinguishes between impairment and disability. Impairment refers to differences in neurological functioning, while disability refers to social barriers that prevent full participation. Many challenges autistic people face arise not from our neurological differences themselves, but from living in environments designed without considering neurological diversity.

This significant shift in thinking has a profound impact on mental health. Studies show that talking about "curing" autism leads to more depression, anxiety, and thoughts of suicide among autistic people. When we think our way of being is wrong, it's hard to feel good about ourselves. The neurodiversity concept offers us something better: pride, community, and acceptance.

Living Under a Narrative That Wasn't Mine

Growing up without a diagnosis, I learned early that my naturel self was essentially not wanted. At the same time, I felt "not good enough" at picking up social cues, at controlling my emotions. This put me in a tough spot, always watching myself closely to make sure my real self did not show through the mask I had built.

Masking became my hardest habit: forcing eye contact, altering my voice, and concealing my upset. I tried to join in small talk when I wanted real conversations, and I hid my excitement about things I cared about. I learned ways to fit in, but acting all the time was very tiring.

Everything changed when I first learned about neurodiversity in my early thirties. Reading stories from autistic people who had experiences a lot like mine, I felt something new: being seen without being called sick. These individuals discussed sensory differences as normal, rather than as problems, and viewed strong interests as strengths, not as obsessions. The same experiences that generate shame under one narrative become sources of strength under another. Reframing personal experiences through a neurodiversity lens can turn shame into empowerment.

The Power of Authentic Storytelling

First-person stories from autistic people have changed how the public sees autism, as well as research and policies. When we tell our own stories, we challenge common beliefs and reveal the disparity between what people assume and how we actually live. Only autistic people can truly share these real stories. It's our job to speak up for ourselves and future generations. Our voices matter, but only if we use them.

This is why autistic people need to lead autism research. When autistic people help plan research, the questions are about what really matters to us. This has helped uncover important aspects that old studies missed, such as how we conceal our traits, sensory experiences, and mental health. It even showed that old ideas—such as the notion that we don't feel emotions —were wrong.

Missing real voices became even clearer to me when my mother died of Amyotrophic lateral sclerosis (ALS). While her mind stayed sharp, her body failed; I remembered my uncle's comment after we watched an autism documentary when I was eleven. He wondered about the "suffering" of non-verbal autistic kids, thinking they were "trapped" and couldn't speak. Later, after I was bullied, I went through a mute period myself. For me, it wasn't a prison—it was a safe place. My mind worked in its normal way, finding patterns and connections that talking might disrupt. It even helped me calm down because I didn't have to worry about what I was saying.

This comparison highlights why authentic storytelling is important. When autistic voices are missing, inaccurate narratives and harmful myths take hold, influencing policies and *opportunities.*

Intersectionality: Expanding the Narrative

One of the most significant problems with dominant autism narratives is their failure to represent diversity across different identities. The voices most heard have predominantly been those of white, middle-class families, leaving enormous gaps in understanding how autism intersects with other marginalized identities.

As previously explained, autistic women are more likely to hide their traits, have interests that seem normal to others, and show their autism in ways that are harder to see. This means we are often diagnosed later, misdiagnosed, or do not get the help we need. Autistic people of color face extra barriers to getting diagnosed, often dealing with stereotypes that make it harder to get understanding and support. LGBTQ+ autistic people also have to deal with the challenges of being both autistic and part of a sexual or gender minority.

These missing stories have real effects on getting diagnosed, finding support, and a sense of community belonging. Inclusive narratives can improve diagnosis rates, support, and community for all individuals on the autism spectrum.

Therefore, liberation narratives must include all autistic voices, not just those of the most privileged individuals.

Practice & Repair: Exercises, Scripts, and Relationship Healing

Narrative Liberation Exercises involve a structured process for rewriting your life story through a neurodiversity lens. The first exercise, the Shame Inventory, requires you to list moments when you felt shame about being "too much" or "not enough," then rewrite each through a neurodiversity perspective—transforming "I monopolized the conversation about marine biology" into "I shared passionate knowledge, creating an opportunity for others to learn."

The Strength Archeology exercise involves identifying traits others have criticized, then researching how these same traits can be strengths in different contexts by creating two columns labeled "Old Interpretation" and "New Understanding."

Through the Environmental Audit, you map environments where you feel most and least like yourself, identifying specific factors that contribute to each experience to help you advocate for supportive environments.

The Letter to Your Younger Self exercise asks you to write to yourself at a challenging age using your current perspective, telling that child what you understand now about their struggles and helping them recognize their strengths.

Finally, the Future Self Visualization involves imagining yourself five years from now living authentically—picturing what your life looks like, what accommodations are routine, and using this vision to set meaningful and authentic goals that align with your true self rather than societal expectations.

Relationship Repair

Understanding my autism at thirty-one required revisiting

decades of interactions through a different lens. Arguments I had attributed to character flaws turned out to be neurological mismatches. My exhaustion after social events wasn't antisocial behavior—it was the natural consequence of extended masking.

With my parents, I began conversations about how their well-intentioned corrections had contributed to internalized shame, while they grappled with the unintended consequences of trying to help me fit into a world they believed would reject difference. The repair wasn't about blame—it was about mutual understanding and moving forward with new awareness.

With friends and people in general, as I became more comfortable sharing my diagnosis, I realized that most people felt uncertain about how to respond. Often, their initial reaction was to downplay or even deny my diagnosis in an attempt to comfort me. However, these responses were ineffective. I found them offensive and irritating. I encourage anyone in this position to refrain from making those statements and consider the alternatives below: Instead of saying "You don't look autistic," a simple "Thank you for sharing this with me" will suffice. Because, ultimately, no one looks autistic, and if there was a proper "autistic look," "don't worry" suggests that we should be ashamed of it. Instead of "You're so high-functioning" or "It must be really mild," please respectfully ask, "What does being autistic mean for you?" or "What challenges do you face?" and we'll be happy to explain the struggles you assumed we did not face because we go out of our way to make you feel comfortable in our presence. And, by the way, you are most welcome. Instead of asking, "What's your special talent?" which might suggest we're candidates for the next season of America's Got Talent, a more supportive question is, "What are you passionate about lately?" This allows us to discuss our strong interests openly. If you would like to change the subject, please let us know. We appreciate honesty and understand when the conversation needs to shift.

Instead of "Everyone feels that way sometimes," consider, "That sounds really challenging."

In my relationships, narrative reconstruction meant renegotiating communication patterns that had been established over years of misunderstanding. My need for routine wasn't rigidity—it was how my nervous system maintained regulation. My direct communication wasn't insensitive—it was authenticity misinterpreted through neurotypical assumptions. Narrative change ripples through every relationship, requiring vulnerability and patience on all sides.

Narrative as Cultural Blueprint: Building the Future

When we rewrite the story, we don't just free ourselves— we free the next generation from ever needing to apologize for who they are. The narratives we construct about autism become cultural blueprints for how future generations understand themselves and how society treats them.

Picture a classroom where a child's need to move while learning is accommodated without question, where intense interests are cultivated as pathways to expertise. Imagine workplaces designed with sensory diversity in mind, where different communication styles are valued and career paths are built around individual strengths. Envision healthcare systems where autistic presentations are understood by every provider, where accommodations are offered proactively.

In this future, diagnosis would be information rather than devastation. Parents would celebrate their child's autism as part of their unique constellation of traits. Teachers would be trained to recognize neurodivergent learning styles. Employers would compete to attract talent with autism.

Switching from systems that expect autistic people to fit in to systems that respect their dignity and authenticity means big changes. Measuring success by supporting authentic autistic expression yields better outcomes. Instead of judging success by how much autistic people act like non-autistic people, dignity-centered systems look at how well places help autistic people do well and be themselves. When authentic autistic behaviors are enabled, success naturally follows.

I extend an invitation to every reader to become a co-author of a better future. Whether you are autistic, love someone with autism, or work with autistic individuals, you have the power to challenge deficit-based narratives and amplify affirming ones. Every time we choose to center autistic perspectives, we contribute to a cultural shift that makes authentic belonging possible.

The story of autism is still being written, and those of us who live it must be the primary authors. The medical model gave us a beginning marked by pathology, but the neurodiversity movement offers us the opportunity to write a different middle and ending—one where difference is celebrated, accommodations are provided without question, and autistic people are valued for their authentic contributions rather than their ability to mask their true selves. Remember, the narratives we tell today become tomorrow's reality for autistic children not yet born. What do you want it to be?

***

INTERSECTIONAL NEURODIVERGENCE

When I received my autism diagnosis at thirty-one, I was keenly aware that privileges had paved my way to understanding. As a white, educated woman with a job, I had access to resources that others did not. I did not need to pursue a private evaluation because our house was located in a good school district with a proper special education department that identified my children's needs early, giving us access to specialized therapists. I then researched autism independently as a parent, trying to imagine my children's futures and how I could support them and came across videos of women and adults with autism sharing experiences that mirrored mine. I took time to process this realization and worked with a therapist to navigate my diagnosis. This forced me to confront a hard truth: my self-discovery was possible due to advantages systematically denied to others based on race, class, gender, sexuality, and other identity markers. Within my own family, I observed my white relatives accepting our diagnosis, while my African and Caribbean family members originally dismissed it.

When Privilege Meets Systemic Barriers

The full weight of this realization struck me when my ex-husband shared a tragedy in our local Haitian community. A six-year-old autistic boy was prone to wandering—a common behavior often overlooked in places with limited autism knowledge. When he went missing one afternoon, neighbors and authorities searched urgently through the night.

With our oldest son deeply interested in water, my ex-husband immediately suggested searching nearby lakes. His advice came from personal experience: many autistic children are irresistibly drawn to water, often disregarding safety. Tragically, that was where the boy was found the next morning.

I couldn't help but feel similar tragedies could be avoided with better autism recognition and support in communities with abnormally low diagnosis rates, reflecting a lack of awareness and resources. For families, educators, medical professionals, and caretakers, understanding wandering behaviors is key to ensuring safety. Instead, this death exposed the deadly inequities in autism awareness and support.

In our mostly white, middle-class neighborhood, children who tend to wander are protected by prompt response protocols and carry GPS watches and safety devices. Parents know to check water sources first. Schools keep detailed safety plans. But in marginalized communities—where mental health resources are limited and autism awareness is scarce—neurodivergent children remain unseen until tragedy occurs.

This Haitian family's loss reveals a larger injustice in how diagnoses are established within our healthcare system. Cultural, language, financial, and medical biases converge, leaving children who need support frequently overlooked.

I saw this bias firsthand. Our children's first pediatrician was from the Caribbean islands because we wanted to keep practicing French at home. When the school raised repeated concerns about my oldest son, our pediatrician dismissed them, blaming delayed speech and unusual fixations on his "bilingual environment." I remember wondering: What does obsessively flushing the toilets have to do with French culture?

Though my son was later diagnosed after a second school recommendation, which also led to my own diagnosis, that Haitian child never received proper accommodations. Despite his diagnosis, basic safety measures weren't in place. The systems meant to identify and support neurodivergent children in less affluent communities were clearly lagging and failing our most vulnerable children from the start.

Luckily, we never faced doubts from schools about whether our children struggles were "real" or "cultural." I never had to choose between seeking help for my child and paying rent. My path to understanding, though challenging, had been eased by advantages I was only beginning to recognize.

Autism itself is impartial, but our diagnostic and support systems are not. Until we address these deep-seated inequities, preventable tragedies will persist in the communities that most need support.

The Intersectional Framework: Beyond Single-Axis Understanding

Developed by legal scholar Kimberlé Crenshaw (1989, 1991), the concept of intersectionality offers essential tools for understanding how multiple systems of oppression intersect to shape individual experiences in ways that cannot be fully understood by examining each identity separately. Crenshaw's framework emerged from her work documenting how Black women faced discrimination that was both racial and gendered, but couldn't be adequately addressed by civil rights law that treated race and gender as separate, non-overlapping categories.

When we look at neurodivergence through this lens, we see how autism, ADHD, and other differences combined with race, gender, class, sexual orientation create unique experiences that only exist at the intersection of all those characteristics.

For example, a Black autistic woman does not just face racism, sexism, and ableism one after the other—she faces a special kind of unfairness that comes from all these parts of her identity combined together. Watching others navigate their own diagnostic journeys illuminated just how much identity shapes every aspect of the neurodivergence experience. I witnessed brilliant Black colleagues whose autism was overlooked or misattributed to behavioral problems, or cultural differences, whose intelligence was questioned rather than their neurological differences explored. I supported friends from working-class backgrounds who couldn't afford the comprehensive evaluations required for adult diagnosis. I learned from LGBTQ+ friends whose gender identity or sexual orientation seemed to eclipse consideration of neurodivergence in clinical settings, as if one could only be marginalized in a single way at a time.

One experience that fundamentally shifted my understanding occurred during a meeting where I met a transgender autistic person who was navigating both gender transition and autism self-discovery simultaneously. They described the impossible task of seeking healthcare that could address both their gender dysphoria and their neurodivergent needs.

"The gender clinic said my autism meant I couldn't really understand my gender identity," they explained. "They wanted me to wait until my autism was 'stabilized' before they'd consider hormone therapy. But the autism specialist said my gender transition was causing too much stress to properly assess my neurodivergence. Neither system could see both parts of my identity as real and valid at the same time."

Another man I met through a group for working autistic adults, openly gay with both autism and Tourette's Syndrome, joked about being a triple unicorn in a world that barely accepts any of his identities, while clearly struggling in every aspect of his life. Those experiences revealed how intersectional discrimination operates through institutional policies that assume people can only belong to one marginalized category at a time. Yet when I witnessed each one connect with other LGBTQ+ autistic individuals online. I also saw the remarkable resilience that emerges when intersectional marginalized people find each other and create a community that honors all aspects of their identity.

Cultural Context and Western Bias

The fact that most autism research and diagnoses are based on Western, male-centered ideas shows a bigger problem about whose experiences are seen as important and whose voices are listened to. In the past, women, people of color, and people from non-Western cultures were often left out of autism research on purpose because of unfair beliefs about whose lives and experiences mattered.

The cultural specificity of current diagnostic criteria becomes apparent when examining how autism traits are interpreted across different cultural contexts. In many East Asian cultures, behaviors that Western frameworks label as "restricted interests" may be viewed as dedication and mastery—valued traits that bring honor to families and communities. Direct communication styles that are pathologized as "social deficits" in Western contexts may be appreciated as a sign of honesty and integrity in cultures that value straightforward interaction.

Indigenous communities often have traditional frameworks for understanding neurological difference that emphasize community support and role specialization rather than individual pathology. Some cultures might even interpret intense sensitivity and different ways of processing information through spiritual lenses, viewing these traits as connections to ancestral wisdom or heightened intuition rather than developmental disorders.

Intersectional Portraits: Complex Lived Experiences

Understanding intersectionality requires moving beyond abstract theory to examine how multiple identities shape real lives in concrete ways. Consider a ten-year-old Black boy whose intense interest in train schedules and routes is interpreted by his teachers as disruptive behavior rather than a sign of cognitive giftedness. His stimming behaviors—hand-flapping and rocking that help him regulate sensory overwhelm—are seen as aggressive or threatening rather than self-soothing strategies within the spectrum of autism.

The school-to-prison pipeline that disproportionately affects Black boys intersects with ableism in ways that create peculiar dangers for autistic children of color. This ten-year-old direct communication style, interpreted as disrespectful in contexts where Black children are expected to show deference to white authority, may lead to repeated disciplinary actions that escalate rather than address his actual needs.

Now, let's imagine a working-class woman in her thirties from Latin America who has never received a formal autism diagnosis but recognizes herself in every autistic experiences she encounters online. Working multiple jobs to support her family, she doesn't have the luxury of taking time off for a comprehensive evaluation or the resources to pay for a private assessment. And even if she did, her family and friends would certainly voice their doubts and convince her that not only would she be wasting her time, but also her hard-earned money that she could use for her own children. Therefore, what are the chances she will still schedule an assessment?

She continues to ignore her acute sensitivity to workplace lighting and noise, finding her retail job draining. Her differences in social communication affect relationships with supervisors and coworkers, while her executive functioning difficulties complicate juggling schedules and family duties.

Without a formal diagnosis, she cannot access workplace accommodations that might help her thrive. Her hopes for advancement fade as her sensory issues hinder her from reaching her full potential and meeting promotion requirements. Still, she perseveres; she has never shied away from adversity, and those around her urge her to keep striving, which exhausts her more each day. Lacking understanding of the neurological origins of her struggles, she blames herself, fueling shame and self-criticism that intensify her daily stress at home. Her mental and physical health, self-esteem, family life, and career all suffer. In turn, her dreams and hopes diminish in a life that feels smaller every day.

Masking and Cultural Code-Switching: The Double Labor

The idea of masking—hiding natural autistic behaviors to seem more typical—becomes even more complicated for people with more than one marginalized identity. For them, masking often occurs alongside assimilation, which involves modifying key aspects of themselves to conform to the dominant culture. This is called "double labor" and means they have to manage both their neurodivergent traits and also change how they act because of their race, gender, or culture, making social situations much more taxing and stressful.

Cultural code-switching, which means changing how you act and talk depending on who you are with, combines with autistic masking in ways that make social situations much harder and more tiring. For example, a Black autistic professional might hide stimming behaviors and also change how they speak, move, and show their culture to fit in at a mostly white workplace. In this situation, after having mastered the art of masking within their community, paying the daily emotional price of this daily performance, they now have to go through this entire process all over again to comply with the new social norms of a white-collar culture, in addition to being Black in a mostly White environment.

They may need to learn the expected ways to behave in meetings, conceal their natural autistic behaviors, and adapt their personality to fit in with the workplace culture. Until they return home and resume their regular masking.

The emotional toll of this compound masking is profound and often misunderstood by providers who lack intersectional competence. Managing multiple stigmatized identities at once can lead to depression, anxiety, or burnout—issues often overlooked when only one aspect of identity is considered.

The Cycle of Medical Misogyny in Autism Diagnosis

The Immediate Breakdown of Trust

When autistic patients—particularly women and minorities —disclose their condition to healthcare providers, they often encounter a response that seems benign but is actually devastating: "You don't look autistic" or "You seem fine to me." When a medical professional dismisses an autism disclosure based on a brief visual assessment, they send three harmful messages simultaneously:

First, they signal that the patient's self-knowledge and lived experience are irrelevant. This fundamentally violates the principle of patient-centered care, implying that the individual's daily struggles will be disregarded rather than addressed.

Second, they demonstrate a troubling overconfidence in their diagnostic abilities. Autism is not a condition that can be diagnosed through casual observation during a routine appointment. The assumption that neurological differences should be visually apparent reveals a profound misunderstanding of how autism actually presents— particularly in women and minorities who have learned to mask their traits. And quite frankly, most medical conditions require elaborate medical screenings; therefore, a medical professional giving the impression they solely rely on their eyesight to spot potential medical issues is quite alarming... Just saying.

Third, they expose their adherence to harmful stereotypes about what autism "looks like"—stereotypes that have historically excluded women, people of color, and anyone who doesn't fit the narrow profile of a young white boy with obvious behavioral differences. My mind then starts to seriously wonder: Have they been refreshing their knowledge since the 90s? Do they satisfy their continuing education requirements... Again, just my two cents here.

The Historical Roots of Medical Bias

The medical community's understanding of autism has been shaped by decades of research focused predominantly on white male children with the most visible presentations. This has created a diagnostic blind spot that systematically excludes women and girls, who often develop sophisticated masking strategies and present with internalized rather than externalized behaviors; people of color, whose cultural expressions may be misinterpreted or whose access to early diagnosis has been limited; and adults, who have spent years developing coping mechanisms that obscure their underlying neurological differences.

The phenomenon of female physicians reproducing or even intensifying misogynistic diagnostic approaches toward autistic women parallels a documented sociological pattern where marginalized individuals sometimes enforce discriminatory systems more rigorously than their privileged counterparts. This paradoxical behavior stems from several interconnected psychological and institutional factors.

Female physicians undergo medical training in systems designed by and for men, where clinical diagnostic frameworks overwhelmingly reflect male presentation of conditions. This creates what Bourdieu termed "symbolic violence": the process by which those subjected to discrimination come to accept and reproduce the very systems that marginalize them. In addition, the Queen Bee Phenomenon describes how women in male-dominated fields like medicine distance themselves from other women and adopt masculine norms to succeed. Research by Derks et al. (2016) found that women in leadership positions tend to distance themselves from other women and enforce stricter standards. The research consistently shows that women who achieve success in male-dominated environments may distance themselves from other women and legitimize gender inequality as a response to discrimination they experience.

The Clinical Consequences of Dismissal

This dismissal isn't just psychologically harmful—it has real medical consequences. Autism affects how individuals process sensory information in medical environments, communicate about pain and symptoms, respond to medications, handle stress and medical procedures, and navigate healthcare systems. When healthcare providers dismiss autism, they lose crucial context for understanding their patients' needs, potentially leading to misdiagnosis, inappropriate treatments, and inadequate care planning.

I experienced this firsthand when I suffered from unbearable temporomandibular joint (TMJ) pain for over two years, losing about 60% of my mouth opening and 20 pounds since chewing was no longer an option. I woke up nightly in excruciating pain, only to have a maxillofacial surgeon explain that I just had to learn to manage my stress and take yoga classes. According to this "excellent" specialist, my symptoms were mostly psychological, and TMJ was mostly a "female affliction.

"After going through the usual first path of treatment for TMJ disorder and wearing a mouthpiece for three months without any improvement, I suggested the surgical option since my symptoms resembled those of UFC fighters who described TMJ injuries and surgeries for dislocated or broken jaws as "the worst a fighter suffers (both physically and mentally)." But doctors were formal: I definitely did not suffer such an injury, as it would be unbearable for me to even talk. I just needed therapy, better sleep with Valium, and maybe consultation with a psychologist for possible anorexia. Finally, a social worker suggested I check Miami School of Medicine. Three weeks later, the diagnosis was clear: an obvious case of dislocated jaw requiring surgery, a surgery I would have to wait for another couple of months because of COVID, thanks to most medical professionals I encountered who delayed my diagnosis by over two years because of decades of internalized medical misogyny.

How many men would have to face the chronic pain of a dislocated jaw, day after day, for over two years, looking like skin and bones, without a doctor immediately investigating a jaw injury instead of entertaining some psychological fabrication? Add to my gender the fact that I disclosed my ASD diagnosis, and you'll be suffering in excruciating pain for years. That's the beauty of intersectionality!

The Broader Public Health Crisis

This pattern of dismissal contributes to a larger crisis in autism recognition and support. When front line medical professionals—often the first point of contact in healthcare —refuse to acknowledge autism in women and minorities, they perpetuate the myth that autism primarily affects white males, delay appropriate interventions and support services, force patients to seek multiple opinions, creating barriers to care, and contribute to mental health crises among unrecognized autistic individuals.

Boundaries, Vulnerability, and Abuse: The Hidden Crisis

This devastating pattern is why diagnosis and proper support matter so deeply. They're not just about academic accommodations or sensory tools—they're about reclaiming our right to exist authentically and safely in the world. In light of my autism diagnosis, a question haunted me: Who were those adults, including my own mother, to tell me how I experienced touch? Why would my mother force herself to kiss me on the neck when I expressed to her multiple times my discomfort: with my words, and through my instinctive reactions and body language (covering my neck and ears with my hands). Still, she would ambush me, arguing it was "her right" as my mother.

In the medical field, professionals assess a patient's pain by asking them to estimate it on a scale of 1 through 10. They do not decide whether it should be a 2 or a 7. They trust their sensory perception. Why was I denied this basic right? And if my own family members, who were supposed to protect me, denied me the right to express and enforce my sensory perception, completely disregarding my physical boundaries, wasn't it normal for others to deny me the right to say, "No"? For many girls and women on the spectrum, most of our "Nos" during childhood were met with forceful resistance, and we got used to it. When boys, then men, groom us, abuse us, or force themselves on us, they use the same tactics—explaining that we cannot say "No" because no one takes our "No" for an answer, not even the family members who are supposed to protect us.

Predators tell us that we don't know what we want, that we always complain or "pretend" things that should feel good are unbearable for us, that no one cares or trusts us anyway. Eventually, they'll explain to our confused selves that we were "asking for it" anyway, that we somehow invited their behavior. We come to wonder: "Maybe they're right. Maybe we gave wrong signals again or interpreted signals incorrectly.

"Thanks to formative years of being told we are not worthy of self-esteem and self-respect, we become the ideal prey for any type of abuser and predator: chronically and socially naive, disarmed shadows of girls and women constantly hiding in shame, whose abuse won't be detected since we've perfected the art of camouflaging and becoming invisible.

Professional Responsibility: The Path Forward

Healthcare providers must recognize that their role is not to be the "gatekeepers" of the autism label, but to support their patients' health and well-being. This requires abandoning visual stereotypes and understanding that autism presents differently across demographics, respecting patient self-advocacy and treating autism disclosures as valuable clinical information, seeking education about the diverse presentations of autism, particularly in women and minority populations, and focusing on functional support rather than diagnostic validation when patients share their autism status.

The statement "you don't look autistic" may seem supportive and reassuring, but from medical professionals, in 2025, it actually represents a heartbreaking failure of the medical system. A failure to care. A failure to look and see the patient standing in front of them. A failure to do their due diligence and give patients a proper examination… Since when do doctors diagnose cancer, diabetes or even hemorrhoids without proper examination? A failure to support a patient asking for help. Because, be assured that no one walks into a medical office to inquire about Autism because it's cool.

True medical care requires proper, up-to-date medical education to move beyond stereotypes and meet patients where they are, with the understanding and accommodations they need to thrive.

Rebuilding Boundaries and Safety

Early Warning System Development: The first step in breaking the cycle of vulnerability involves developing an early warning system that helps autistic women recognize when situations feel unsafe, even when they can't articulate why. This requires learning to identify physical signs of discomfort, unease, or danger that the body registers before the mind can process the threat. Common signals include tension in the shoulders, jaw, or stomach, changes in breathing patterns, feeling "frozen" or unable to speak, sudden fatigue or confusion, or simply a vague sense that something feels "wrong.

"Pause Protocol Implementation: When something feels "off" but you can't identify why, implementing a "Pause Protocol" can provide crucial safety space. This involves saying "I need a moment to think about this," stepping away physically if possible, texting a trusted friend that "something feels wrong, but I can't pinpoint it," and most importantly, trusting the feeling even without a logical explanation.

Boundary Scripts and Practice: Boundary reconstruction requires systematic practice, starting with low-stake situations and building confidence through success. Developing scripts for common situations provides concrete tools for challenging moments. Phrases like "I'm not comfortable with that," "I need to think about it," "That doesn't feel right to me," and "I'm going to leave now" should be practiced until they become automatic responses rather than difficult decisions.

Safety Network Creation: Creating a robust safety network requires identifying two to three trusted individuals who understand your autism and communication style, won't dismiss your concerns as "overreacting," can provide an objective perspective when you're confused, and will support your decisions even if they don't fully understand them.

The Intersectional Identity Map: Self-Understanding

Understanding your intersectional neurodivergent identity requires a systematic examination of how different aspects of who you are interact to shape your experience. Begin by creating an intersectional identity map that includes all the ways you identify—your race, gender, sexuality, class background, religion, nationality, family structure, and any other aspects of identity that feel significant to your experience.

Next, examine how these identities interact with your neurodivergence. How might your cultural background influence how your autism is expressed or perceived? How do gender expectations in your community affect your ability to show autistic traits authentically? How does your economic situation impact your access to diagnosis, support, and accommodation?

Journal prompts for deeper self-reflection might include: What aspects of my identity do I feel most comfortable expressing authentically, and which do I feel pressure to hide or modify? How has growing up with multiple marginalized identities affected my relationship to my neurodivergence? What messages did I receive about each aspect of my identity, and how have these shaped my self-perception?

Building Inclusive Systems: Institutional Best Practices

Healthcare System Reform: Healthcare systems that serve intersectional populations effectively require fundamental changes in how services are designed and delivered. This means providing interpretation services not just for language but for cultural context, training providers to understand how different communities express distress and seek help, and creating intake processes that capture the full complexity of intersectional experience.

Educational Transformation: Truly inclusive educational environments move beyond accommodation as an afterthought to design that welcomes neurodivergent students from diverse backgrounds from the beginning. This involves hiring teachers and support staff who reflect the diversity of the student population, offering ongoing training in both autism understanding and cultural competence, and developing policies that explicitly address the needs of multiply marginalized students.

Inclusive workplaces: recognize that neurodivergent employees from diverse backgrounds may require accommodations that address multiple aspects of their identity simultaneously. This might mean flexible dress codes that accommodate both sensory needs and work culture, communication styles that honor both autistic directness and cultural expectations around hierarchy, or workspace modifications that address both sensory sensitivities and cultural preferences.

Research and Future Directions

The research foundation supporting intersectional approaches to neurodivergence continues to grow. Cascio et al. (2020) provide comprehensive frameworks for applying intersectionality to autism research, highlighting the importance of examining how race, gender, class, and other identities interact to create unique presentations and support needs. Mandell et al. (2009) document persistent racial disparities in autism services while offering concrete recommendations for creating more equitable systems of care. Dewinter et al. (2017) explore the intersection of LGBTQ+ identity and autism, revealing both challenges and strengths that emerge from navigating multiple minority identities.

This growing body of research provides essential evidence

for the need to move beyond single-axis approaches to understanding and supporting individuals who are neurodivergent. It documents the real-world consequences of failing to address intersectional needs while also highlighting resilience factors and community-based solutions that can inform more effective intervention approaches.

Prevention Through Empowerment: Breaking Generational Cycles

Rebuilding self-worth requires daily practices that counter years of negative messaging about autistic value and validity. This includes listing three things you did well each day, practicing self-compassion when making mistakes, celebrating authentic moments when you didn't mask your emotions, and connecting with other autistic women who understand your experiences.

The key insight underlying all prevention strategies is that they require rebuilding the foundation that was damaged in childhood by teaching autistic women that their perceptions are valid, their boundaries matter, and their safety is paramount. This work cannot be accomplished through individual effort alone but requires systemic change in how we raise, educate, and support autistic girls and women.

The ultimate goal is to transform autistic women from "ideal victims" into empowered individuals who trust their instincts, enforce their boundaries, and refuse to carry shame that rightfully belongs to their abusers. This transformation serves not only individual healing but also creates generational change that protects future autistic girls from experiencing the same cycles of vulnerability and victimization.

Future Vision: Intersectional Inclusion as the Norm

When we dismiss autism in women and minorities, we don't just fail individual patients, we perpetuate a healthcare system that serves only a narrow slice of the population.

Imagine educational systems in 2040 where intersectional neurodivergent students are celebrated for the unique perspectives and strengths their multiple identities bring to learning communities. Envision healthcare systems where providers routinely consider how multiple identities impact the expression of autism and support needs. Imagine workplaces where neurodivergent employees from all backgrounds are recruited, retained, and promoted based on their unique strengths and contributions.

In this future, research on autism and other forms of neurodivergence is conducted by and with multiply marginalized communities, ensuring that findings reflect the full diversity of human experience. Advocacy organizations are led by intersectional voices, policy recommendations address systemic barriers that affect multiple marginalized communities, and resources are designed to serve the needs of individuals whose experiences don't fit into single-category frameworks.

The future of neurodivergence support depends on embracing intersectional frameworks that honor the full complexity of human identity and experience. This means moving beyond universal approaches based on dominant group experiences to creating flexible, responsive systems accommodating the diverse ways neurodivergence intersects with other aspects of identity.

Most fundamentally, it recognizes that neurodivergence liberation cannot be separated from broader struggles for racial justice, gender equity, economic fairness, and LGBTQ + rights—because many of us are fighting all these battles simultaneously, with brains that process the world differently and hearts that refuse to accept that anyone should have to face marginalization alone.

IDENTIFYING ENVIRONMENTAL TOXICITY

Where we learn to stop shrinking ourselves to fit mental and physical spaces that were never designed for us.

The Conference Room That Broke Me

The conference room had no windows, fluorescent lights that buzzed like angry wasps, and walls painted the color of institutional despair... Don't we all know it? Twenty-three people crammed into a space designed for twelve, talking over each other while someone's cologne competed with the smell of microwaved fish from the kitchen next door. My skin crawled. My jaw clenched. Every cell in my body screamed to flee. I could feel the blood in my temple pulsing while I was slowly getting nauseous, clearly starting a major migraine.

However, as the project lead, I had to run this meeting. So I stayed, trying to look engaged and professional while my body felt completely out of control. By the time we got to the third topic, I couldn't understand what people were saying anymore. The overwhelming sights, sounds, and smells took over my ability to think, so I just nodded and "took notes" that turned out to be unreadable scribbles.

That meeting lasted forty minutes. Forty minutes of sensory

aggression leading to nothing, except the fact that it took me three days to recover from it. However, what struck me most was that I wasn't the only one struggling. As I stood in the hallway recovering, I watched others periodically step out, rub their temples, or shift uncomfortably in their seats. The difference was that my nervous system had reached its breaking point faster and more dramatically than theirs.

I wasn't difficult. I wasn't high maintenance. I was a canary in a coal mine, alerting everyone to an environmental design that wasn't working for anyone, but that most people had learned to endure.

Later, when I told a coworker without autism about this, they brushed it off as just a bad day. But for me, that conference room was more than just uncomfortable—it felt like an assault on my senses, leaving me drained, out of balance, and doubting whether I could continue doing my job if I had to attend daily meetings like this one. The environment turned a normal meeting into something that felt traumatic.

This is the hidden problem of ignoring neurodivergent needs in how spaces and systems are set up. These places don't just leave us out—they actually hurt us. The harm spreads, affecting how we work, our ability to focus and be productive, our relationships, and our sense of self-worth, in ways that are rarely recognized or addressed. That day marked a turning point in my understanding. Instead of asking, "What's wrong with me that I can't handle this?" I began asking, "What's wrong with this environment that it's causing distress?"

The Infantry Metaphor: Neurodivergent Individuals as Early Warning Systems

Years later, I would come to understand this experience through a different lens—one that reframes neurodivergent individuals not as defective, but as essential early warning systems for environmental toxicity. We are like infantry on the front lines of sensory warfare, experiencing immediate casualties from environmental hazards that will eventually reach the neurotypical artillery advancing behind with heavier armor.

Our hypersensitivity makes us the first to fall, but the toxic design elements—noise, lighting, crowding, sensory chaos—don't discriminate in their ultimate impact. Just as infantry units provide critical intelligence about enemy positions and hazards ahead, neurodivergent individuals serve as an early warning system for workspace toxicity.

Reframing The Question: What's Wrong with This Toxic Environment?

The traditional approach to neurodivergent workplace challenges focuses on fixing the person: teaching better coping strategies, prescribing anxiety medication, and recommending mindfulness apps. But what if we asked a different question entirely? Instead of "What's wrong with this person?", what if we asked, "What's wrong with this environment?"

Just as the Radium Girls were told their work environment was not only safe but beneficial—with companies claiming radium paint would "add years to our lives" and make them more beautiful—autistic employees are often told that overwhelming open offices, constant interruptions, and sensory chaos are simply" modern workplace culture" that everyone must adapt to.

The radium companies were aware of the dangers—male scientists wore lead aprons and used ivory-tipped tongs to handle radium—but the female workers were given no protection and told that the exposure was harmless. Similarly, neurotypical managers often work from private offices with controllable lighting and sound while expecting autistic employees to thrive in sensory-overloaded cubicle farms.

The dial painters developed "radium jaw"—their bones literally disintegrating from the inside—while companies denied any connection between their deteriorating health and work conditions. Autistic employees experience neurological burnout, chronic stress responses, and mental health deterioration while being told their struggles are personal failings rather than environmental toxicity.

As the Radium Girls were instructed to use their lips to point paintbrushes—unknowingly ingesting poison with every stroke—autistic employees are instructed to "just adapt," "be more flexible," and "try harder" in environments that are systematically depleting their cognitive and emotional resources.

By themid-1920s, the dial painters were "falling ill by the dozens," with legs breaking under them and spines collapsing. Many died within years of exposure. Similarly, autistic employees in hostile work environments show dramatically higher rates of burnout, depression, and early career exit.

The crucial difference? The Radium Girls' lawsuits in 1927 were "among the first instances in the United States in which employers were held liable for the health and safety of their employees," leading to occupational safety standards that protect all workers today. We're still waiting for that recognition when it comes to neurological environmental safety.

The Hidden Costs of Hostile Environments

Environmental hostility forces neurodivergent individuals into three distinct but related adaptive strategies, each with different psychological costs and implications for environmental design:

Masking: Hiding natural reactions like fidgeting, not making eye contact, or not showing discomfort with sights and sounds to seem more like everyone else in places that don't fit your needs. This involves actively hiding autistic traits to appear neurotypical, like forcing eye contact or suppressing stimming behaviors.

Assimilation: Changing who you are and how you act to fit in, such as adapting to work in open offices even when it feels overwhelming. This involves changing core behaviors to fit social norms, like suppressing sensory needs to endure open office environments.

Compensation: Developing alternative strategies to function effectively despite environmental barriers, like wearing noise-canceling headphones or working unusual hours to avoid peak sensory chaos. These involve learning specific strategies to navigate social situations, such as developing scripts for professional interactions.

While compensation strategies can be helpful tools that enhance our abilities, masking and assimilation come with huge mental and physical costs. Research by Bradley et al. (2021) documented what many autistic individuals have experienced firsthand: prolonged camouflaging leads to identity erosion, while forced assimilation in hostile environments causes burnout and increased risk of mental health crises. Their qualitative study found that "time spent camouflaging is what seems to be most damaging for the participants' mental health," with autistic adults reporting that camouflaging leads to "exhaustion, isolation, poor mental and physical health, loss of identity and acceptance of self." Supporting this, Hull et al. (2021) found in their large-scale study that "camouflaging was associated with greater symptoms of generalized anxiety, depression, and social anxiety" in autistic adults. A comprehensive systematic review by Zhuang et al. (2023) reinforced these findings, identifying that camouflaging leads to being "overlooked, under-supported, and burnt out" as well as "low self-esteem and identity confusion." Even compensation strategies become exhausting when environments demand constant adaptation rather than providing basic accessibility, with camouflaging being "seen as necessary to survive in a world designed for the neurotypical majority."

I think of assimilation as emotional strip mining—being forced to suppress your core neurological needs to extract what others expect from you, while masking hides the caused damage, leaving behind a depleted landscape that takes years to restore. Compensation strategies become survival tools in this toxic environment.

The Science of Environmental Impact on Performance

A systematic review of 31 studies found that working in open-plan workplace designs is associated with more negative outcomes on many measures relating to health, satisfaction, productivity, and social relationships (James et al., 2021). The constant interruptions, random noise, and lack of private space that make it hard for autistic people to focus also break up attention and raise stress for everyone else. The difference is that people without neurodivergence often adjust without thinking about it, while neurodivergent people feel the problems more strongly and obviously.

The research on open office design perfectly illustrates this phenomenon. Harvard Business School's Ethan Bernstein found that face-to-face interactions actually dropped by 70% after companies adopted open office plans, while digital tool usage increased dramatically (Bernstein & Turban, 2018). A systematic review of 31 studies found that open designs are associated with more negative outcomes on measures relating to health, satisfaction, productivity, and social relationships (James et al., 2021). Workers reported a 34% increase in sweat response and 25% increase in negative mood after just eight minutes of simulated open-office noise (Sander, 2021, July 4).

These findings reveal that neurotypical workers struggle too—they just have more armor, so the damage accumulates more slowly.

When we start designing environments that work for neurodivergent nervous systems, we often discover that we've created spaces that work better for everyone. This isn't charity—it's intelligent design that begins with the most challenging use cases to create universally better solutions.

Deep Work vs. Interruption and Multitasking Culture

Harvard Business Review research following 20 teams from Fortune 500 companies found that workers switch between different applications and unique websites nearly 1,200 times per day, totaling 5 working weeks or 9% of their annual work time.

Am I the only one concerned here? As we all know, modern workplaces expect people to be always available and respond promptly, which can be especially challenging for neurodivergent workers who often perform their best work when they can focus for extended periods. "Prompt answers" are especially important in remote positions, where most in-house managers feel the constant need to obtain regular proof that their remote team is working during business hours, and consider "flexibility" a worker's ability to jump and focus instantly on any task thrown at them.

Daily thread chats with messages that require immediate attention to avoid suspicion are sent to remote workers daily. Failing to provide an answer within the next 15 minutes will usually result in an additional message suggesting that the "Good morning" they just received in the team's thread is a time-sensitive matter (obviously, it will no longer be relevant after noon), reminding them of the company's expectations and best practices. A second delayed response, and the worker will face an impromptu call with a vocal recap of the company's expectations and best practices, followed by the passive-aggressive: "Does this make sense?" Meanwhile, our neurodivergent workers are now completely out of their deep focus, stressed about their job being potentially threatened, and unable to regain their focus in time to meet the deadline they were initially focused on. However, the reality extends far beyond neurodiversity in the workplace: If companies opt to hire remotely, they must trust their remote workers. Unless a worker has a history of delivering projects late with quality concerns, the way they process them is irrelevant.

Under the right conditions, I can maintain deep focus for approximately 6 hours, tackling an entire week's worth of work. Unfortunately, the constant Slack pinging, emails, and receipt confirmations required by companies within a certain time frame, as well as random questions, keep me away from reaching my deep focus state and working efficiently.

The Mathematics of Cognitive Destruction

Just think about the fact that research by Dr. Gloria Mark (2023) indicates that it takes approximately 23 minutes to regain focus after just one interruption. Let's multiply this number by 275. Why? Precisely because Microsoft's latest research, involving 31,000 workers, found that employees are interrupted every two minutes during core work hours, amounting to 275 interruptions per day when accounting for extended work hours beyond the standard 9-to-5.

• Dr. Gloria Mark with Irvine researchers at the University of California also found that the typical office worker is interrupted or switches tasks every three minutes and five seconds on average.
• Corporate employees are interrupted at least 12 times per hour, with interruptions happening every 12 minutes and 40 seconds on average, usually lasting 10-15 minutes each.

- Employees in knowledge-intensive professions are interrupted 15 times per hour—every 4 minutes—resulting in a loss of 3 full days per month.

The Cognitive Damage of Multitasking

A Stanford study found that heavy multitaskers performed worse on cognitive control tasks and were more susceptible to interference from irrelevant environmental stimuli. Another study from the University of Cambridge found that participants who multitasked while performing cognitive tasks experienced significant IQ drops similar to what you see in individuals who skip a night of sleep or who smoke marijuana. For men, multitasking can lower IQ by as much as 10 points, essentially rendering them the cognitive equivalent of an 8-year-old. I don't know about you, but I'm certain that workers who are "cognitively" performing under a middle school level, under the influence, or after an all-night party are not the ones companies' HR departments are after. But the working conditions created in the name of productivity made it impossible for most workers to perform, by design. How embarrassingly stupid and counterproductive is that? I suppose it might be the logical result of decisions made in workplaces that literally drain people's brainpower, one interruption at a time. Ping!

The Educational Pipeline Problem

Ironically, despite neurodiverse people being equally intelligent and needing the least number of interruptions possible, those "knowledge-intensive professions" are typically dominated by neurotypical individuals. Educational systems indeed discriminate, again by environmental and instructional design, against neurodivergent learning styles, creating systemic barriers that prevent talented individuals with autism, ADHD, and other neurological differences from accessing these prestigious careers. Not convinced?

• Only 73.6% of autistic students earn a high school diploma compared to 86% of all students.

• Just 15% of the young adults with ADHD held a four-year degree compared to 48% of among those without the condition.

• "Despite the overall increase of individuals with disabilities in higher education, in 2021 only 4.5% of law school graduates reported having a disability." (Kelly, 2025). In this fantastic article that I would recommend, Kelly (2025) illustrates the challenges of masking through a student's experience with classroom seating, explaining how Eden had to manage classroom seating throughout law school due to sensory needs. During 1L year, two large classes had assigned seating based on where students sat the first day. Eden arrived early but still had to sit in the back of one class where they struggled to hear. To secure better seating in the second class, Eden spent lunch breaks sitting in the empty classroom. For three years, Eden scouted rooms early and arrived as soon as possible to find seats away from distracting ambient noise that neurotypical students wouldn't notice. Consider how much extra time, effort, and energy Eden expended to maintain achievement levels. For neurodiverse individuals, sensory overload is like having an intense rash you can't scratch or acknowledge. Imagine sitting in class for an hour daily all semester, acting normal while taking notes, listening, answering questions, and learning material for exams worth 95% of your grade. This is masking—a survival strategy that requires enormous energy and has negative effects including exhaustion, reduced achievement, and lower quality of life. Neurodivergent people may mask so effectively that others won't believe they need accommodations (Kelly, 2025).

• In higher education, approximately 17.2% of undergraduates report having ADD or ADHD and 4.9% report having autism.

- Recent surveys indicate that 25% of law students identified as neurodivergent (Blaemire, 2024), suggesting growing recognition but persistent underrepresentation in professional programs.

These statistics reveal how educational discrimination systematically excludes neurodivergent minds from knowledge-intensive careers in law, medicine, academia, and other fields that could greatly benefit from diverse cognitive approaches to complex problems, and who need more favorable deep-work conditions to function effectively.

The Recovery Nightmare

As seen beforeMicrosoft. (2025), it takes 23 minutes and 15 seconds to regain focus after an interruption. Factor in the recovery time needed, and workers end up with very little actual productive time, if any at all.

When I used to attend school or go to work in person, I had to bring work home to learn what I had been "taught" during the day (I know, it sounds just as ridiculous as it is!), complete my homework, or finish my work projects. Time spent at school or at the office was a complete, utter waste of my brainpower, time, and energy. I would go home depleted yet still had to make up an entire day of learning at school to catch up. This "second shift" would reduce my sleeping hours, cut into my weekend relaxing time, and push me over the edge a little more each day. In high school, to balance my personal and academic life, I started sleeping at school during the day to catch up on my studies at night. During the weekend, I was finishing up homework, taking naps, and going on walks, mostly alone, to "save" my social energy for the week. My parents thought I was a "mystery." Occasionally, I would be asked: "Are you sure you don't want to see friends this weekend?" Truth is, even if I did have friends, my basic survival depended on this strict routine, without which I would face an autistic burnout.

So, no, as a neurodivergent woman, I am not being difficult when I refuse to take an office job. I am being realistic, considering a situation that is not only unsustainable but also unfair: Why should a 40-hour job impede on my evenings, weekends, mental health, and family time because of my neurodivergence when I have proven over the last 17 years that I can sustain daily quality work, meeting every single deadline? The only word that comes to my mind is discrimination. If someone cannot perform a job without experiencing debilitating headaches or making mistakes because they struggle to read small characters, no one would ever question whether they should be wearing their glasses. What's the difference?

The Perfect Storm for Neurodivergent Workers

Let's reframe:

• 275 daily cognitive assaults for someone whose brain needs sustained focus to function.

• Recovery periods of 23+ minutes for individuals whose hyperfocus is their superpower.

• Constant task and apps switching for minds that excel at deep, sustained attention.

• Double-digits IQ point drops for people already fighting stigma about their cognitive abilities.

It's no wonder that neurodivergent workers do not last long in the workplace. A 2023 study by Waltower shows that 60% or less of work time is actually spent productively, with interruptions causing employees to take 27% more time to complete tasks, commit up to twice as many errors, and experience twice the anxiety. For neurotypical workers, modern workplaces turn into productivity murder. For neurodivergent workers whose strengths lie in sustained attention and pattern recognition, it's cognitive genocide—death by a thousand interruptions, each one stealing not just focus but the very cognitive architecture that makes them exceptional contributors.

Modern workplaces aren't just unfriendly to neurodivergent minds; they're toxic and systematically designed to prevent them from doing their best thinking.

The Corporate Contradiction

Just as the radium dial painters were told their exposure was beneficial while their bones were literally disintegrating from radiation poisoning, modern workers are told that constant availability and multitasking are signs of productivity and engagement, while their cognitive capacity is measurably deteriorating.

The IQ research shows that working in constantly interrupted environments doesn't just feel exhausting—it literally makes people, at best, temporarily less intelligent. For neurodivergent individuals whose cognitive strengths often depend on sustained focus and deep processing, this cognitive impairment can be even more devastating. Both the radium exposure and constant interruptions cause measurable, cumulative damage to essential systems (bones vs. cognitive function), are promoted as beneficial by those who profit from the harmful conditions, have effects that compound over time, and disproportionately harm those who are most exposed.

The difference is we now have the Occupational Safety and Health Administration (OSHA) standards for radiation exposure, but no equivalent protection for cognitive assault in the workplace. In fact, big companies often provide a perfect ironic backdrop for workplace toxicity, despite their emblematic values. While tech giants preach frugality and efficiency, spending millions on "productivity consultants", they create work environments that can literally damage employees' brains with hundreds of daily interruptions per employee and constant multitasking. Meanwhile, big retailers champion "efficiency" and "productivity" while forcing employees to work in sensory-chaotic retail environments, handling constant interruptions and task switching, and operating under a "manufactured crisis culture."

Those same companies will micromanage a 20-dollars expense report but ignore the millions lost to cognitive assault. They will also take pride in having their employees share a hotel bedroom, in the name of frugality, thereby depriving their neurodivergent employees of the ability to take their mask off at the end of the day to recover from the sensory and social assault of their business trip.

The contradiction between stated values and actual workplace design couldn't be more striking.

Identifying Toxic Environments: Red Flags and Warning Signs

Sensory Red Flags

- Fluorescent lighting with no alternative options
- Open floor plans with no quiet spaces
- Constant background noise without sound control
- Strong scents, air fresheners, or chemical odors
- Temperature extremes without individual control
- Visually cluttered or overstimulating environments

Communication Red Flags

- Expectations for immediate responses to non-urgent communications
- Unclear or constantly changing expectations
- Reliance on unspoken rules and implicit understanding
- Punishment for asking clarifying questions
- High-pressure meeting environments with no processing

time

Schedule and Structure Red Flags

- Constant "urgent" requests and manufactured crises
- No protected time for deep work
- Frequent last-minute changes without notice
- Expectation to be available outside designated work hours
- Multitasking requirements and constant task-switching

Social and Cultural Red Flags

- Forced participation in social events
- Open criticism of accommodation requests
- "Flexibility" defined as accepting dysfunction
- Productivity measured by face time rather than output
- Disability accommodation treated as special favors rather than legal rights

The Path Forward

Creating areas where people won't be interrupted is not just a special favor—it's recognizing that good work requires long periods of focus, which most workplaces fail to provide. Companies that set aside time for deep work see better new ideas, finish more projects, and have happier employees, both neurotypical and neurodivergent.

The answer is to make real changes, such as setting quiet hours when only urgent messages are allowed, using tools that allow people to reply when they're ready instead of immediately, and planning projects so that people can work for longer periods without constantly switching tasks. And for everyone's sake, please stop the constant notifications!

Just as we now recognize that exposing workers to radiation requires protective equipment and safety protocols, we must recognize that exposing workers to cognitive toxicity requires environmental accommodations and neurological safety standards.

The next chapter will explore how to design environments that support rather than assault neurodivergent nervous systems, moving from identification of problems to implementation of solutions.

***

THE FUTURE IS INCLUSIVE WITH SAFE DESIGN

Beyond Inclusion: The Science of Psychological Safety

For decades, diversity and inclusion efforts have focused on getting neurodivergent people into spaces—schools, workplaces, communities. But inclusion without safety is just organized suffering. Being in the room isn't enough if the room itself is causing harm.

Dr. Amy Edmondson's groundbreaking research on psychological safety defines it as "a belief that one can speak up without risk of punishment or humiliation" (Edmondson, 2019). For neurodivergent individuals, this concept extends beyond verbal communication to encompass the fundamental right to exist authentically without constant adaptation or masking.

Recent brain research reveals why a calm, predictable environment is particularly crucial for autistic individuals. Brain imaging studies show that autistic brains process sensory information differently—they receive more unfiltered sensory input from their surroundings, which can overwhelm attention and contribute to sensory sensitivity. Think of it like having a broken filter on your sensory system: where neurotypical brains automatically tune out background noise, flickering lights, or nearby conversations, autistic brains receive all of this information at full intensity. This isn't a deficit—it's a neurological difference that requires environmental accommodation.

Multiple studies show that autistic people in stressful environments experience serious health impacts. Research consistently finds that autistic individuals report significantly higher stress levels than non-autistic people. Studies measuring stress hormones found that autistic children had higher levels of both short-term and long-term stress markers, which negatively affected their thinking abilities. For autistic adults who "mask" or camouflage their autism at work, the constant effort to appear neurotypical often leads to severe burnout—complete physical and mental exhaustion that affects their ability to think clearly and handle everyday tasks. But here's the crucial insight: neurotypical workers suffer too, just more gradually. Studies show that office noise reduces thinking ability and increases stress responses, with research finding that open-plan office noise increased negative mood by 25% and physical stress reactions by 34%. Employees lose an average of 21.5 minutes per day due to conversational distraction. Multiple research reviews conclude that open-plan offices consistently harm employee health and well-being, leading to more sick days and higher stress levels.

The SPACE Framework: Designing for Neurological Safety

Creating safe spaces isn't about building autism-only environments. It's about applying universal design principles that recognize human neurological diversity as natural and valuable. The SPACE framework provides a systematic approach to evaluating and improving environments: Sensory considerations, Predictability and structure, Autonomy and choice, Communication clarity, and Emotional regulation support.

Sensory Considerations

Research by Balasco et al. (2020) found that about 90% of individuals diagnosed with autism spectrum disorder have atypical sensory experiences, with these differences confirmed across the lifespan and cross-culturally. Additionally, studies show that sensory processing impairments are associated with significant challenges in social, linguistic, and adaptive skills, with recent estimates suggesting prevalence rates of sensory differences ranging from 42 to 96% among autistic individuals. Research by van den Boogert (2022) demonstrates that "sensory processing difficulties are relevant predictors of stress and occupational burnout, also in healthy employees". This finding deserves additional investigation, since relatively minor modifications to workplace conditions could have significant protective benefits.

Conducting an environmental sensory audit is key to assess the cognitive safety of an environment. Multiple critical factors affect autistic individuals' ability to function comfortably in a space:

- **Lighting Quality**: Harsh fluorescent lights can be replaced with warm LED alternatives, and dimmer switches provide essential control over brightness levels. Natural light should be maximized where possible, with options to control glare and intensity.

- **Sound Management**: This requires assessing ambient noise levels and incorporating sound-absorbing materials where possible to reduce overwhelming auditory input. The minimum should be to allow workers to wear noise-canceling headphones with or without white noise. Recording weekly volume levels and displaying real-time noise levels can help create collective awareness and responsibility for acoustic comfort.

- **Texture and Comfort**: Providing various seating options and ensuring individuals can avoid materials that cause distress. This includes considering fabric choices, furniture textures, and tactile elements throughout the environment.

- **Temperature Control**: Many autistic people struggle with thermal regulation and need the ability to adjust their immediate environment. Individual control over heating, cooling, and air circulation becomes essential.

- **Movement Opportunities**: Space to stand, pace, or use fidget tools when needed for self-regulation. This also includes privacy considerations—autistic workers need spaces where they won't feel subjected to potential scrutiny, as constant social monitoring drains cognitive resources.

- **Spatial Organization**: Reducing visual clutter and creating clear, logical organization systems that support navigation and reduce cognitive load.

At home, sensory refuge zones can feature blackout curtains, weighted blankets for deep pressure input, noise-canceling headphones for auditory relief, and collections of fidget tools for tactile regulation. These environmental modifications benefit neurotypical individuals as well, even if they don't immediately recognize the sensory harm they were previously experiencing in poorly designed spaces.

Predictability and Structure

Uncertainty is kryptonite for many neurodivergent brains. The anterior cingulate cortex, which processes uncertainty and prediction errors, shows altered activity patterns in autistic individuals when facing unpredictable situations (Sapey-Triomphe et al., 202). This isn't about being inflexible —it's about conserving cognitive resources for what matters most.

People feel safer when their environment is steady and they know what to expect. This means:

- **Consistent Schedules**: Keeping routines the same and providing advance notice of changes. This includes posting schedules visibly and maintaining predictable timing for regular activities.

- **Clear Organization**: Organizing spaces logically with consistent labeling and filing systems. Items should have designated places, and these systems should be maintained consistently. More importantly, the organization system must make sense to the neurodivergent individuals using it. It might seem obvious, but trust me, the "tiny detail" is often disregarded,

- **Routine Establishment**: Having routines everyone can count on, from daily workflows to emergency procedures. This provides cognitive scaffolding that reduces the mental energy needed for navigation and decision-making.

- **Change Management**: When changes are necessary, providing maximum advance notice with clear explanations of what will be different, why the change is happening, and what support will be available during the transition.

- **Protected Deep Work Periods**: Establishing quiet hours when only urgent messages are allowed and creating tools that allow people to reply when they're ready instead of requiring immediate responses.

Control isn't about getting your way—it's about having agency in your environment. In their comprehensive 2017 book, Ryan and Deci present their complete self-determination theory framework, including the three basic psychological needs: the need for autonomy, the need for competence, and the need for relatedness. All of them are crucial for motivation and are considered essential nutrients for psychological growth, integration, and general well-being (Deci & Ryan, 2017).

- **Seating Choice**: Allowing individuals to position themselves where they're most comfortable, whether near a wall for security, away from high-traffic areas to reduce overstimulation, or in spots with optimal lighting and temperature.

- **Participation Options**: Ensuring multiple ways to engage with activities or discussions, recognizing that some people contribute better through written responses, one-on-one conversations, or alternative formats rather than traditional group discussions.

- **Timing Flexibility**: Enabling individuals to take breaks when needed for sensory regulation, processing time, or to prevent overwhelm before it becomes unmanageable.

- **Method Choice**: Empowering people to complete tasks in ways that work for their specific neurological wiring, whether that involves using different tools, following alternative sequences, or employing strategies that may look unconventional but produce superior results.

- **Environmental Controls**: Providing options to adjust lighting, sound, temperature, and workspace configuration based on individual needs and preferences.

These autonomy considerations aren't accommodations or special treatment—they're fundamental recognition that different brains work optimally under different conditions, and providing choice creates environments where everyone can contribute their best work.

Communication Clarity

Indirect communication and hidden meanings create unnecessary cognitive load for neurodivergent individuals who often excel at processing explicit information but struggle with implicit social codes while it's important to remember that communication breakdowns between autistic and non-autistic people often stem from different communication styles rather than deficits in social understanding. To improve communication with neurodivergent workers, the following points should be taken into consideration:

- **Direct Language**: Using communication that conveys meaning without relying on subtext or expecting others to read between the lines. This includes clear, specific instructions and feedback.

- **Written Follow-up**: Providing written confirmation of important information and reference points that reduce anxiety about misunderstanding or forgetting critical details.

- **Processing Time**: Recognizing that some individuals need additional moments to formulate responses, and that rushing or filling silence with pressure can actually impede communication.

- **Multiple Communication Channels**: Offering various ways to communicate—verbal, written, visual, and digital—to accommodate different processing preferences.

- **Clear Expectations**: Posting clear rules for shared areas, establishing set formats for meetings and collaboration, and making implicit social expectations explicit.

Emotional Regulation Support

Emotional regulation isn't about controlling or suppressing emotions—it's about having adequate resources and strategies to navigate them skillfully when they arise. Samson et al. (2015) found that autistic individuals often have intact emotional awareness but may use different regulation strategies than neurotypical peers.

- **Quiet Spaces**: Providing dedicated areas for decompression when overstimulation or stress builds to unmanageable levels. These should be easily accessible and free from social demands.

- **Movement Options**: Explicit permission to pace, step outside, or engage in physical self-regulation to process emotions through the body rather than forcing sedentary positioning during distress.

- **Comfort Items**: Making fidgets, weighted objects, or noise-canceling headphones available as immediate sensory regulation tools that can prevent emotional escalation.

- **Reduced Social Demands**: Creating opportunities for solitary processing, recognizing that some people need to step away from interpersonal interaction to effectively regulate before rejoining group activities.

- **Regulatory Tools**: Providing access to resources like breathing exercise guides, sensory tool kits, or calming activities that support emotional self-management.

Creating Safety at Home: The Foundation

Home should be where you can drop all masking and assimilation, where your compensation strategies become choices rather than survival requirements, and where your nervous system can rest and restore.

The Sensory Home Audit

- **Lighting Transformation**: Replace every overhead bulb with warm, dimmable LEDs and add table or salt lamps for ambient options. The harsh brightness that causes daily headaches can be eliminated through thoughtful lighting design.

- **Sound Sanctuary**: Use blackout curtains that also dampen noise, white noise machines, and strategic workspace positioning away from high-traffic areas.

- **Texture and Comfort Assessment**: Evaluate every surface regularly touched—replace scratchy towels with bamboo alternatives, add weighted blankets, and create a "texture library" of soothing fabrics.

- **Temperature and Air Quality**: Ensure good ventilation, temperature control options, and air purification to create a comfortable atmospheric environment.

Homes as Co-Regulators

Research by Black et al. (2022) found that factors related to the interiors of buildings, including the layout of rooms, colors, smells, noises, temperature, ventilation, color and clutter, among other things, can change the way we interact with our environment and the people around us. Autistic individuals can have differences in processing sensory information and may find aspects of the built environment (BE) overwhelming and difficult to navigate. A literature review also allowed the identification of three main factors to be considered when designing for people with ASD—the sensory quality, the intelligibility, and the predictability of the built environment Daffara et al. (2021).

Effective home design involves picking simpler styles, reducing clutter, and adopting a purposeful minimalist approach where items serve specific functions like calming or focusing. This includes lights that can be adjusted, elements that create peaceful rooms, quiet spots for breaks, and organizing space to support predictable routines.

Workplace Safety: Beyond Legal Compliance

Low-Cost, High-Impact Modifications

The Job Accommodation Network reports that 56% of accommodations cost nothing, and the average cost of those that do require investment is around three hundred dollars (Jan 2024), dispelling the myth that supporting neurodivergent employees requires significant financial burden.

- **Sensory Modifications:**
- Desk lamps to supplement or replace fluorescent lighting ($15-50 per workspace)
- Noise-canceling headphones or white noise machines ($50-200)
- Flexible seating options, including stability balls, standing desks, or cushioned chairs ($100-400)
- Removable visual barriers or desk screens to reduce peripheral distractions ($25-100)

- **Schedule and Structure Support:**
- Protected deep work blocks with clear, visual communication about availability
- Meeting-free time zones that allow for sustained focus
- Advance notice protocols for schedule changes or workplace modifications
- Written agendas and follow-up summaries for meetings to support information processing

- **Communication Accommodations:**
- Email or written communication options for employees who struggle with phone-based interaction
- Clear, direct feedback that focuses on specific behaviors

rather than personality traits
- Structured check-in formats that reduce ambiguity about expectations and performance

- **Environmental Accommodations**:
- Noise-canceling headphones to manage auditory sensitivities
- Adjustable lighting options to reduce visual overwhelm
- Workstation positioning away from high-traffic areas or other sources of distraction

- **Social Accommodations**:
- Optional social events with clear communication expectations
- Alternatives to small talk that allow for more meaningful professional connections
- Reduced expectations for forced interpersonal interaction

The Acoustic Revolution

One of the most helpful changes involves managing the overwhelming sounds in modern workplaces and public spaces. Open offices, constant background noise, and sudden loud sounds cause stress and make it difficult to focus or stay calm.

Effective sound management includes providing noise control options from white noise that covers distractions to quiet areas for deep focus. Companies can record weekly volume levels and display real-time noise levels visually, helping everyone become aware of their volume and making noise reduction a collective effort for everyone's well-being.

Community Spaces: Building Belonging

Community involvement presents unique challenges for neurodivergent individuals, as many spaces operate on unspoken social rules and feature sensory-rich environments that can quickly become overwhelming rather than welcoming.

Finding Neurodivergent-Friendly Communities

When evaluating potential community spaces, examine several critical factors:

- **Sensory Environment Assessment**: Can you regulate sensory input through available accommodations? Are quiet spaces accessible when overstimulation occurs?

- **Communication Style Evaluation**: Is direct communication valued over indirect social cues? Are written options available for those who process information better through text?

- **Flexibility Considerations**: Can you participate in ways that work for your specific energy levels and processing style, rather than being forced into neurotypical participation models?

- **Organizational Awareness**: Do organizers demonstrate genuine understanding of neurodivergent needs through their policies, physical space design, and interaction styles?

Communities that successfully include neurodivergent members typically provide agendas in advance, offer multiple ways to participate, maintain predictable structures, and create space for different communication and social interaction styles without requiring extensive self-advocacy.

Creating Change in Existing Communities

Rather than abandoning communities that matter, advocate for neurodivergent-friendly changes that reduce the need for masking and assimilation. This might involve suggesting modifications like dimmed lighting, providing education about neurodiversity, or modeling authentic participation by using fidgets and taking breaks.

When framing requests as improving the environment for everyone—which they genuinely do—resistance decreases significantly.

Guidelines for Community Organizations and Event Planners

- Provide detailed sensory information about venues in advance (lighting, sound levels, crowd size)
- Offer quiet spaces or break areas for sensory regulation
- Use clear, specific communication about schedules, expectations, and changes
- Consider multiple engagement formats (verbal, written, hands-on) to accommodate different processing styles
- Train staff to recognize and respond supportively to neurodivergent behaviors like stimming or need for breaks

Educational Environments: Building Safety from the Beginning

Home Environment for Neurodivergent Children

Parents of neurodivergent children have the opportunity to create safety from the ground up. Research by Cage et al. (2018) shows that when parents create accommodating environments, their neurodivergent children present better self-advocacy skills, higher self-esteem, and improved mental health.

- **Multiple Lighting Options**: Allow children to adjust brightness levels throughout the day, accommodating fluctuating sensory sensitivities and supporting natural circadian rhythms.
- **Sound-Dampening Materials**: Area rugs, heavy curtains,

and soft furnishings help manage acoustic overwhelm, creating spaces where children can think clearly without battling background noise.

- **Varied Seating and Positioning Options**: From traditional chairs to floor cushions, standing desks, or swings— different bodies and brains require different physical arrangements for optimal learning and regulation.

- **Designated Quiet Spaces**: Essential retreat areas where children can decompress from sensory or social demands without being isolated as punishment, helping them develop self-awareness about regulatory needs.

- **Child-Centered Organization Systems**: Organizational systems that make sense to the child's specific brain rather than imposing adult logic, achieved through visual labeling, color-coding, or spatial arrangements that match natural thinking patterns.

Recognize that environmental modifications benefit all family members. Prioritize function over aesthetics when designing family spaces, create designated areas for different energy levels, establish family routines that provide predictability while maintaining flexibility, and understand that resistance to certain environments may reflect genuine neurological incompatibility rather than behavioral problems.

School Advocacy Strategies

- **Understanding Rights**: Learn about IDEA regulations, 504 plan provisions, and IEP processes to navigate systems confidently and ensure children receive legally mandated supports.

- **Documentation**: Keep detailed records of both challenges and successful interventions, creating an evidence base that helps school teams understand what works.

- **Collaboration**: Work with school teams as partners rather than adversaries, recognizing that most educators want to help but may lack training or resources.

- **Education**: Provide school staff with current resources about neurodivergent learning styles and evidence-based interventions, helping bridge the gap between research and classroom practice.

Guidelines for Educators

Research consistently demonstrates that classroom environmental modifications designed with universal accessibility principles benefit all students, not just those with identified learning differences. Almeqdad's (2023) study found that Universal Design for Learning (UDL) can improve student learning across diverse populations, with UDL principles enhancing students' academic ability from diverse backgrounds in contemporary classrooms to acquire and use new knowledge. This approach recognizes that by focusing on making spaces, content, and learning activities accessible to those with disabilities, UDL benefits all learners, including those without disabilities, as even small environmental adjustments can make a significant difference in learning outcomes. The framework creates learning environments that are least restrictive and most culturally responsive for all students, providing multiple means of engagement, representation, and expression that create opportunities for every learner to succeed. These findings support evidence-based educational practices demonstrating that UDL applications effectively assimilate diverse students and illustrate the impact of designing and implementing effective learning environments that minimize barriers in education for all learners through:

- **Multiple Information Presentation**: Visual displays, auditory explanations, and kinesthetic activities ensure students can access content through their strongest processing channels.

- **Flexible Seating and Movement**: Learning doesn't require stillness—allow students to find physical positions that support attention and cognitive processing.

- **Predictable Routines with Change Notice**: Provide structural security while reducing anxiety and behavioral challenges that emerge when expectations shift unexpectedly.

- **Quiet Regulation Spaces**: Essential support for students who become overstimulated or need processing time without social or sensory demands.

- **Clear Expectations and Success Criteria**: Eliminate guesswork and reduce anxiety by helping students understand exactly what constitutes successful performance.

Universal Design Principles for Spaces

Creating spaces that work for everyone means starting with the needs of those who have the most difficulty. This approach challenges the traditional notion of designing for an "average" person and making changes only for those who are different.

After Hurricane Andrew devastated South Florida in 1992, the state revolutionized building standards by designing every structure to withstand Category 5 hurricane conditions. This became the baseline standard statewide. When you design for hurricanes, you automatically create superior buildings for all conditions: doors that open outward prevent wind pressure while making emergency evacuation easier year-round, impact-resistant windows that survive flying debris also resist break-ins and improve energy efficiency, reinforced structures handle extreme forces while creating homes that last decades longer.

This exemplifies universal design thinking: when you engineer for the most demanding users, you create environments and systems that enhance everyone's experience. Neurotypical people benefit from the clarity, flexibility, and multiple pathways built for autism and ADHD, while those with cognitive differences get exactly what they need to thrive. Build for the storm and be ready for any weather.

The Ripple Effect: Universal Environmental Benefits

Environmental modifications designed for neurodivergent individuals consistently produce benefits that extend to entire communities and organizations. Reduced sensory chaos improves concentration for anyone dealing with stress or distraction. Clear communication and predictable routines support individuals with anxiety, learning differences, or temporary life disruptions. Flexible workspace options accommodate parents, caregivers, people with chronic health conditions, and anyone whose peak productivity doesn't align with traditional schedules.

Research consistently demonstrates that environments incorporating neurodivergent-conscious design principles enhance satisfaction and usability for all users, extending benefits beyond the target population to individuals experiencing various challenges. Universal design approaches create environments that are "user-friendly and accessible, especially for people with neurodiversity/physical disabilities," while simultaneously improving functionality for all users. Studies on quiet space design for neurodivergent populations reveal that environmental modifications addressing sensory needs—such as optimized sound and lighting considerations—create restorative environments that benefit anyone experiencing sensory overload or stress. Research in workplace environments shows that universal design principles, when applied to support neurodivergent employees, "improve learning outcomes for all employees, not just those who disclose a need," particularly benefiting individuals facing temporary challenges or transitions. This aligns with broader findings that environmental supports designed for neurodivergent individuals enhance resilience and positive outcomes across diverse populations, particularly during periods of stress or major life changes.

The economic benefits are measurable: companies implementing environmental modifications see reduced sick leave usage, higher employee retention, and improved productivity metrics. Schools report decreased behavioral incidents and improved academic outcomes. Community organizations experience higher participation rates and more diverse engagement.

Scentsy Inc.: A Universal Design Success Story

Scentsy Inc. in Meridian, Idaho, exemplifies universal design thinking by creating an environment that addresses diverse employee needs, resulting in a space where people genuinely want to be. Forbes named Scentsy among America's Best-In-State Employers, offering flexible work options and remote work possibilities.

Rather than designing for the never-met-before "average" employee and offering accommodations, Scentsy built its culture from the ground up to support diverse working styles. Their Scentsy Commons campus features open floor plans with suspended chairs for thinking, individual soundproof booths for private calls, outdoor balconies, panoramic mountain views, an affordable corporate cafeteria, a convenience store, a café, a fully equipped gym with family-friendly fitness classes, and an employee game room. This universal approach means whether you're a parent needing flexible hours, someone who thrives with physical activity during workdays, an introvert in need of a quiet space, or an extrovert enjoying collaborative environments, the workplace naturally accommodates your needs. Direct Selling News listed Scentsy among the seven Best Places to Work in the U.S. for the fourth time, and Forbes has recognized them multiple times as one of America's Best Midsize Employers.

This demonstrates that when you design for the full spectrum of human needs rather than retrofitting for differences, you create a workplace so compelling that attendance becomes a choice rather than an obligation.

Moving Forward: Your Environmental Revolution

Creating neurologically safe environments begins with recognizing that your sensory and cognitive needs are valid design requirements, not personal shortcomings to overcome. Start by auditing your current environments: What energizes you versus what depletes you? Where do you perform your best work, experience genuine rest, or feel most authentically yourself?

Document the environmental factors that support your regulation: lighting preferences, sound levels, spatial organization, scheduling patterns, and social interaction structures. Use this information to advocate for modifications in existing spaces and to design new environments that work with your neurology.

Remember that environmental change often requires systemic advocacy rather than individual adaptation. Connect with other neurodivergent individuals to identify shared environmental barriers and collaborative solutions. Collaborate with employers, schools, and community organizations to implement modifications that benefit all parties. Your nervous system's responses to environmental factors are data, not deficits. When you feel overwhelmed, agitated, or unable to focus, consider whether the environment might be the problem rather than automatically assuming you need to adapt better. Environmental ableism is real, but so is your power to create and advocate for spaces that nourish rather than drain your neurological resources. The goal isn't perfect environments, but environments that are flexible, responsive, and designed with awareness that human neurology varies significantly. When we stop shrinking ourselves to fit hostile spaces and start designing spaces that accommodate human diversity, everyone benefits from more thoughtful, humane, and effective environmental design.

Your voice matters. Your needs are valid. Your brain deserves environments that help it thrive. Your sensitivity isn't a burden—it's reconnaissance that could save the entire battalion. The goal isn't to eliminate compensation strategies —these can be valuable tools that enhance our abilities. The goal is creating environments where masking becomes unnecessary and assimilation is replaced with genuine accommodation, allowing our compensation strategies to enhance our natural strengths rather than merely enabling survival in toxic spaces.

It all starts with recognizing that you're not too much for the world, the world just hasn't been designed for enough of us yet. When we speak up about environmental toxicity, we protect everyone advancing behind us. Designing for safety isn't a favor, it's a foundation. This environmental lens scales beyond spaces to products, business models, and cultural innovation, showing how designing from neurodivergent insight creates market advantages and competitive innovation. But that's another book!

To be continued...

***

CONCLUSION

Throughout this book, I have shared my journey of discovery, struggle, and ultimately, transformation. But there is one final piece of this story that I must address—the very language I use to describe myself and why it matters so profoundly to who I am today.

I am autistic. Not a person "with autism," but autistic. This is not merely a semantic choice or a trendy linguistic preference —it is a declaration of identity that represents decades of searching for the missing piece of myself that, once found, finally allowed my life to make sense.

My autism and ADHD are not accessories I carry or conditions I manage—they are integral threads woven into the very fabric of who I am. Just as I am a white, tall woman, I am an autistic woman. The intersectionality of all these characteristics creates the unique tapestry of my identity, and I am proud of each thread. My neurodivergence cannot be separated from my core self without fundamentally altering who I am, how I think, how I experience the world, and how I contribute to it.

For thirty-one years, I lived without understanding this crucial aspect of my identity. Those decades were marked by confusion, failed relationships, abandoned opportunities, and an exhausting performance of neurotypicality that left me depleted and invisible—even to myself. I was a shadow of a person, constantly trying to decode a world that seemed to operate by rules no one had taught me, surrounded by people who appeared to effortlessly navigate social complexities that felt impossibly alien.

My life only began to take the direction I consciously chose once I finally unveiled my neurodivergence. Before my diagnoses, I couldn't function properly because I was trying to operate with incomplete information about my own cognitive architecture. I was attempting to force my square-peg brain into round-hole expectations, wondering why nothing ever felt natural or sustainable.

The moment I received my autism diagnosis—and later, my ADHD diagnosis—everything shifted. Not because anything about my brain had changed, but because I finally had the context to understand why I processed information differently, why certain environments energized me while others depleted me, why my interests ran so deep, and why my approach to communication and relationships followed patterns that made perfect sense once I understood my neurological blueprint.

This revelation allowed me to reclaim my life entirely. I stopped apologizing for my intensity, my need for detailed communication, my preference for written over verbal interaction, my sensory sensitivities, and my passionate focus on topics that fascinated me. Instead of constantly trying to mask or compensate for these traits, I learned to leverage them as the strengths they actually were. I developed pride in my autistic mind and let my authentic identity shine through for the first time in my life.

I understand that others may prefer person-first language (PFL)—"person with autism"—and I deeply respect their choice. For some, this language emphasizes their humanity first, or helps them conceptualize autism as something manageable rather than all-encompassing. These perspectives are entirely valid, and I would never invalidate someone else's experience or preferred terminology.

However, I suspect that preference for person-first language often stems from experiences vastly different from my own. Those diagnosed early in childhood—who grew up with understanding families, appropriate support systems, and never spent decades lost in a maze of self-doubt and failed neurotypical performance—may not fully grasp how profoundly diagnostic recognition can transform a previously incomprehensible life.

For late-diagnosed individuals like myself, autism isn't just a characteristic we have; it's the missing foundation that explains why our entire life structure kept collapsing.

Consider this analogy: A person living in a properly built house with foundations engineered to withstand hurricanes will never question why their home remains standing after storms. The foundation is invisible, taken for granted, yet absolutely essential. Meanwhile, their neighbor—whose house repeatedly collapses during every weather event—must desperately investigate what critical structural element is missing. They dig deeper, replace pieces, move components around, searching for that one essential element that will finally allow their house to stand strong.

When you receive an early diagnosis with proper support, autism doesn't feel defining because that foundational knowledge empowers you to build your identity from the ground up with full understanding. But when you're late-diagnosed, discovering your autism isn't just information—it's the missing cornerstone that suddenly explains decades of structural failures. It's the difference between living with invisible support and living without it entirely.

For those of us who spent years watching our lives collapse at every level—relationships, careers, self-esteem, mental health

—finally understanding our neurological differences isn't limiting. **It's liberation.** We're not just people who happen to have autism; we're people whose autism fundamentally shaped every aspect of our existence, and recognizing that truth is what finally allows us to build lives that won't collapse under pressure.

For those of us who lived for decades in ignorance of our diagnoses, the impact reaches far beyond simple accommodation needs. It affects our core sense of self, our relationships, our career trajectories, our mental health, and our fundamental understanding of our place in the world. When you spend thirty-plus years trying to exist as someone you're not, finally discovering who you actually are feels less like acquiring a diagnosis and more like coming home to yourself.

My autism and ADHD are not burdens I carry or challenges I overcome—they are the neurological foundation that makes my greatest strengths possible. My ability to detect patterns others miss, to maintain focus on complex projects for hours, to notice details that escape typical observation, to think systematically and logically—these capabilities exist because of, not despite, my neurological differences.

But this is not a debate I wish to perpetuate. Whether you identify as autistic, as a person with autism, as neurodivergent, or with any other terminology that feels authentic to your experience, what matters most is that we recognize our shared humanity and common goals.

We face far more significant challenges than semantic preferences. We confront employment discrimination, educational inadequacy, healthcare disparities, social isolation, and systemic misunderstanding that affects our entire community. We need research that includes our voices, policies that reflect our actual needs, and representation that showcases our full spectrum of experiences and capabilities.

To address these substantial issues, we must present a united front. We cannot afford to fragment our community over language choices when we have legislation to influence, stereotypes to dismantle, accommodations to secure, and understanding to build. Our diversity of perspectives, experiences, and identities is our strength, not our weakness.

I call on all of us—regardless of how we choose to identify—to live by the principle of radical inclusion. Let's embrace the full neurodiversity of our community, including the intersectionality of race, gender, sexuality, socioeconomic status, and life experience that makes each of our stories unique and valuable.

Let's create space for the early-diagnosed and the late-discovered, for those who mask and those who never learned to, for those who speak and those who don't, for those who need significant support and those who appear to need none. Let's acknowledge that our autism manifests differently across genders, cultures, ages, and circumstances, and that this variation enriches rather than diminishes our collective voice.

Most importantly, let's lead by example. Let's demonstrate that neurodivergent individuals can be researchers, advocates, entrepreneurs, parents, partners, and leaders. Let's show the world that autism is not a tragedy to be cured or a deficit to be overcome, but a natural variation in human neurology that brings unique perspectives and capabilities to every field we enter.

My life truly began when I stopped trying to be someone else and started being authentically me—an autistic, ADHD, passionate, intense, detail-oriented, pattern-recognizing woman who sees the world through a distinctive lens. This authenticity has not limited my life; it has expanded it beyond anything I thought possible.

To those still searching for answers, still struggling to understand why the world feels so complex and exhausting, still wondering why they don't fit the molds they're supposed to fill—keep looking. Keep advocating for yourself. Keep believing that your differences might not be deficits but features. Your authentic self is worth discovering, and your unique perspective is needed in this world.

To families and allies, please understand that accepting and celebrating neurodivergence doesn't mean lowering expectations or abandoning goals—it means aligning support with authentic strengths and creating environments where different kinds of minds can thrive.

And to my fellow autistic individuals, however you choose to identify: you are not broken. You do not need to be fixed. Your mind works differently, not deficiently. Your perspective matters. Your voice deserves to be heard. And your authentic self—whatever that looks like—is exactly who the world needs you to be.

This is what it means to reclaim autism beyond stereotypes: to recognize that we are not defined by limitations others project onto us, but by the remarkable capabilities that emerge when we're finally free to be ourselves.

Our lives are not upside down—they're right-side up, perhaps for the first time. And from this authentic foundation, we can build not just better lives for ourselves, but a more inclusive world for everyone.

**

BONUS CONTENT AND BIBLIOGRAPHY

If you haven't done it already, scan this QR Code to download your Bonus Content and access the Bibliography.

www.ingramcontent.com/pod-product-compliance
Lightning Source LLC
Chambersburg PA
CBHW060456090426
42735CB00011B/2011